When Love Is Not Enough

When Love Is Not Enough
A Theo-Ethic of Justice

Mary Elsbernd, O.S.F.
and
Reimund Bieringer

A Michael Glazier Book

THE LITURGICAL PRESS
Collegeville, Minnesota

www.litpress.org

A Michael Glazier Book published by The Liturgical Press.

Cover design by Greg Becker. Photos: Skjold Photographs.

The quotations from documents of Catholic Social Teachings are from Michael Walsh and Brian Davies, eds., *Proclaiming Justice and Peace: Papal Documents from* Rerum Novarum *through* Centesimus Annus (Mystic, Conn.: Twenty-Third Publications, 1991).

1   2   3   4   5   6   7   8

Library of Congress Cataloging-in-Publication Data

Elsbernd, Mary, 1946–
    When love is not enough : a theo-ethic of justice / Mary Elsbernd and
    Reimund Bieringer.
        p.   cm.
    Includes bibliographical references and index.
    ISBN 0-8146-5960-8 (alk. paper)
    1. Christianity and justice—Catholic Church.   2. Catholic Church—
Doctrines.   I. Bieringer, R. (Reimund)   II. Title.

BX1795.J87 E57 2002
241'.622—dc21

                                                    2001038060

*To our parents,
our first teachers of justice*

Contents

Acknowledgments

We would like to thank a number of people who were instrumental for the coming into being of this book. We thank the students among whom we taught, some of whom were also readers of the various manuscript versions. In particular we thank Shannon Green, Mark LaBoe, Matt Lohmeier, Gail Ross, Maria Lucia Serrano, and Frederique Vandecasteele-Vanneuville. We also thank and are indebted to the ministers and practitioners of justice who thoughtfully allowed us entrance into the world of their faith, reflection, and practice of justice. Mary would like to express her gratitude to Loyola University Chicago for a study leave in fall 1997, which allowed her to do substantial thinking as well as an initial version of her parts of the manuscript. She also thanks the Gannon Center for Women in Leadership for a research support grant that assisted in the preparation of the final manuscript.

Reimund thanks the "Fonds voor Wetenschappelijk Onderzoek —Vlaanderen" (Fund for Scientific Research—Flanders) for a grant ("Krediet aan Navorsers") that helped to get the research off the ground.

We are pleased to thank the editors of The Liturgical Press, the acquisitions editor for theology, Ms. Linda Maloney, and the managing editor, Mr. Mark Twomey. It was a pleasure to work with them, and we learned so much in the process.

Abbreviations

BETL	Bibliotheca Ephemeridum Theologicarum Lovaniensium
BTB	*Biblical Theology Bulletin*
EDNT	*Exegetical Dictionary of the New Testament*
ETL	*Ephemerides Theologicae Lovanienses*
EvTh	*Evangelische Theologie*
JBL	*Journal of Biblical Literature*
JSNTSS	Journal for the Study of the New Testament, Supplement Series
LAUD	Linguistic Agency University Duisburg
NovT	*Novum Testamentum*
NTS	*New Testament Studies*
NTSuppl	Supplements to Novum Testamentum
SBL	Society of Biblical Literature
TDNT	*Theological Dictionary of the New Testament*
WUNT	Wissenschaftliche Untersuchungen zum Neuen Testament

Documents of Catholic Social Teachings:

CA	*Centesimus annus*
GS	*Gaudium et spes*
JW	Justice in the World
LE	*Laborem exercens*
MM	*Mater et magistra*
OA	*Octagesimo adveniens*
PP	*Populorum progressio*
PT	*Pacem in terris*
QA	*Quadragesimo anno*
RN	*Rerum novarum*
SRS	*Sollicitudo rei socialis*

Other:

std.	standard deviation
ch.	chapter

Introduction

The gospel call to do justice has inspired Christians to practice justice throughout the centuries. Yet popular usage has tended to associate justice with the legal system, with due process, and with fair treatment. In this book we address the practice of justice at the dawn of the new millennium through the lens of seven dilemmas which confront middle-class Christians in their concrete efforts to do justice. After an initial description and analysis of these dilemmas, the text draws on four resources to develop a comprehensive, faith-based approach to justice that will contribute to a resolution of the dilemmas. These resources include experience, the Hebrew and Christian Scriptures, Catholic Social Teachings, and contemporary theories of justice.

Stimulating the interaction and mutual complementarity of these resources, we developed an approach to justice as participation in the human community. In the just and inclusive community which we envision, all persons count, contribute, and participate in building the city of God. Our approach expands the understanding of justice as participation in the human community through attention to seven dimensions. The relational dimension underscores the essentially social nature of justice. A second dimension of justice concerns access to resources which are necessary for human thriving. A just community also requires that structures and procedures facilitate the participation of all. In addition, because well-meaning intentions are not enough, justice as participation necessitates skills for effective action. A sixth dimension reminds us that existing unjust structures and practices must be transformed if a just community is to result. Finally, the dimension of accountable agency recalls the role of individual persons in the transformative process and the practice of justice.

We then return to the seven dilemmas with which this book begins to illustrate how this particular approach to justice contributes to their resolutions. These suggested responses to the justice dilemmas are rooted in the seven dimensions of justice as participation and reflect a theological, eschatological, sacramental, and ethical worldview.

The approach to justice taken in this study occurs within a five-fold context. First, we are convinced that the practice of justice is integrally connected to our images of God. Sociologists of religion have shown that images of God as relational and engaged in this world promote action on behalf of justice. Our own interviews and contacts with practitioners of justice demonstrated that about 90 percent of the time, these practitioners described God in relational and engaged terms. Many of the multiple images of God in the Scriptures reflect relational and engaged understandings of God. For instance, in the Hebrew Scriptures we encounter a God who intervenes on behalf of the oppressed. In the Gospel of John we meet the Indwelling Spirit who enables believers to take up the mission of Jesus and put it into practice in ever-new situations. Finally, in the documents of Catholic Social Teachings on justice, God is sometimes portrayed as engaged and relational and sometimes as distant and unengaged. As our research demonstrates, these changing images of God have shaped the practice of justice throughout the last century.

Second, we believe that the practice of justice is integrally connected to our understanding of the human person. Theological anthropologists, philosophers, and sociologists have proposed various understandings of the constitutive dimensions of the human person. The practitioners of justice whom we contacted articulated a firm belief in the goodness and dignity of human persons. Consequently they expressed outrage at disrespect for persons and their dignity. In the Gospel of John relationality is highlighted as constitutive of being a human person and a significant place is given to embodiment. Catholic Social Teachings emphasize the preeminence of human intellect and agency over what they present as secondary dimensions of the human person such as embodiment, historicity, and difference. In contemporary approaches, the choice of either an individual or social anthropology has critical implications for an understanding of justice.

Third, we start from the presupposition that the world is sacramental, that is, persons encounter God in and through materiality. In the Gospel of John, flesh becomes a place of encounter with God. In some documents of Catholic Social Teachings, poverty and hunger are presented as hindering human relationships with God.

Fourth, we hold that a vision or the imagination of a just and inclusive community is a necessary part of just practice, for vision engages the affective dimension of the human person for transformation. As a result, injustice is in part a failure of imagination. The work with practitioners revealed a deep desire for a better world which inspired just actions. Christian traditions in both the Scriptures and Catholic Social Teachings are replete with eschatological visions built on justice. Some contemporary theorists of justice are beginning to articulate an awareness of the importance of imagination for the practice of justice.

Fifth, we believe that the vision of justice can provide values and principles to guide actions today. Some of the practitioners of justice found guidelines for their concrete daily choices in the vision of a better world or the endtimes city of God. The eschatological inclusion of persons who were blind, poor, and marginalized in the narratives of the Scriptures still calls for a reversal of social destinies now. In some documents of Catholic Social Teachings, the endtimes vision of the city of God is used to invite Christians to implement that vision today.

These five dimensions—theology, anthropology, sacramentality, vision, and eschatological implications for ethics—provide the framework within which we develop our understanding of justice as participation and spell out its practical demands. With this framework as well as the definition of justice as participation, we hope to make a contribution to the practice of justice and theological reflection on it.

Our framework and definition of justice emerges from those with whom and among whom we write: (1) practitioners and ministers of justice; (2) believers haunted by the gospel call to act justly; (3) persons of good will troubled by encounters with those who are homeless or abandoned by society; and (4) middle-class Christians reluctant to let go of their privileged social location. This decidedly middle-class and Christian social location out of which we write shapes our understanding of justice.

This social location presents us with four challenges vis-à-vis justice. First, what do we do about middle-class privilege? Elisabeth Schüssler Fiorenza comments, "those privileged by ordination, education, wealth, nationality, race, gender, age or sexual orientation must use their privilege to bring about change."[1] Some Christians have renounced or tried to reject privilege, while others deny that their social location includes privilege. Still, privilege remains a challenge with which middle-class Christians must struggle.

Second, although conversion to justice is a challenge for all Christians, the contours of conversion are shaped by social location. Conversion for Christians with economic power and political influence may well take the form of a call to use power for those treated unjustly. Conversion for Christians excluded from the above power may rather come as a call to devise initiatives which claim what is justly theirs. But

---

[1] Elisabeth Schüssler Fiorenza, "Equality: A Radical Democratic Ekklesial Vision," *Spirituality Justice Reprint* (November/December 1998) 1–6, esp. 3.

what does conversion look like for middle-class Christians with some voice, but with limited power and influence?

Relationships or solidarity with persons treated unjustly introduces a third challenge for middle-class Christians. Persons who have survived unjust structures and practices often do not live in middle-class neighborhoods or shop in middle-class malls or become involved in middle-class Church life. Such invisibility challenges middle-class Christians to establish relationships with survivors of injustice.

Marginality presents a fourth challenge to middle-class Christians. As persons of the middle-class we are socialized for progress up the socioeconomic ladder. Such socialization conflicts with at least some dimensions of the gospel message and with some insights emerging from feminist and womanist ethics, community organizing, social and organizational change. Insights from these fields highlight a potential for change which exists at the margins of social systems.[2] In addition, life at the margins requires persons to function both in the dominant and alternative worlds. Consequently, they are able to think beyond socially acceptable patterns and to access resources outside established paradigms. Whether middle-class Christians embrace, resist, or transform marginality, the challenge remains. Our work seeks to address these four challenges presented by middle-class Christian social location.

Chapter 1 describes and comments on situations that have come out of the experiences of the middle-class Christians who are struggling with solidarity, privilege, and downward mobility. In these instances questions arise: How can Christians respond to persons who are homeless? How can Christians move justice to the center of their faith communities? How do Christians practice just marital relationships in a society which supports men's roles as public providers and women's roles as domestic nurturers? How do Christians confront racism in their hearts and communities? What kind of economic decisions are Christians called to make?

Chapters 2 through 5 probe available Christian, Catholic, and contemporary resources. Through personal conversation, interviews, and surveys, we tapped into and analyzed the experiences of Christian practitioners and ministers of justice in Chapter 2. We analyzed their experiences for four things: (1) the practices in which persons engaged when acting on behalf of justice; (2) the connections between these practices and their beliefs about God, Jesus, and the Spirit; (3) their

---

[2] Walter Brueggemann, "The Call to Resistance," *The Other Side* 26 (November/December 1990) 44–6; 44 notes the significance of "the vision of a faith community at the margins of empire" for the courage, freedom, and imagination necessary for transformative action.

understandings of the human person; and (4) the meaning of justice which they have embraced. These practitioners described God as relational and engaged in this world. They further stressed access to basic human needs, dignity, relationships, and recognition of difference as essential for human living. They primarily understood justice as membership in the human community, as the fair distribution of resources, and as an obligation or duty emerging from their identity as Christian.

In Chapter 3, we searched the Hebrew and Christian Scriptures for the vision of a just community (Gospel of John), as well as the just practices of God and of the covenant communities (Hebrew Scriptures). The scriptural approach to justice is based on particular understandings of God and of the human person. God is always more than humans can ever imagine or hope for. God seeks ways of being in relationship with human persons and with peoples. The human person lives in a network of relationships with God, with the people they belong to, with families, and with strangers. Justice cannot be understood apart from the context of God's covenants. Thus God's inclusion of human persons, participation in human living, and invitation to share in God's own life and mission provide a framework for understanding God's justice. God's justice includes intervention on behalf of the oppressed, judgment of the oppressor (both a call to conversion and, when necessary, condemnation), and a new beginning (new creation, city of God, resurrection, messianic banquet). These understandings provide a critical resource for an adequate understanding of just practices.

We explored Catholic Social Teachings as a resource for the practice of justice in Chapter 4. The official magisterial documents provided additional insights with regard to the beliefs about God and understandings of the human person as the contexts for descriptions of justice. This analysis of justice in the documents of Catholic Social Teachings emphasizes that justice develops in response to particular situations, is rooted in a social anthropology, and begins to rely on a theological framework, including an eschatological future from which norms can be derived.

In Chapter 5, we turned to eight contemporary theories of justice from the philosophical and theological arenas which significantly impacted current thinking and practice. We posed the same ten questions to each of these contemporary contributors in an attempt to understand and analyze their contributions. In addition to Catholic Social Teachings, we analyzed Reinhold Niebuhr, John Rawls, Robert Nozick, Alasdair MacIntyre, Michael Walzer, liberation theologies, and approaches to justice as law.

Drawing on these four kinds of resources and our own insights, Chapter 6 describes the contexts which support the understanding of justice as participation in the human community. Justice as participation relies on a social anthropology, a relational God who is engaged with persons and their world, a world where materiality bears divinity and a vision of the city of God at the end of time from which norms for just practices in these times can be derived.

Chapter 7 then develops our approach to justice as participation in a community where all persons count, contribute, and participate in building up the city of God. Our approach is developed initially as a vision of a just and inclusive community, followed by a systematic articulation of seven dimensions of justice as participation. The chapter concludes by describing the values and mediating principles which flow from this approach to justice.

Chapter 8 illustrates how justice as participation can sort out some just practices that respond to the seven dilemmas with which the book began. Each of the dilemmas in the first chapter is revisited and concrete proposals for just practices are given. The point of the chapter is to show how justice as participation can be used to think through and to do justice.

The book began as a dream of collaboration in constructive theology which drew on the authors' own expertise in the Gospel of John and in Catholic Social Teachings, as well as our ministry of teaching. In this regard it is an effort to develop the relationship between the Scriptures and ethics in the specific area of justice. Within the context of our ministries, this working experiment in the relationship of the Scriptures and social ethics is not only concerned about the transformation of thinking, but also about the transformation of practices related to justice.

Our collaboration included an exchange of ideas, of experienced instances of justice and injustice, of successes and failures in teaching justice. We also were able to team-teach a course in the summer of 1995. As interactive collaborators we are mutually accountable for the content and the shape of the book. When we came to the point of writing the text, one of us wrote a section or a chapter. The other did an initial editing before we sat down together for a joint, final editing and rewriting.

Our collaboration led to our own transformation as teachers and scholars. This intra-disciplinary work changed how we view our primary discipline. Now the Gospel of John shows forth its justice dimensions and the documents of Catholic Social Teachings are situated in a Christian scriptural tradition. Our study brought home an awareness that we are not guardians of museum collections, but are accountable to today's faith and human communities. We are both challenged to become constructive theologians and not merely philologists or documentors of changes in Church teachings. Our work has highlighted the critical nature of passages which have potential to provide a future for humanity beyond the intention and words of the original authors. For these passages might be the in-breaking presence of the Indwelling Spirit today. Through our work we have become concretely convinced that the experience of Christians is a true resource for constructive theology. The wisdom of the ministers and practitioners of justice with whom we came in contact showed itself to be profound. Finally, we came to understand that our beliefs and images of God and the human persons decisively impact the Christian understanding and practice of justice.

January 15, 2001
The Feast of Dr. Martin Luther King Jr.

Contemporary Experiences of Justice

The following case studies and commentaries surface some of the dilemmas which white, middle-class Christians encounter when they try to live with an awareness of justice in their lives. These vignettes may well raise an awareness of the pervasive nature of injustice in communities and households like their own. Although many of the cases have an urban setting, the issues which they raise are not limited to urban Christianity. While the case studies raise issues of race, class, and gender, they do so primarily from the perspective of white, middle-class, Catholic Christians. These limitations come from the social location of the authors and the decision to remain as concrete and particular as possible. The authors hope that these situations and this book will encourage authors in other social locations to enter into the dialogue about the understanding and practice of justice in this world at this time.

CASE STUDY: A CHANCE ENCOUNTER

As they came out of a board meeting for a neighborhood food pantry, Mary and Julie met a couple walking in the cold March night. The couple knew Julie from the food pantry and asked if they could stay overnight in the pantry because they had been locked out of their apartment until they paid the rent and it was too cold to sleep outside. Insurance regulations prohibited overnight guests in the pantry, so Mary and Julie tried to find a place in an area shelter. There weren't any beds left in one. Another didn't take people after nine P.M. The couple had been in a third when they were locked out the last time and couldn't return for two months. Another shelter only took women and children. Both Mary and Julie considered inviting them home with them, but neither had talked to the people they lived with about such a possibility and didn't feel they could make such a decision individually. By this time the couple decided to ride the subway all night to stay warm, leaving Mary and Julie engulfed in ambiguity, guilt, and self-blame for their individual failures in responding to the gospel call of justice.

Similar stories recurred in conversations with people who questioned their responses to unjust situations: a person at a busy intersection with a sign "Will work for food"; an intoxicated man sleeping on the sidewalk in front of one's home; a woman with children begging outside the grocery store; a panhandler on the street corner selling peanuts; street musicians playing for disinterested passersby. The middle-class Christians who told these stories most typically dwelt on guilt, self-blame, and ambiguity in the face of these situations. Although guilt and self-blame may be appropriate moral responses, more often they illustrate the individualization of justice in today's world. Justice becomes an individual response to an immediate interruption of daily routine.

Individualization urges persons to interpret the inherent ambiguity of such encounters as individual responsibility for the outcome of the encounter. Thus Christians as individuals are called upon to develop their own criteria in determining how to act justly. Some attempt to judge the worthiness of those asking or of the request. Others help only women. Some give food coupons, but not money. Others have decided to support agencies, but not individuals. Still others give to persons whose story or performance moves their hearts. Some simply give a predetermined amount to the first person who asks or to a favorite group. Some stress the human encounter and so engage in conversation or share a meal in a restaurant. Whatever the criteria, as individuals they stand alone and they judge alone.

Self-blame and guilt, in turn, make it hard for individuals to ask the structural questions: Does this neighborhood need a shelter? How have citizens been socialized into fear or distrust of those different from us? Self-blame and guilt do not urge individuals to address the dilemma from a community perspective: Can social service providers work with apartment managers/owners to develop alternatives to temporary eviction? Do churches need to develop a community network to respond to temporary emergency homelessness? Without a structural and communal framework, guilt and self-blame serve to isolate and reinforce powerlessness in such situations. Such internalization of isolation and powerlessness protects the status quo from change; that is, it is in the interest of the current system that situations similar to those above are interpreted as individual invitations to do justice. As long as individuals are socialized into shouldering guilt or blame for failures, then existing structures do not have to change. As a result, middle-class Christians like Julie and Mary experience situations of injustice as a source of guilt, self-blame, and a feeling of powerlessness.

CASE STUDY: ENCOUNTERING POWERLESSNESS

Holy Family is a suburban parish comprised primarily of blue-collar and professional families with a parish staff of six ministers providing a wide range of social, educational, and religious opportunities. A group of interested parish volunteers makes up the social justice committee. The members stay involved as long as they want. Leadership roles are determined by consensus and time availability. The committee chair is not part of the finance committee or of any decision-making body of the parish. In the past year the committee has organized and sponsored some highly successful projects, including a Christmas giving tree for an inner city sister parish, a Thanksgiving dinner for the needy and lonely in the neighborhood, holiday food baskets, and a children's winter coat drive. However, a lenten speaker series on "Justice in the Scriptures and Catholic Social Teachings" averaged eight persons an evening, most of whom were committee members. Publicity about a "Justice in the Marketplace" ministry formation program brought one inquiry. A subsequent social justice committee meeting surfaced frustrations and concerns about the viability of the committee, its mission, and its place in Holy Family Parish.

The story of the social justice committee at Holy Family finds resonance in a variety of urban, suburban, and rural parishes. Social justice committees of churches typically provide informational programs on current issues to a voluntary audience, but are rarely invited to explore the ritual presence or absence of justice with the ministers responsible for Sunday worship. Social justice committees of churches typically develop limited food and clothing projects, but are rarely part of finance committee meetings when salaries or annual budgets are determined. In addition, the typical voluntary nature of such committees includes no accountability to parish staff or the parish council, as well as no mutual sharing of resources or expertise. Parish structures such as the above signal the peripheral nature of social justice to the parish mission.

Rather, social justice committees tend to be constituted as a voluntary coming together of some like-minded persons in a local church for

neighborhood outreach work. Since membership is voluntary, involvement tends to be dependent on a sense of success or accomplishment.
Frustration, disagreements, or crises typically lead to dropout or non-
involvement. Often Christians do not even expect their local churches
to provide opportunities for formation and for the practice of justice.
Rather, they turn to what John Coleman calls para-denominational
groups such as Pax Christi, Bread for the World, or Habitat for Humanity.[1] Their national profiles, paid staff, and clearly-defined goals furnish
strong competition to local church operations. This structural and voluntary constitution of social justice committees locates justice at the
margins of ecclesial and social living.

The typical agenda of social justice committees links action on behalf
of justice with specific projects for the Christmas and Easter seasons.
Such an approach reinforces an understanding of just action as an extraordinary event rather than a daily practice. In addition, the provision of
food and clothing, particularly at holiday times, easily becomes associated with benevolence and charity rather than a requirement of justice.
Furthermore, this approach allows the benevolent volunteer to maintain a protective distance. Three reasons limit the involvement of
middle-class Christians to well-circumscribed voluntary charity: (1) a
reluctance to be identified with persons at the margins of society; (2)
the fear of economic and social repercussions; and (3) an unwillingness
to confront those economic and political structures which have provided a livelihood. The interpretation of justice as "extraordinary
benevolence" further marginalizes justice from public and daily living.

This marginalization of justice is reinforced in contemporary U.S.
social arrangements connected with both volunteerism and separation
of Church and state. In the last decades political officials have called for
volunteers to meet basic human needs for those whom the system has
failed. Religious persons and Church are seen as primary providers of
such volunteers. President William J. Clinton specifically called on
churches to employ persons who were being moved off welfare.[2] When
these remarks are read in light of the official interpretation of separation of Church and state as mandated by the Constitution, we are confronted with a complex process which moves justice to the margins of
public life.

The official policy of separation of Church and state excludes the
Church from the public arena and silences the public voices of Chris-

---

[1] John Coleman, "Discipleship and Citizenship in America Today," video recording of a talk given on April 14, 1994, at Loyola University Chicago.

[2] William J. Clinton, "State of the Union Address," January 23, 1996, Washington,
D.C.

tians. This policy urges Church membership and religious beliefs as matters of voluntary decisions and private choices, that is, not part of public life. The political call for churches and their members to meet basic human needs on a volunteer basis thus moves the meeting of basic human needs out of the public arena to the private domain of Church volunteerism. The very possibility of such Church activity, however, relies on the equally voluntary decisions of people choosing how to spend resources of time and money. Consequently, meeting basic human needs becomes either a work of charity or is relegated to the margins of political life.[3]

Thus middle-class Christians today experience action on behalf of justice as a marginal or even optional activity within both their churches and the sociopolitical order. This experience is a logical outgrowth of ecclesial and public structures linking justice concerns with an extraordinary response by volunteers.

CASE STUDY: HABITS OF THE HEARTH

After some ten years of friendship and being professional colleagues, Sarah and Adam committed themselves to each other in a mutual and egalitarian marriage. Sarah and Adam had become friends while working on their doctorates in English literature. After finishing their degrees they found good positions in neighboring universities. Because their research interests overlapped, sometimes they collaborated on research and writing projects. They quickly learned that their personal commitments to a just love in their marital relationship was not enough. Even though Sarah and Adam decided to keep their birth names, marriage congratulation cards and mail came addressed to Mr. and Mrs. Adam Smith. Even Sarah's medical records ended up filed under Adam's name. Whether through socialization, practice, or personality, Sarah was an excellent cook and had an artistic sense for beauty in the home. Whether through socialization, practice, or personality, Adam's energies focused on his work. Consequently, Sarah found herself volunteering to cook when it was Adam's turn because he had a pressing deadline at work. Adam found this a precious expression of Sarah's love, to which he responded with gifts and gratitude. Casual conversation with colleagues reflected similar patterns in their relationships. Sarah's colleagues took it for granted that she would go home

---

[3] One positive dimension of such Church involvement consists in the opportunity to further blur the traditional distinction between charity in the private sphere and justice in the public sphere. In fact the reliance of federal and state governments on private and ecclesial agencies to meet basic human needs for its citizens blurs the official interpretation of the separation of Church and state.

early to take care of household affairs. Adam's colleagues expected that his wife would be the affirming presence as he worked through the emotions of professional politics and workload. Work and social contacts assumed that Adam's activities would take precedence in conflicts of date and time. Sarah was surprised when professional colleagues construed their professional collaboration as her secretarial and research assistance for Adam's ideas. Adam and Sarah's commitments to just marital love required constant vigilance and careful listening to one another's experiences in their relationship. Without these efforts, justice risked subversion by their own socialization and habits, as well as by socially expected patterns of domination, gender role expectations, and institutional structures.

Families speak of additional struggles to live justly when children are part of the network of relationships. Can parental efforts to model justice in relationships offset the socialization into patterns of domination and gender role expectations provided in children's books, on television programs, and in daycare or school? Can their mother's public roles and their father's domestic roles compensate for "Father's" public liturgical and leadership roles, especially when women's secretarial and domestic roles support "Father"? Can explicit conversations with their children about why parents opt for justice in their family relationships make a difference when the language and practice of Church and society promote patterns of injustice? Can their effort and love as a couple and family counter the patterns of domination and injustice present in the larger social order and its institutions? These questions and stories like that of Sarah and Adam surface the growing awareness that with justice issues love is not enough.

When good and well-meaning persons who seek to embody mutual, egalitarian relationships in marriage or in friendship experience both the power of and their own complicity with socialization into patterns of injustice and domination, a certain loss of innocence results. This loss of innocence invites them to abstain from a bitterness born of disillusionment and to engage the emerging truths about justice. Although love is not enough, justice is itself inherently relational and consequently requires reciprocity, mutuality, and equality in relationships, whether those relationships are personal, intimate commitments or public, standardized arrangements.

The relational nature of justice further blurs the dualism of the past which links domestic relationships with love and public alliances with justice. The blurring of these distinctions, however, also demonstrates the futility of attempting to bring about just communities through an exclusive focus on face to face relationships, while avoiding attention to social language, patterns, and structures.

The same blurring of distinctions between domestic love and public justice does not mean that resistance to domination in the name of justice is supported in the public life. Understandably the dominant culture responds to resistance aimed at its demise with massive outpourings of resources, both to maintain its patterns of injustice and to discredit the resistance efforts of individuals or groups. Social analysis, mobilizing time and personnel resources, engagement in public discourse, allowing oneself to be touched by the call for respect of another's dignity, celebrating difference, and community building are required skills if patterns of domination are to be transformed into patterns of justice.

In the midst of their efforts to create just marital and family relationships, middle-class Christians today experience that good will and love are not enough to bring about justice in either the civic or the domestic sphere, even though justice is inherently relational.

CASE STUDY: HOSPITALITY IN DIVERSITY

Bethany is a Catholic faith community in a major university. A local parish's decision to exclude lay involvement and leadership within their community birthed this group. In response to this exclusion, the group sought to become a community resisting exclusionary structures and embodying inclusion of diverse peoples.[4] The initial leadership team provided for collaborative ministries and leadership opportunities for members through a structure of volunteerism. The team itself included a diversity of persons, some of whom may well have been excluded from membership in other Catholic communities. Although the official language of the community was English with a variety of accents, efforts were made to include music and readings in the native languages of the members. In keeping with the hospitality for which the scriptural Bethany is remembered, each liturgical event was followed by a simple reception for informal community building. This initial phase of becoming a community of resistance centered on the development of structures which would facilitate inclusion and diversity. Some signs of the success of this phase were seen in the following: (1) the leadership team was comprised of ten persons from six nations and was responsible for organization, decisions, and events;

---

[4] The printed materials from this community state: "The goal of our community is to welcome people from various parts of the world who are bound together by English as a common language. We want to foster an atmosphere where people from different backgrounds and countries, people of different ages and walks of life, people affiliated with the university and people who have other affiliations can meet and experience Christian community together."

(2) community membership grew in numbers and in cultural, ethnic diversity; and (3) the per capita contributions of the community exceeded that of any other faith community in the university. But the story does not end here because an origin as a community of resistance differs from continuation as a community of resistance. The struggles to resist unjust, exclusionary practices have begun to change form. In spite of its diversity, the leadership team primarily consists of white Western persons. As a team they are committed to an inclusive, just community, but their perspective remains Western. For example, in the Western approach a structure of volunteerism affords opportunities for collaboration, inclusion, and participation. This policy, however, clashes with cultures where appointment empowers persons for service. Again in the Western perspective, potluck meals signify a coming together of equals; such an approach, however, excludes those who fear that their non-Western food is inferior and non-acceptable. These new struggles offer new opportunities to resist these more subtle exclusionary practices.

The experience of Bethany Catholic Community is not unique in the Western world. Rather, a plethora of small groups trace their origin to the resistance of an injustice. Community organizations emerge in resistance to a political decision to locate a toxic landfill in the community. Church groups arise to oppose the closing of a parish school. Ethnic initiatives counter the loss of culture and heritage. Such communities of resistance invite the broader community to engage the process of learning how different people can live together well. For the most part, however, Western culture does not have the interpretative myths or foundational paradigms to facilitate such an engagement.

Rather, the religious, political, and social paradigms of the Western world dismiss resistance because the power to define reality is at stake. The stories of persons and groups who resisted are silenced or are retold as examples of traitors. In reality, resistance does critique present social arrangements which enable persons to recognize the failures of social arrangements. Criticism of what has afforded privilege and status does not come easily to middle-class Christians.

Resisters are typically labeled crazy or different, enemy or heretic. These labels serve to discredit resistance efforts and to avoid grappling with the question of how difference and community can interact, without absorbing either into the other. Both the labels and the opposition of "difference" with "community" connect difference with individuals and community with the whole. To resist or to struggle, then, is to be outside the whole, isolated from the homogenous community. Resistance entails a loss of identity, at least the identity shaped by the interpretative myth of a harmonious community. Thus to sustain resistance and discover a new identity, persons must become members of "communities of resistance." The dominant interpretative myth, however, frustrates the formation of communities of resistance by retelling stories of resistance as tales of individuals who are different. It is no wonder then that persons find it challenging, or even impossible, to struggle against injustice in the ecclesial or social orders.

Church teachings and scriptural interpretations emphasize harmony, continuity, and compromise in an effort to obscure the struggles from which the texts arose. For example, the Gospels are typically harmonized into the one story of Jesus the Christ, rather than diverse christological statements arising out of quite different communities. The differing ethical statements on divorce in the Christian Scriptures are harmonized into a single universal norm. Catholic Social Teachings stress their continuity with previous statements by the often-erroneous introduction "as the Church has always taught" or with multiple footnotes to prior documents. Seemingly contradictory statements, for example, on the nature of the Church in the documents of Vatican Council II, are presented as the product of gracious compromise, rather than of unmitigated resistance.

Even the traditional emphasis on the oneness of God serves as a theological legitimization of harmony. Renewed interest in personal difference in Trinitarian theologies offers a counterweight to this focus on unity. But for the most part, the stories of struggle, resistance, and difference are not considered part of formation into the ecclesial communities. As a result, Christians who struggle, resist, and represent diverse points of view are unaware that they, too, have foremothers and forefathers in the Christian traditions. Without such models they are profoundly torn between faithfulness to a gospel of justice and faithfulness to traditions of harmony and conformity.

When communities of resistance begin as intentional and voluntary groupings in response to an injustice, certain transitions must be negotiated if they are to become more permanent groups. Bethany Catholic Community is beginning to look at these transitions. The initial self-interest which brought the group together must be transformed into an abiding commitment to justice for all. Hence Bethany needs to reexamine the formation of its leadership team. Similarly, communities of resistance must negotiate the transition from applauding a first success to noticing and resisting the new forms of injustice. Thus Bethany needs to turn its focus to more subtle forms of exclusion. Bethany tries to resist the dominant interpretative myth which associates superiority with Western, non-student and inferiority with non-Western, student. In becoming a congregation where difference and conflict are allowed or even encouraged, Bethany may transform hierarchy into community of diversity. Finally, Bethany's option to link itself with the University

Parish has given it a certain public presence which cannot be allowed to co-opt its resistance paradigm.

Given the above theologies of Church, models of social interpretation, and required transitions, middle-class Christians as a whole are understandably ambiguous about a move from a paradigm of harmony to a paradigm of resistance. Such a move critiques a dominant paradigm which has in fact provided some protection and privilege. The move also entails a change of identity and of interpretative myth. Identity as a resister within a community of resisters calls for new evaluations of difference. The shift from an interpretative myth founded on harmonization to one which validates struggle calls for an open-ended worldview. Ambiguity seems an accurate description of middle-class Christians with regard to action on behalf of justice.

CASE STUDY: PASSIONATE COMMUNITY

A group of young single and young married persons in their twenties meets biweekly for a meal, prayer, theological reflection, and sharing of concerns. The majority of the group spent at least a year after their undergraduate education as part of various Christian young adult volunteer programs. There they lived in community and volunteered in economically disadvantaged settings. Their volunteer experiences nurtured a longing for a just and inclusive community. Today the group struggles together about how to live simple lives. They purchase only what they need so as to provide jobs and income for the persons who are poor. They invest so that their savings can benefit persons and companies practicing justice. They support affordable housing, fair lending practices, and sustainable communities of diversity. Together they are organizing a local cooperative which buys durable chemical-free food in bulk from the producer at fair prices. In their biweekly meeting times they are consciously trying to connect their lives and just actions with the Scriptures and Catholic Social Teachings. They are trying to articulate foundations and to surface inspirations for how they live. They struggle to create images and to uncover principles which give language to the vision drawing them to its concretization. The group has found that coming together has fueled the desire for a just and inclusive community and developed real, concrete ways to live that vision already now.

This affective passion for what could be can be named a "holy passion," that is, the indwelling presence of the promised Spirit drawing believers to the just and inclusive community. Yet there is a certain discomfort about admitting one is led by passion, even if it is a holy passion. A more reasonable approach would count such longings as utopian projections of unrealizable ideals. The dismissal of a longing for community in the name of reason isolates persons and reinforces individualism. A more spiritualistic approach could recognize that the desire for justice might come from the Holy Spirit, but finds the efforts to do justice odd. The dismissal of the desire for tangible justice reinforces dualistic oppositions and reduces sacramentality to ecclesial rituals. The longings of Christians for just communities, which transform the social order, recall scriptural images like reign or city of God.

These desires are more than negative contrast experiences.[5] These longings are not only responses to suffering and injustice. They are not only exclamations that "there is something wrong with this picture." The Indwelling Spirit is both ground for the imagination of an alternative future and the power to make that future incarnate now.[6] The passionate pursuit of "what could be" may be an awareness that excessive reliance on past traditions and teachings has failed to provide motivations, principles, or models for our living today. These longings may be the invitation to look to the ever-receding eschatological horizon for adequate models, principles, and motivations.

Although middle-class Christians today may not be able to name their desires holy or link their longings to the Indwelling Spirit, the passion for justice and community makes them restless for the concrete realization of a more just community. Connecting concrete longings with religious traditions of the Spirit and the endtimes challenges both churches and Christians.

Case Study: Inviting the World Home

Angela and Peter live with their three children in a modest home which they own in a neighborhood of white-, pink-, and blue-collar families. After a lenten homily urging church members to participate in Operation Ricebowl, they start watching where the food they eat is produced and where the clothing they wear is made. Their amazement at inviting the world to the family table turns to dismay as they learn about the poverty in these same countries. Their coffee comes from Kenya, a country with an annual per capita gross domestic product of $1,200. Their bananas come from Honduras and Nicaragua, countries with annual per capita gross domestic products of $700 and $410 respectively. Their sugar comes from Haiti, a country with an annual per capita gross

---

[5] Edward Schillebeeckx, *God among Us: The Gospel Proclaimed* (New York: Crossroad, 1983) 149.

[6] Johan DeTavenier, "Eschatology and Social Ethics," *Personalist Morals: Essays in Honor of Professor Louis Janssens*, ed. Joseph A. Selling, BETL 83 (Leuven: University Press, 1988) 279–300, esp. 295–8.

domestic product of $1,000. Angela's silk blouses come from China, a country with an annual per capita gross domestic product of $494. The children's turtlenecks come from El Salvador, a country with an annual per capita gross domestic product of $1,000, and where 2 percent of the population controls 90 percent of the country's wealth. Peter's flannel shirt comes from Guatemala, a country with an annual per capita gross domestic product of $980. In her closet Angela finds a dress from Sri Lanka, where the annual per capita gross domestic product is a mere $500, and skirts from Pakistan and India, countries with annual per capita gross domestic products of only $434 and $350 respectively. Even though the family does not consider themselves well off by U.S. standards, they know that it is financially difficult to raise their family on their annual income in a country where the per capita gross domestic product is $14,420. But how can they improve these economic realities for people half a world away whom they do not know? How can they engage the struggle to end global economic injustice?

The dilemma of families in the United States profiting from depressed wages and export crops in countries of the Two-Thirds World is complex, overwhelming, and as immediate as families gathered around their dinner table. On the one hand consumer demand for inexpensive food, a variety of fruits or vegetables available year round urges grocery store chains to import food products as cheaply as possible. In the Two-Thirds World hunger is often the result of vast lands set aside for export crops. The investors who control the production and export of food focus on consumer demand in the United States, rather than provision of food needs for the Two-Thirds World.

Similarly the demand for inexpensive clothing responsive to quickly changing fashions supports the shift to overseas labor where wages are a few dollars per day and workers' unions are virtually non-existent. This shift increases unemployment in the United States for unskilled and semi-skilled workers. For example, in February 1999 Levi Strauss announced the closure of half of its plants in North America which had employed six thousand workers, due to competition from Tommy Hilfiger and J.C. Penney. The news release specifically mentioned that Levi Strauss' decision included a shift to a labor force outside of the United States. Consumer demand for inexpensive jeans contributes to the loss of jobs for workers in the United States when corporations make the option to compete for a market share by employing workers in the Two-Thirds World.

The complexity of the issue surfaces again in the effort to respond to such injustices. How can Christians disengage themselves from complicity in global economic injustices brought about by demand for available, inexpensive food products and fashionable, disposable clothing? If efforts to reduce demand for inexpensive products are too minimal, the effect may witness to the issue, but may have little impact on corporate economic policy. If efforts are too effective in reducing demand, the per capita gross domestic product in the Two-Thirds World could actually decline.

An awareness of complexity recognizes that some of the economic injustices are connected with the internal structures of countries in the Two-Thirds World. How can the United States foster efforts for sustainable food production and the creation of alternative employment? Can citizen pressure to end human rights abuses in employment actually protect the most vulnerable? Can support of worker unionization actually bring about the wages and benefits which are legitimately theirs? This complexity is heightened by the collusion of multinationals with oligarchies in the Two-Thirds World to exploit the existing system.

CASE STUDY: THE FAITH DIFFERENCE

St. Augustine's Catholic Parish resembles other urban parishes. Located in a large metropolitan area, its membership had shifted over the years from a homogenous to a heterogeneous population of European Americans, African Americans, Asian Americans, and Hispanic Americans. The transition had occurred with minimal white flight and racial hostility. Yet there were rumors that some parishioners refused to put money in the collection basket when African Americans passed it. Other parishioners would not receive from the communion cup when someone of another race drank from it ahead of them. The attitude that minorities ought to know their place surfaced when a vocal Indian American woman was labeled "obnoxious and out of line" for her contributions on the parish council, while a similarly vocal European American man was commended for his leadership. Two incidents brought existent racial tensions to the surface. Two young Hispanic men fiddling with a CD player in a car were accosted and questioned by local police officers for allegedly trying to steal the CD player. Their subsequent arrest made the headlines when it was learned later that the young men were in a car owned by a parent in front of their apartment near a local seminary that they attended. One of the police officers was a parishioner and one of the students arrested helped out in the parish religious education program. A couple of months later three teenage members of the parish were implicated in a hate crime directed toward African American students from the neighborhood school. The three young men had attended the parish elementary school and graduated from a Catholic high school in the area. After discussion, the parish Peace and Justice Committee made the following proposal to the parish council: (1) the parish council adopts a "zero tolerance" policy with regard to racial discrimination for all parish institutions and programs, and (2) through the Peace and Justice Committee, the parish collaborates with other religious groups, elected officials, and block clubs in the neighborhood in the implementation of an anti-racism education program.

Although the specific factors of racial and ethnic discrimination may vary from urban to suburban and rural neighborhoods, an overarching question remains: How do local Catholic communities respond to racism? The credibility of churches to end injustices has roots in a long historical tradition of meeting basic human needs. Yet some of this credibility has been tarnished through practices and teachings which allowed for slavery and segregation. Are specific instances of racial discrimination the sinful choices of individuals for which the local Catholic community cannot be held accountable? Is the local Catholic community's mission exclusively to its membership or to the broader neighborhood in which they are located?

In addition to these questions, the parish discussion brought racist social attitudes to the fore which shocked even the council members who caught themselves admitting a twinge of fear as they rode public transportation or ate in neighborhood ethnic restaurants where white persons were clearly a minority. They acknowledged that they locked their car doors in certain blocks of the neighborhood. They lamented that the old buildings and yards just didn't look the same once "those people" started moving in. They were amazed at their own deep worry that their children's friendships with classmates of other ethnic backgrounds might develop into a dating relationship. The council struggled to make sense of these racist attitudes co-existing with the desire to build just and inclusive Christian communities.

Furthermore, the proposal's response to racism would require collaboration with political officials, with ecumenical and interfaith representatives, and with school boards. Such collaboration would not be easy. Political players tend to be wary of churches getting involved in so-called secular affairs. Separation of Church and state, as it is currently understood, and uncompromising religious righteousness contribute to this state of affairs. The residue of "making converts" and the language of the "only true Church" still linger in the minds of other religious bodies. Some faith traditions and Christian denominations intentionally focus on the needs of their own membership in preference to interfaith, ecumenical, and social collaboration. Underneath these realities rests the theoretical question: Can differing traditions cooperate on common issues without attention to the differing beliefs and values connected to the common issue?

On top of all these issues, the parish council seemed overwhelmed with existing ministries, education, and building maintenance needs in a time of decreasing financial and membership resources. Does parish survival take precedence over a politically and socially charged issue like racism? Furthermore, while individual council and parish members may be drawn to social and political involvement, they feel themselves restrained by the knowledge that the parish as a whole is divided on questions like: Is racism really incompatible with the Christian faith? Would the proposed education and policy strategies actually make a difference? How does a local Catholic community respond to racism in its midst and in its neighborhood?

Concluding Themes and Issues

A number of themes and issues related to the practice of justice emerge from the above situations and commentaries:

- Guilt and self-blame reflect efforts to relegate justice to the response, choice, or action of individuals.

- Social structures, volunteerism, and the justice agenda positions action on behalf of justice at the margins of Western society.

- Although justice is inherently linked to relationships, love is not enough.

- Justice is about resisting injustice, i.e., moving from a worldview of harmony and conformity to a worldview which encourages resistance and struggle. People are ambiguous and challenged by such a change of worldview.

- The longing and desire for just communities reflects the potential of the eschatological horizon to both inspire and enable the building of just communities here and now.

- Personal economic decisions cannot be separated from global economic injustice.

- Social injustices challenge local faith communities to find ways to address issues of racism, classism, and sexism in keeping with their religious traditions, their social context, and their interdependence with other religious and social bodies.

In the final chapter of this book, we will return to the issues which these dilemmas raise, after having explored the understandings and practices of justice in current experience (Chapter 2), in the Jewish and Christian Scriptures (Chapter 3), in Catholic Social Teachings (Chapter 4), and in contemporary theories of justice (Chapter 5). Chapters 6 and 7 set forth our resulting theological framework and understanding of justice, before we return in Chapter 8 to the practice of justice which these situations and issues generate.

The Experience of Ministers and Practitioners of Justice

Ministers and practitioners of justice call upon a variety of resources in determining a just response to the dilemmas posed in the previous chapter. This chapter explores images of God, the understandings of the human person, and the operative notions of justice which ministers and practitioners highlighted as central to their activity on behalf of justice. This exploration is based on an analysis of survey responses from fifty-one persons[1] engaged in justice activity in the Archdiocese of Chicago, in the Diocese of Joliet, and in ministry education at the Institute of Pastoral Studies, Loyola University Chicago.

The survey was comprised of five open-ended questions, six descriptive statements about God, five descriptive statements about the human person, and six descriptions of justice. The open-ended questions asked respondents to delineate their justice activities, talk about why they were involved, how God fit into the picture, and what they had come to believe about the human person. The descriptive statements will be treated in later sections of this chapter.

---

[1] We recognize that the sample of respondents is small and geographically similar. Yet it does represent the face of ministers and practitioners of justice in the Roman Catholic Church of the greater Chicago area. Additional research with specific focus on other geographic areas, rural or small city dioceses, as well as other ethnic and racial Roman Catholics would benefit this study.

A PORTRAIT OF THE SURVEY RESPONDENTS

Over 90 percent of the respondents were ethnically European American, Roman Catholic by denomination, and socioeconomically middle class. An almost equal number of women (twenty-seven) and men (twenty-four) completed the survey.

In articulating their motivation for engagement in justice activities, 35 percent (eighteen) of the survey respondents referred to areas connected with personal integrity. For instance: "I can't not do what I do"; "I find it imperative to link behavior and beliefs"; "I cannot say that I am a follower of Jesus if I do not act on my beliefs"; "They make me who I am . . . these are constitutive to who I am"; "I can more easily live with myself if I attempt to live according to my ideals." Twenty percent (ten) of the survey respondents[2] described their justice activities as providing meaning, purpose, or an integrated wholeness for their lives.

Fifty-nine percent (thirty) of the respondents explained their engagement as at least partially inspired by their emotional response to injustice or by a heartfelt desire for a more just world. The injustices which persons experienced surfaced feelings of anger, frustration, outrage, revenge, guilt, empathy, or compassion. The experience of injustice left others "disturbed" or "personally troubled." Some respondents also were led by a desire, heart-knowledge, or a sense of fairness which inspired action on behalf of justice. Still others felt satisfied, good, and rewarded by their work. The importance of an emotional engagement was perhaps best summarized by a community organizer who found that persons with strong feelings including anger about injustice were the best leaders because intellectual conviction complemented by emotional investment sustained persons for the long haul.

Forty-five percent (twenty-three) of the respondents did refer to reason or intellectual convictions as a source of their motivation. A couple of respondents called justice activities the rationally correct or the right thing to do. Others specifically mentioned some of their intellectual convictions which motivated their activities, such as the dignity of the human person, the equality of all, a need for the redistribution of resources, the family of God, service, God as Creator of all, and stewardship. The sources of intellectual convictions or beliefs included the teachings of Jesus and God as well as the Scriptures, Church teachings in general, Catholic Social Teachings, and contemporary writings.

Virtually all the respondents explicitly linked their motivation for activities on behalf of justice to their experience. Sometimes that experience was the source of motivating emotions or intellectual convic-

---

[2] Three of these ten also used the language of integrity to describe their motivation for justice action.

tions or a meaningful worldview. Occupations with persons who are treated unjustly, encounters with persons who were disadvantaged by social systems, personal experiences of injustice, or the realities of poverty, racism, and sexism were the most frequently mentioned experiences which inspired action on behalf of justice. Nine persons mentioned the awareness of their gifts and blessings as a motivation to share these gifts and blessings with others. Family upbringing, education, personal and communal prayer were also regularly mentioned. Several respondents described the impact of an extraordinary event such as the birth of a differently-abled child, a talk, or a book on their transformation. These survey results suggest that the call to justice has a basis in personal experience, although that experience is further interpreted through intellectual convictions or through heartfelt responses or through the search for integrity and purpose.

The activities on behalf of justice in which the survey respondents engaged were diverse. Some persons were employed full-time in social justice work, while others worked as volunteers. Some persons have spent their lives in social justice arenas, while others have become involved more recently. Their activities comprised six general areas with many persons working in more than one area. The six areas identified are systemic and structural change (twenty-nine), direct service (twenty-two), networking (twenty-one), education (sixteen), witness (eleven), and lifestyle (nine).

Systemic and structural change activities include community organizing actions (thirteen) such as social analysis, leadership development, mobilizing grass roots groups, and designing change. Other practitioners influenced the political system (eleven) through letters, lobbying, phone calls, attending meetings, establishing legislative networks, and proposing action plans to political players. Other activists described their action as advocacy (nine) for a wide variety of underrepresented groups. Six mentioned economic change through socially responsible investment, direct marketing of Two-Thirds World products at just prices, and Campaign for Human Development projects. Twelve served on boards of parish or diocesan justice groups as well as church or not-for-profit direct service providers. Other individuals prosecuted institutions engaged in unjust practices or designed public systems or worked to bring about the closure of the School of the Americas.

Direct service activities included meeting basic human needs (eighteen) such as food, clothing, shelter, health care, literacy, or special projects like the Catholic Construction Corps. Although much of the direct service activities took place locally, some took place internationally. Some of the practitioners were engaged in creating possibilities of direct service through fund raising (two), grant-writing (two), sharing personal resources, or organizing service opportunities (three) for others. Other justice ministers engaged in the ministry of hospitality (five) with persons who were imprisoned, homeless, refugees, or poor.

About half of the survey respondents understood networking and convening groups as part of their cultivation of justice. Sometimes the networking was with (inter)national groups such as Campaign for Human Development, Bread for the World, Pax Christi, or Eighth Day Center for Justice. Sometimes the networking was with a sister parish, other parishes, churches, or organizations. Other times groups were convened to address a social issue or work together toward a goal. Some justice activists saw their work as linking persons to needed services or building long-term partnerships to address issues of common concern. Others deliberately fostered the inclusion of persons underrepresented on the basis of some "difference" in culture, race, or class. Still others mentioned the intentional effort of networking behind decision-making processes.

Education activities on behalf of justice encompassed making information available (two), consciousness-raising (five), presentations on issues (two), and teaching (three) in parish, school, religious education, or teacher training settings. Other activists (seven) spoke of the need to form their own social conscience and educate themselves or their families about the requirements of justice.

Justice practitioners described their action as witness in presence, words, or deeds (five). Some more specifically mentioned denouncing evil contrary to the gospel (two) and speaking the truth of unjust structures (three). Others spoke of demonstrations, civil disobedience, or resistance (five). The final group of justice practitioners spoke of doing justice in and through their daily living by being fair to those with whom they came in contact (two), by living low on the consumer chain (three), and by their choice and practice of work (three).

Before exploring the images of God and the understandings of the human person which this diverse group of ministers and practitioners highlighted as central to their activity on behalf of justice, we will contextualize these survey responses in previous research on the connections between social activism and images of God. The next chapters assess the Scriptures and the documents of Catholic Social Teachings for their potential to nurture and resource the understandings of God and the human person which emerged from the survey results.

IMAGES OF GOD AND JUSTICE IN PREVIOUS RESEARCH

A number of theologians and sociologists of religion have asked questions about the relationship between people's images of God and their involvement in social justice concerns. Their research has demonstrated that certain images of God foster engagement in social justice concerns.

Marie Augusta Neal, a sociologist of religion, did three studies between 1965 and 1975. Her first study focused on the response of local ministers in Little Rock, Arkansas, to the mandate from their national church organizations to integrate schools. Since the national church positions highlighted the sinfulness of segregation, the research team hypothesized that socially and financially secure ministers with relatively permanent appointments would support the national church mandate for integration. The results of the study, however, showed that these ministers tended to be the most resistant to integration. But other ministers without such security risked their future careers by supporting the local integration effort. Not the security of the minister, but rather the image of God preached in the churches was the determining factor for the local integration effort.[3]

In the aftermath of Vatican II's call to act on behalf of justice, Neal studied the beliefs and behaviors of the priests of the Archdiocese of Boston in the wake of pressure to support causes which violated the principles of social justice. Neal learned that the understanding of God was the most significant predictor of action for social justice. When the priests experienced God as immanent, involved in the world, and acting through people, they supported action for social justice. However, when God was experienced as remote, outside the world, and lording it over people, then the priests resisted social justice causes.[4]

In a third survey sent to 80 percent of the congregations of women religious, Neal studied the relationship between religious belief and social change.[5] Two distinct belief orientations were demonstrated which Neal called pre-Vatican themes and post-Vatican themes. The pre-Vatican orientation understood God as other-worldly and remote or in family terms. God was experienced as calling people out of the world into designated sacred places and away from potential contamination of social issues to an afterlife of salvation. The post-Vatican orientation understood God as active in history, through people and in

---

[3] See Marie Augusta Neal, "Social Justice and the Right to Use Power," *Journal for the Scientific Study of Religion* 23 (1984) 329–40. See also Thomas Pettigrew and Ernest Campbell, *Christians in Racial Crisis* (Washington, D.C.: Public Affairs Press, 1959).

[4] Neal, "Social Justice," 330. See also Marie Augusta Neal, *Values and Interests in Social Change* (Englewood Cliffs, N.J.: Prentice-Hall, 1965).

[5] Marie Augusta Neal, "Part II. The Relation Between Religious Belief and Structural Change in Religious Orders: Some Evidence," *Review of Religious Research* 12 (1971) 153–64.

ever new ways. God was encountered in the protest against evil, in the building of just structures, in risk-taking, and in working with people for the transformation of the world. Based on these survey results, Neal concluded that the post-Vatican belief orientation supported actions of social change and structural transformation. Living and working with persons who shared this belief orientation further facilitated social activism.

Adair Lummis and Allison Stokes surveyed 3,746 women to determine the relationship between a personal feminist spirituality and involvement in social justice activities.[6] The authors concluded that the more women espouse a feminist spirituality, the more they tended to be active in social justice concerns. Similar to Neal, Lummis and Stokes learned that, when feminist spiritual orientation included membership in supportive spirituality or action groups, social justice activism was further facilitated and increased.

Yet another sociologist of religion, Andrew Greeley,[7] asked Catholics to locate themselves on a seven-point continuum for four pairs of possible images for God: (1) father/mother, (2) master/spouse, (3) judge/lover, and (4) king/friend. The resulting score was a more accurate indicator of social and political positions than age, sex, or geographic location. The more the score tended toward the relational images of God as mother, spouse, lover, or friend, the more likely the respondent voted democratic, opposed capital punishment, supported civil liberties, advocated government aid for minorities, favored neighborhood integration, and promoted the participation of women in economic and political arenas.

Systematic theologian Kathryn Tanner raises the question of which images of God can and do support a Christian social ethic.[8] She holds that Christian belief in a transcendent God and in God's continuing creating presence in the world (providential agency) urges social change. She explains that belief in God as transcendent legitimates Christian suspicion of social, political, or economic orders which claim to be unalterable as well as of any human institution which identifies itself as God. Belief in God's continuing presence legitimates Christian suspi-

---

[6] Adair Lummis and Allison Stokes, "Catholic Feminist Spirituality and Social Justice Action," *Research in the Social Scientific Study of Religion* 6 (1994) 103–38. Lummis and Stokes describe feminist spirituality as the embrace of divine attributes typically connected with women (compassion, loving) and of womanly images for God (mother, midwife).

[7] Andrew Greeley, *The Catholic Myth: The Behavior and Beliefs of American Catholics* (New York: Scribner, 1990) 41–3.

[8] Kathryn Tanner, *The Politics of God: Christian Theologies and Social Justice* (Minneapolis: Fortress Press, 1992).

cion of attitudes which decry social, political, or economic orders as unredeemable or completely devoid of any possibility for encounter with the divine. Tanner additionally maintains that God's transcendence and providential agency support universal community as well as equal regard and respect for others. Consequently, these images of God challenge social systems based on fixed hierarchies with superiors and inferiors, on relationships of exploitation or domination, or on intolerance toward others.

Another theologian, Charles Davis, laments the exclusive identification of religion and spirituality with the interior life which has resulted from modern individualism and the separation of Church and state.[9] Rather, God's transcendence can be encountered in and through knowledge of the external world or cosmos, in the political, social, and economic creation of cultural meaning and values, and in the inner world of integration, interiority, and self-awareness. Consequently, Davis urges believers to expect and anticipate encounter with God in objective reality, cultural meaning, and interiority.

The above sociological and theological research demonstrates that beliefs and images of God impact Christian ethics including action on behalf of social justice. This research has arrived at the conclusion that images of God as remote, outside the world, and acting over people obscure the call to change the world's unjust structures and practices. Images of God as immanent, involved in the world, and acting through people foster transformation of unjust structures and engagement in the social order.

IMAGES OF GOD AND JUSTICE IN THE VOICES OF PRACTITIONERS OF JUSTICE

Against the backdrop of the above research, this section examines the images of God which move and inspire Catholics who are actually engaged in the works of justice. We turn to survey responses concerning the questions about their beliefs and the images of God in connection with their action on behalf of justice.[10] Eighty-four percent

---

[9] Charles Davis, "From Inwardness to Social Action: A Shift in the Locus of Religious Experience," *New Blackfriars* 67 (1986) 114–25.

[10] This part of the survey consisted of six descriptions of God which we developed on the basis of conversations and discussions with practitioners and ministers of justice over the years. The respondents were asked how these descriptions resonated with their own experience and spirituality on a scale of 1 to 5. They rated the images as follows: 1 = mostly untrue; 2 = somewhat untrue; 3 = somewhat true; 4 = generally true; 5 = definitely true.

(forty-three) of the respondents referred to God in their replies. Half of these responses used God as a name with no further explanation, or as part of an expression, such as kingdom/reign/city of God or family/children of God. Most frequent among the remaining descriptions were Creator God (seven), God as Love (six), God as Mercy and Compassion (four), and God as Abba/Prodigal Parent (three).[11] Noticeably absent were references to images of God as Father, as Omnipotent, or as Almighty. The God whom ministers and practitioners know is a God capable of relationships.

Fifty-nine percent (thirty) of the respondents referred to Jesus in their answers. Two-thirds of these used Jesus as a name with no further comment or as part of a predetermined expression, such as the teachings, mission, ministry, example, message, or disciple of Jesus. The name Jesus was preferred to Jesus Christ (two) or Lord (one), although four respondents referred to both Jesus and Christ on separate occasions. The few remaining descriptions of who Jesus was were singular.[12] The Jesus whom the ministers and practitioners of justice know is the Jesus whose ministry and mission took place in this historical world and was recorded in the Gospels. The practitioners of justice noted Jesus' passion for human persons, Jesus' relationships and human experiences, including suffering. Christological statements and "Son of God" understandings seem to have little influence.

In replies to the questions, five respondents referred to the Spirit as one who directed and guided their actions or as the source of encouragement, desire, inspiration, and opportunities. In the words of one practitioner: "My primary image of God is of the Holy Spirit dwelling within each person. Because of the Spirit within, every person deserves to live in dignity. Thus we are called to create a society and world where that is possible." An additional five respondents attributed characteristics to God which are traditionally associated with the Spirit, namely, Energy, Guide, Power, and Indwelling Instinct. Although Spirit language is noticeably infrequent from the survey responses, the roles associated with the Spirit are mainstream Catholic teachings.

In addition to these general comments, the survey sought specific assessment of six images of God which had emerged from informal

---

[11] Lord God and a Just God were mentioned twice. Mystery, Source, Companion on the Journey, and Guide were each mentioned once.

[12] Two respondents spoke of Jesus' love for them. One described Jesus as the Good Shepherd and a Wounded Healer. One described Jesus as the "embodiment of human potential and challenge." Another described Luke 4 as presenting Jesus as an "author of his own life and of a new society," when he stood up and dared to assume authority for his vision of a different way where captives are free and the poor have the Good News preached to them.

conversations and discussions with ministers and practitioners of justice. The survey asked participants to rate on a scale of 1 to 5 the degree to which each of the six descriptions of God held true for them in their action on behalf of justice. In addition to the rating, we also probed the written responses for evidence of these images in their own words and experience. All the descriptions were assessed in the range of "generally true" by the justice practitioners.[13]

God as Transformative Action[14] received the highest composite rating of 4.36 with a standard deviation[15] of 0.8980. In addition, 51 percent (twenty-six) of the survey respondents spontaneously described God in ways reflective of this image. They explicitly recognized that human activities, especially collective efforts, can transform injustice into a more just social order (six). The survey respondents linked their transformative activities to the Scriptures in which Jesus transformed the typical patterns of his time and culture. For example, Jesus' proclamation at Nazareth (Luke 4) and the Sermon on the Mount (Matthew 5) turned upside down the dominant religious expectations. The miracle at Cana (John 2) altered the distribution of resources. In addition, these ministers expected that God continues to hear the cry of the poor and to raise up prophets to respond to their needs.

These ministers and practitioners of justice spoke of their actions on behalf of justice as a participation in building the city of God here (six) or as participation in God's own ongoing creation (four). They spoke of participating in Jesus' transformation, healing, liberation, or historical project as described in the Gospels (five). Throughout these responses a sense of mutual responsibility and accountability from both divine and human persons was apparent.

God as a Longing for the Dream[16] tallied a composite score of 4.18 (std. 1.1008). Thirty-nine percent (twenty) of the survey respondents talked

---

[13] The scores ranged from 3.55 to 4.33. As we will see later in this chapter, these composite scores are somewhat lower than the composite scores for authentic human living and descriptions of justice.

[14] In the survey the description of this image of God read as follows: "Some ministers and practitioners of justice experience their own work on behalf of justice as a participation in God's own creating, liberating and transforming activities. They speak of their justice activities as 'doing what Jesus would have done,' as 'making God present' or as 'God's gracious intervention in the lives of others.' They recognize that human activities can be transformative."

[15] The standard deviation shows the range of diversity within the responses. The larger the standard deviation, the more diversity exists in the responses.

[16] In the survey the description of this image of God read as follows: "Some ministers and practitioners of justice may name their dream the reign of God or a better world. The names convey the sense that the longing for this dream is fundamental, sustaining in the dark days and somehow stretches beyond their own creation. The

about the dream which inspired their activities on behalf of justice. Most frequently (thirteen) this dream was identified with images drawn from the Scriptures: the city or reign of God (six), the vision of the prophets and Gospels, the worldview of the Beatitudes, the egalitarian community who breaks bread and washes one another's feet, Jesus' proclamation at Nazareth (Luke 4), feeding the lambs and tending the sheep (John 21), and unity in God (John 17). In the words of one respondent:

> I am called to make life holy and whole for those oppressed by injustices. I know in my heart, soul, and mind that we must redistribute the earth's goods, give power to the powerless, and access ways to bring life to those who are dying. I am called to communicate hope and imagination. . . . I believe God still hears the cry of the poor and raises up prophets and enables ordinary people to respond, take risks, and act courageously.

Others spoke of a vision of a better world without injustice or a world "in which there are no marginated and all are one" (six). Or, in another's words, "Mostly I think God was there as part of the same voice that drew me to the job. It was a voice that always pointed out how things could be better. It was a voice that I think still calls me to work for ethics and social justice." Although often the content of the scriptural vision of the better world was not specified, the following characteristics were specifically mentioned: love (three), justice (three), equality (two), solidarity (two), unity (two), mutuality (one), hospitality (one), nonviolence (one), and fairness (one).

God as Reciprocal Relationality[17] scored a composite rating of 3.92 (std. 0.9441). In their comments to open-ended questions, 50 percent (twenty-five) of the survey respondents described their relationship with God, including Jesus or the Spirit, as connected with their activities on behalf of justice. Their own personal relationship with God as well as God's "intimate relationship with the world and its people"

---

longing emerges from outrage at injustices or from an abiding hope which remains in spite of frustrated efforts or bone-deep tiredness. Their longing for the dream keeps them and their lives open to a future which changes how they live today."

[17] In the survey the description of this image of God read as follows: "Some practitioners and ministers of justice concretely identify encounters with God or the Divine in their relationships with others. These relationships include meeting and working with others whose social location and experiences are very different from their own; they include long-term relationships with kindred spirits similarly engaged in action on behalf of justice. God is encountered in working through misunderstandings and in confronting unilateral decision-making as well as in friendship and shared successes."

called them to justice, supported their actions on behalf of justice, and showed them how to love and do justice with and for the oppressed and marginalized. The images which were used to describe their relationships with God highlighted intimacy and love of others (fourteen). God is like the womb which nourishes a growing, separate child. God is like the Good Shepherd whose unconditional love makes love of others possible. God is like a caring parent whose generous love shows how others ought to be treated. These practitioners of justice with a single exception talked about God's love as including love of others. These relationships with God were also described as reciprocal and mutually engaging (seven). One respondent described God as a Companion on the Journey: "Together we have talked about the meaning of life, walked in ghettos, South American Barrios and Haitian Villages. We have asked people to give of their time, talents and resources to better life for others. We challenge each other with the whys of life often." In the words of another respondent, "my relationship with God is beyond passive."

These ministers of justice explicitly identified the doing of justice as a dimension of their relationship with God (seven). "When I see God as love, I know that I am called to be love where that love is often suppressed and struggles to survive. That love calls me to a mutuality, solidarity and a dream of equality." "My activity on behalf of justice is an outgrowth of my relationship with God. To follow Jesus is to follow both the person and the historical project of Jesus which is the reign of God, i.e., justice-making." "Without this relationship I would not see injustice, nor feel compassion to serve, nor have the strength and authority to do action." "I feel loved by God and I need to give that love to others to be part of bringing about God's kingdom on earth." For a couple of respondents, justice was defined in terms of right relationships.

The image of *God as Gracious Resistance*[18] also received a composite score of 3.8 (std. 1.142). Only about 25 percent of the respondents (thirteen) in their own comments described God in terms of gracious resistance. These comments linked justice with the need to resist poverty, overconsumption, racism, classism, exploitation, violence, slavery,

[18] In the survey the description of this image of God read as follows: "Some ministers and practitioners of justice experience God in their resistance to patterns of injustice, particularly when they stand with the marginalized against economic, political or social powers. Divine assistance and strength makes it possible to confront such powers. They understand their resistance to injustice as taking up God's work in the world or continuing God's preferential option for the poor. In the face of systemic complexity and easy conformity, they experience God as the source of their consistent, gracious resistance."

ignorance, prejudice, unfairness, inequality, and institutional disregard of human dignity. Persons like Nelson Mandela and Mahatma Gandhi were held up as models of resistance. The stories of Jesus banishing the moneychangers from the Temple and of the proclamation in Nazareth were noted as examples of Jesus' resistance of the evils of that century. Although God as Gracious Resistance was recognized as a viable image of God, these practitioners of justice spontaneously made fewer links to this image on the basis of their experiences of God.

God as a Call to Conversion[19] received a composite score of 3.76 (std. 1.1349). Fifty-one percent (twenty-six) of the survey respondents described God in terms reflective of this image in their own comments on the questions provided. On the basis of the survey responses, practitioners of justice understood their justice activities as a response to a God-given call (sixteen): "As a child I heard about priests and nuns being called, having a vocation. This is my vocation: I have unswerving strength when it comes to standing up for those whom I sense are at a disadvantage." These same respondents encountered their vocational call in personal experiences, the Scriptures, Catholic Social Teachings, in baptism and confirmation, through a desire or haunting images.

These ministers of justice understood their call as a call to conversion (sixteen), although they tended to speak of a challenge or of the call to change, to see differently, to make a better world, and to act justly. For some respondents the call was not yet completely clear: "I continue to wait." Other respondents articulated a more specific content to their calls: "I am called to be with poor, marginalized people." Another wrote:

> As a Christian I have been called to look beyond my own self-interest and to view all people as children of God and precious to God. If I have been given access to power, privilege and resources, I am called to use them for the building of God's kingdom on earth.

One of the respondents spoke of the birth of her differently-abled daughter:

> I promised God that moment that I would teach my child to live her life with dignity and courage. I also realized then that if I wanted this for my

---

[19] In the survey the description of this image of God read as follows: "Some practitioners and ministers of justice experience God as a multi-faceted Call to Conversion away from all those personal and communal patterns or attitudes which prevent the in-breaking of justice. God is named the grace which breaks down personal complicity with injustice. God is experienced as the call to turn away from trust in superpowers to reliance on the little people. God is experienced as the call to avoid exploitation, injustice and exclusivity in order to build just communities."

baby, then I could not allow ignorance or prejudice to be in my heart about other people, not just little people, but all people. This was a promise, but also a challenge.

Practitioners of justice, then, do understand activities on behalf of justice as a call; they have encountered the call in a wide variety of situations.

The image of *God as Performative Ritual*[20] received the lowest composite score: 3.50 (std. 0.9529), even though less than two-tenths of a point separated it from the previous image. The comments in response to the open-ended questions provided virtually no consciousness of God's presence or activity in enacted communal ritual. One respondent noted, "If people are thirsty, it diminishes my baptism. If people are hungry, it diminishes the Eucharist." Another spoke of footwashing as "excellent symbolism for people ministering in peace and social justice." The apparent absence of God as Performative Ritual surfaces several questions: Does this image of God not emerge from the experience of ministers and practitioners of justice? Does individualism have such a strong hold on Catholicism in the United States that communal celebrations can no longer represent the presence of God? Has the experience of mechanized rituals conditioned believers to expect little meaning in them? Or has action on behalf of justice become marginalized from the communal celebrations associated with Roman Catholicism?

Even though communally enacted ritual was not articulated as an experience of God, the survey responses did demonstrate a strong awareness of the sacramentality of the world and of an incarnate God, which provide the foundation for communal ritual enactment. Sixty-seven percent (thirty-four) of the respondents articulated a clear sense of a God incarnate in this world and its people. This awareness was rooted in a Creator God who made human persons in God's own image and likeness and in the scriptural identification of God with neighbor (see Matt 25:31-46). As a result human persons need to be treated with dignity and whatsoever they do to their neighbor, they do to Christ.

[20] In the survey the description of this image of God read as follows: "Some practitioners and ministers of justice call ritual actions an experience of God's Justice. They experience the Justice of God in programs marking anniversaries of Hiroshima; or in candle light vigils remembering persons killed in violent crimes; or in non-violent gatherings calling for an end to racism; or in contemporary stations of the cross; or in Eucharistic liturgies recognizing Dr. Martin Luther King, Jr.; or in walks raising money for food pantries. Singing songs together forges common dreams; aesthetic beauty moves hearts to conversion; telling the stories of survivors fashions courage for collective action; marching together transforms isolation into community."

In addition, God was explicitly identified with the unjustly treated (the hungry, poor, immigrants, American Indians, etc.) as a call to do justice. God was also identified with persons who practiced justice, especially political leaders—Mahatma Gandhi, Martin Luther King, Dorothy Day, Edwina Gately, Desmond Tutu, Nelson Mandela, Oscar Romero, and even the bishop in Victor Hugo's *Les Misérables*. Also mentioned, albeit less frequently, were recognitions of God's incarnate presence in the very practice of justice, in the coming together as community as well as in colleagues and co-workers. These ministers of justice also understood that they, too, were the incarnate love of God and the healing hands of Jesus in this world. Thus it seems that practitioners of justice are acutely sensitive to a sacramental world and an incarnate God, but do not spontaneously link this sensitivity to communal rituals.

The survey results thus far seem to coincide with the results described in the previous section of this chapter: relational and engaged images of God call believers to action on behalf of justice. In order to follow up on the theories of this previous section, the open-ended answers were examined for evidences of a distant and disengaged God. Some of the practitioners spoke of their actions on behalf of justice as doing God's will or finding their place in God's plan (ten) or following the teachings of the Church (two), the Scriptures (six), or Jesus (five). Other ministers spoke of justice as a duty or obligation (seven); however, the source of the obligation was frequently not a distant Plan of God or abstract teachings. Rather, the obligation emerged from family upbringing, the unmet needs of people, the desire for integrity as a Christian disciple, or from personal blessings and gifts.[21]

A small number of respondents (five to six) seemed to prefer more distant and disengaged images of God. For example, "God created the nature of things according to infinite and eternal Wisdom. I seek to know the nature and needs of others. I do what I find to be my place in this schema of things." "I am only trying to save my soul. Most people don't understand that what I do has much less to do with the rest of the world, than it does with my desire to be in relationship with God." A couple of respondents described themselves as instruments or tools for God's plan. Another prefaced a description of the Indwelling Spirit with this contrasting image of a distant God:

---

[21] An obligation to give to others arising from an abundance of gifts and blessings can have a different meaning than the obligation arising from other's unmet needs. The first could be motivated by charity, while that latter could be motivated by justice. The first could be individual, while the latter could be structural. Consequently the first could be paternalistic care, while the latter could be a grassroots claim from those in need. The surveys offer too little information to make a judgment.

> My image of God is of a very distant being, not very involved in or aware of the nitty-gritty of the world. I see God as just having a general sense of whether things in the world are balanced more on the just or more on the unjust side. I have the sense that my image isn't very accurate because the faith-filled people I talk to see God as very involved and personal.

Although about 10 percent of the respondents seemed to know a distant and disengaged God as the source of their activities on behalf of justice, the majority of the respondents described an incarnate God in intimate relationship with people whose activities were God's own continuing works of creation, liberation, and transformation into the city of God. The ministers of justice experienced their call to engage in justice-making and to resist injustice as well as their vision of a just world as God-given.[22] Although this research seems to confirm the research findings in the previous section, further study of the images of God in the lives of persons who are not engaged in action on behalf of justice could be helpful.

AUTHENTIC HUMAN LIVING AND JUSTICE IN THE VOICES OF PRACTITIONERS OF JUSTICE

This section examines the understanding of authentic human living[23] which emerged from the activities on behalf of justice as described by the above survey respondents. The questions invited them to narrate their convictions about authentic human living as well as to evaluate the accuracy of five summary dimensions of authentic human living from their experience of engagement in just action.[24] The summary

---

[22] Comparisons of the images of God with specific understandings of justice, however, showed no correlation. For instance, those who ranked God as reciprocal relationality did not necessarily give a similar ranking to justice as membership in the human community.

[23] We use the term "authentic human living" to refer to an adequate anthropology. See the section in Chapter 6 entitled "An Anthropological Context for an Ethic of Justice as Participation" for a full description of our understanding of the term.

[24] The scale is as follows: 1 = mostly untrue; 2 = somewhat untrue; 3 = somewhat true; 4 = generally true; 5 = definitely true. The five dimensions were rated as "generally true" or "definitely true," with those numbers given at the beginning of each paragraph. The analysis of the responses to the open-ended question ("Describe what you have come to believe about human persons or about authentic human living through your activities on behalf of justice") provides the basis for the description of each dimension. The description, which the respondents rated, appears in the footnote.

dimensions were assessed as an accurate expression of the understandings of authentic human living as held by the justice practitioners.[25]

These survey respondents rated highest (4.60; std. 0.8061) access to what is needed to meet *basic needs*[26] as an essential dimension for authentic human living.[27] In addition to food, shelter, health care, clothing, education, and employment, the practitioners named love, compassion, respect, and self-determination as basic human needs. They described access to basic human needs as a human right and included the right to organize and to participate in decision-making.

Dignity[28] was also widely recognized (4.58; std. 0.7309) as an essential dimension of authentic human living. These faith-based practitioners connected dignity with creation in the image and likeness of God, with the Indwelling God or with the human longing to see God's image in human likeness. Human dignity and worth must, however, be recognized by others, be experienced by the person, and be protected by social structures. The personal experience of self-worth emerges from recognition and fair treatment by others. The works of justice were called the recognition of the dignity of those who were poor or marginated.

Practitioners and ministers of justice spoke about *difference and diversity* (4.4; std. 0.8081) as part of authentic human living.[29] Sometimes differences were viewed as "fragments of God's beauty" and other times as confusing complexities. Differences emerged between persons, but also across time and space. For example, difference was mentioned to explain personal and communal changes over time and to address the

---

[25] The composite scores ranged from 4.16 to 4.61.

[26] In this book the expression "access to basic human needs" is used as a short form to refer to "access to what is needed to meet basic human needs."

[27] Basic human needs were described as follows: "Ministers and practitioners of justice insisted that authentic human living required access to basic human needs, such as food, shelter, health care, clothing, education and employment."

[28] Dignity was described as follows: "Practitioners and ministers of justice spoke of the inherent value and worth of persons connected with human dignity and creation in the image of God. They saw this dignity in persons who underwent experiences of exploitation, violence or discrimination and survived with a resilient sense of themselves as deserving better. They spoke of the creativity, ingenuity and skill which persons exhibited in order to survive, thrive or develop. Their experiences taught them that this dignity required recognition, respect and systemic protection."

[29] This dimension was described as follows: "People were not the same and what worked for some would not work for others. Differences were attributed to culture, physical abilities, gender, race, class, religious beliefs or personal experiences. This diversity provided remarkable richness and sometimes overwhelming difficulties for human living. Yet differences ought not be the basis of discriminatory practices nor of determining inferiority."

gulf between classes and the mutual enrichment between cultures. A couple of the respondents stressed the similarity of human persons. People are all the same except for some circumstances. "Human traits cross over differences." "All people want a better life and to help others." In addition, the responses tended to see others as those who were different, as if the writer somehow did not contribute to diversity. In U.S. settings white, middle-class persons do not perceive their social location as such. Rather "white" and "middle class" are perceived as "neutral" or "the point of comparison." All others, by virtue of being other, are seen as socially located and as contributing to diversity.

Authentic human living simply requires *relationships* (4.38; std. 0.8302), working together, or community.[30] Persons are connected to one another and to God by virtue of needs and being human. Therefore, persons need to love and be loved by one another. The practitioners of justice pointed out some ethical implications of connectedness. "If we experience a bond with others, we can't accept injustice." "Our actions affect others." Human relationships must recognize the worth of others and be based on mutual respect. Coalition building even between unlikely partners and solidarity are expected ways of acting. These same ministers of justice spoke of redemptive dimensions of relationality. Through relationships they were "pulled to wholeness." They spoke of being shaped by their relationships and experiencing God's saving activity in the passion and love of persons who are poor. "Life eternal happens through each other." Engagement in just actions caused "a hunger for relationship with God."

While the respondents did describe a *potential for inhumanity* (4.20; std. 0.9035), a more prevalent theme was the basic or intrinsic goodness of human persons. According to the justice activists, this goodness is apparent in the capacity for sacrifice and dedication, in efforts to do the good and the just, in care and sensitivity, and in desiring good for others. A couple of them stated that persons act unjustly because they are taught to act that way or are treated unjustly first. A few practitioners noted that even innate goodness needs encouragement and sometimes the need to blend into the society deters persons from doing the good. Others stressed that persons were basically good, but capable of choosing evil.

---

[30] This dimension was described as follows: "Ministers and practitioners of justice held that authentic human living necessitated community, collaboration and working together. At times this insight emerged more as a lament about what ought to be if persons were to be authentically human. These actors on behalf of justice spoke of their own sense of needing to work with other persons and groups to bring about humane conditions for living. They recognized the necessity of communal support and collaboration in order to continue to work for justice."

The potential for inhumanity[31] was seen in selfishness, in nearsighted-
ness, in the rationalization of inhumanity, and in collaboration with
systemic injustice. The experience of the potential to act inhumanly
was a challenge to these justice ministers to act with compassion, to
withhold easy judgment, and to stop romanticizing poverty.

The respondents also spoke about authentic human living as requir-
ing *responsible agency*. Human persons are capable of making hard
choices and of exercising self-determination, whether they are practitioners of justice or persons who have been marginated by class and
racial systems. Commitment, freedom, and equality were noted as important for responsible agency. A sense of powerlessness, the reluctance to change lifestyles, and the persistence needed to transform
injustice were viewed as threats to responsible agency.

The surveyed practitioners of justice noted that personal just actions
were not sufficient. Structures were necessary to make full humanness
possible, to acknowledge human dignity and worth, and to build a
"sustainable economy so all have basic human needs met." These
activists noted that some structures actually made just actions and
authentic human living difficult because they threatened integrity or
co-opt people.

JUSTICE IN THE VOICES OF PRACTITIONERS OF JUSTICE

This section examines the understanding of justice which emerged
from the activities on behalf of justice as described by some fifty survey
respondents. The specific survey questions asked them to narrate their
operative description of justice as well as to evaluate the accuracy[32] of six
summary descriptions which had been drawn from their earlier survey
comments about justice and action on behalf of justice. These summary
descriptions were also assessed in the range of "generally true."[33]

[31] Potential for inhumanity was described as follows: "Ministers and practitioners
of justice experienced human persons as very capable of evil, sin, inhumanity, ego-
tistical behavior and viciousness. They cautioned against stereotypes of the greedy
rich and the noble poor, because their experience showed that rich and poor alike
were capable of both inhumanity and virtue. They also stressed that non-exposure
to difference as well as blind complicity in inhumane structures make it easier to act
inhumanely and viciously."

[32] The respondents were asked to rate "the degree to which the statement articulates a description of justice" which informs their activities on behalf of justice. The
scale used was: 1 = mostly untrue; 2 = somewhat untrue; 3 = somewhat true; 4 =
generally true; and 5 = definitely true. The generally high ratings seem to reflect an
accurate analysis and articulation of their earlier statements.

[33] The composite scores (3.9 to 4.47) showed stronger agreement than the composite scores for the God descriptions (3.55 to 4.33), but not as strong as the descriptions
for authentic human living (4.16 to 4.61).

The survey respondents gave the highest ratings (4.62; std. 0.8023) to an understanding of *justice as membership in the human community*,[34] which resembles a foundational concept of justice in the U.S. Bishops' statement on the economy (#77). Membership in the human community was called constitutive of justice and the only long-range solution to injustice. These practitioners of justice maintained that justice as membership in the human community entailed participation in decision-making, voice, collaboration, recognition of dignity, solidarity, or the realization of the unity of the human family. Tools which would realize this ideal encompassed nonviolent conflict resolution, the replacement of dependency with interrelatedness, and the creation of an environment which enhanced human dignity. The survey respondents recognized that the embrace of justice as membership in the community required conversion and promoted a relationship with Jesus. They also mentioned that the embodied practice of justice as inclusion in the human family was a transforming spiritual experience.

Justice as righting wrongs[35] scored 4.34 (std. 0.7722). In their assessment, the survey respondents described righting injustices as including advocacy activities, denouncement of injustice, education, encouraging others in their efforts, and structural systemic change. Examples of systemic change included policies and institutions which would end hunger as well as current practices of restorative justice. This understanding of justice was deemed a goal capable of ridding society of injustice. At the same time the practitioners of justice recognized the difficulty of this approach to justice because these ministers themselves were so embedded in unjust structures like nationalism and the global economy that the righting of injustices challenged them to radical change.

---

[34] *Justice as membership in the human community* was described as follows: "Ministers and practitioners speak about justice as the inclusion of all persons in the human community, with particular attention to the embrace of the marginated and powerless. This description of justice entails deliberate efforts to build relationships across differences through hospitality and friendship. This community-oriented description of justice also requires the creation of patterns and structures which foster rich and diverse participation in the human community." Seventy-one percent of the respondents ranked inclusive justice as definitely true.

[35] *Justice as righting wrongs* was described as follows: "Ministers and practitioners of justice speak about justice as righting what is wrong in society. The wrongs most often mentioned include violence, racism, classism, sexism and inhuman treatment. The ministers and practitioners talk about individual and collective intervention to stop these wrongs from continuing. These interventions can consist of standing up for 'the right' or advocating for someone or engaging in political and social change of unjust practices." Forty-nine percent of the respondents ranked justice as righting wrongs definitely true.

Justice as fulfilling one's obligation[36] (4.32; std. 0.8437) received a similar composite score. These ministers of justice described the source of their obligation as their relationship with Jesus, whose mission they continued. They spelled out the obligations of continuing Christ's mission as including the marginated, as helping others to live in dignity, as providing access to resources, as promoting voice in decision-making and the establishment of structures, as sharing the gifts they had received, as loving their neighbors, as living the Golden Rule, as building up communities, as proclaiming good news to the poor, liberty to captives, sight to the blind, release to prisoners, and as announcing a Jubilee year. For these practitioners this understanding of justice could not be separated from their faith in Jesus. Justice was an ethical imperative emerging from their participation in the mission of Jesus.

The next highest composite rating was given to *justice as fair distribution of resources*[37] (4.25; std. 0.9606). Distributive justice was described as acting equitably toward every person or as some fair (not necessarily equal) sharing of resources, power, rights, information, and opportunity. The respondents acknowledged that persons who had access to more resources than those required to meet basic human needs could legitimately be expected to relinquish some of their access and resources. From their perspective, justice as fair distribution was rooted in human dignity of all persons created in the image of God. These practitioners saw distributive justice as both a goal of human living and a basic principle of economic well-being.

Justice as prophetic announcement/denouncement[38] received a rating of 3.94 (std. 1.1501). Ministers who identified with this understanding of

[36] *Justice as fulfilling one's obligation* was described as follows: "Ministers and practitioners speak about justice as carrying out the duties and obligations inherent in their identity as human persons and disciples of Jesus Christ. These obligations are stated in the teachings of the Scriptures, in God's Plan, in Catholic Social Teachings and even in civil laws. Fulfilling these obligations entails not only adherence to these teachings, but also influencing change particularly in public policy and legislative agenda." Fifty-four percent of the respondents ranked justice as duty definitely true.

[37] *Justice as fair distribution of resources* was described as follows: "Ministers and practitioners speak about justice as the fair distribution of natural and economic resources with a particular emphasis on those resources necessary to meet basic human needs such as nourishment, shelter, health care, protection and education. Ministers and practitioners typically suggest various criteria as the basis for the distribution, such as need, strict equality, dignity or deservedness." Fifty-one percent of the respondents ranked distributive justice as definitely true.

[38] *Justice as prophetic announcement/denouncement* was described as follows: "Ministers and practitioners speak about justice as announcing the values of the reign of God and denouncing what opposes these values. Justice as well as equality, mutuality, non-violence, inclusivity, love, compassion and solidarity are the values most

justice used the language of faith, conversion, and Christian beliefs to describe their position. "My prayer life gives me courage to stand up and be prophetic and to suffer if necessary." "Justice is advocating for the reign of God and its values in our world." Because this understanding of justice called believers to conversion, some practitioners spoke of announcement and denouncement as constitutive of justice.

A similar rating was given to *justice as access to power*[39] (3.88; std. 0.9612). Respondents described justice as access to power in one of two ways. For some, the emphasis fell on empowerment of the disadvantaged, for example, in providing opportunities for persons to speak on their own behalf. For others the emphasis fell on using power to influence policies and change structures for the sake of the oppressed and powerless. The power to which this understanding of justice sought access was variously named opportunity, resources to meet basic human needs, participation, and relationships. When justice was discussed according to this pattern, access to power was understood almost exclusively in structural and systemic terms. Practitioners did acknowledge that justice activists themselves are sometimes so enmeshed in power games that they end up replacing some unjust structures with different unjust structures.

As shall be seen in subsequent chapters, virtually all of these approaches to justice are at home in the scriptural or Catholic Social Teachings traditions of Roman Catholic Christianity. Still these evaluations of justice are significant for at least three reasons. First, they suggest that the Scriptures and Catholic Social Teachings actually do have a formative power in the Roman Catholic Christian community. The survey respondents were not asked to evaluate descriptions of justice which came directly from these traditions, but descriptions which came from their own experience of doing justice. Yet their preferred descriptions reflected the Catholic Christian traditions in which they were steeped. Second, the preferred description of justice according to both

---

often associated with this reign of God. The practice of denunciation includes truth-telling, demonstrations condemning injustice and civil disobedience of unjust laws or practices." Only 37 percent of the respondents ranked prophetic justice as definitely true.

[39] *Justice as access to power* was described as follows: "Ministers and practitioners speak about justice as access to a power which promotes the common good and the practice of non-harm. Justice so understood requires access to information for persons often marginated from access to power. It also requires a voice in decision-making for persons dismissed as incompetent and ineffective in the exercise of power. Reliance on this description of justice stresses the development of self-governing, local communities with sustainable local leadership which create patterns of a power which serves the common good." Only 34 percent of the respondents ranked justice as power definitely true.

composite average and number of "definitely true" responses was justice as membership in the human community. Although this description has its roots in the essentially social nature of the human person, its first developed articulation came in the pastoral on economics of the U.S. Bishops. Both the survey and the pastoral on economics then suggest that this understanding of justice may well be a distinctive contribution of the Church of the United States to the ongoing dialogue about the nature and practice of justice. Third, these survey results in general point to a definite wisdom which comes from the practice of justice.

Conclusion

Four quite distinct constellations of images of God, beliefs about the human person, and approaches to justice can be discerned in the survey responses. No one constellation received uniformly high ratings, which suggests the complex interconnection between just actions, beliefs about God, and convictions about what constitutes authentic human living. Rather, sometimes the practice of justice has led to an understanding about justice which is still shaping images of God and dimensions of authentic human living. Other times the justice implications of an image of God have not yet found a home in the hearts of practitioners. Still other times, understandings of justice emerge out of convictions around what it means to be human, with little apparent link to God.

First, the understanding of justice as membership in the human community stresses inclusion of all persons with special attention to differences and structures which facilitate participation. The understanding of justice as access to power focuses on the structures which promote inclusion and participation in the human community. This approach to justice has its foundations in convictions that human persons are essentially relational and richly diverse. God is encountered in reciprocal relationships with persons whose life experiences are both different and similar to their own. The image of God as Reciprocal Relationship causes practitioners of justice to identify God with their neighbor. The inclusion and participation of all persons in the human community could facilitate an understanding of God as essentially relational.

Second, the approach to justice as righting wrongs was described as including intervention, advocacy, and social change. The need to right what is wrong suggests an awareness that human persons have potential for inhumanity. Two of the descriptions of God ground this understanding of justice. God as Gracious Resistance images God as the one who resists injustice in this world by continuing creation and liberation. God as Transformative Action describes a God who continues to transform the world through the creating, liberating, and transforming activities of human persons. Here it seems that the preferred image of God as Transformative Action may well be the catalyst for an emerging description of justice as transforming injustice.

Third, the understanding of justice as fulfilling one's obligations did not seem to be linked to proposed descriptions of God or the human person. The sources of these duties were explicitly mentioned as personal identity and a God who gave laws, teachings, and gifts to direct and encourage disciples along the ways of justice. This infrequent mention of God and Christian discipleship as sources of obligations of justice does not fit with the relatively high composite score given to justice as duty. This is an instance where more relational images of God and understandings of the human person still need to transform lagging conceptions of justice.

Fourth, justice was also described as fair distribution of resources. This description of justice seems to be more explicitly linked to the two most highly rated dimensions of the human person: basic human needs and dignity. Authentic human living requires access to the fair distribution of resources to meet basic human needs. Human dignity, in turn, is a recurring criterion for distribution of resources. The survey respondents rooted human dignity in creation in the image of God. Hence Creator is the corresponding image of God. This image of God was used almost exclusively when addressing human dignity. Independent of this link, God as Creator was not a recurring image for God.

The description of justice as prophetic announcement/denouncement has links to God imaged as Call to Conversion. The image of God as Longing for the Dream provides content to a vision which grounds several approaches to justice, namely, the right in righting wrongs, the city of God which is prophetically announced, and the inclusion in the just human community. The high ranking given to this image of God suggests as well a certain resonance with an affective dimension of God as longing and desire which moves ministers of justice to action.

3

Justice in the Scriptures

In contemporary Western societies the term "justice" is associated with the juridical sphere or the sociopolitical arena. Many Christians therefore perceive justice as a thoroughly secular concept. They are no longer aware that justice has deep roots in the earliest Jewish and Christian traditions as they are handed down to us in the Scriptures. Both the Jewish and the Christian faiths see justice first and foremost as a quality of God. Belief in a just God has important consequences for the way the Jewish and the Christian faiths see God and the human person. In the previous chapter we already saw that the Scriptures feed the vision of justice practitioners and thus play an important role in their justice commitment. In this chapter we will unearth the scriptural roots of the Christian justice tradition. After a short survey of the Hebrew Scriptures and the Christian Scriptures in general we will turn to the Gospel of John.

JUSTICE IN THE HEBREW SCRIPTURES

Justice plays a central role in Hebrew Scriptures, yet no one Hebrew word conveys justice as it is used or understood in English. An exploration of justice in the Hebrew Scriptures brings the contemporary Western reader into unfamiliar and fruitful territory.

Justice in the Hebrew Scriptures is essentially linked to relationship, which is reflected in the typical translation of the Hebrew word *ṣĕdāqâ* as "right relationship." The covenant relationship between YHWH God and the Hebrew people provides the defining context for justice. God entered into relationship with the Hebrew people through creation (Isa 45:11-13, 18-19), the Exodus from Egypt (Exod 13:17–15:21), and the formation of the people Israel (Psalm 98). God chose to enter into a covenant with the Hebrew people, which established particular relationships with resulting obligations and duties in justice. God is justice and acts justice (Isa 45:21) through the covenants with creation (Psalm 96) and with the Hebrew people (Exod 19:1–24:18).

The Law, the Torah, delineated actions and behaviors which characterized a right relationship between God and the people Israel (Exod 18:5-9). The prophets, in particular, were insistent that these same actions and behaviors could neither create a relationship with God, nor were they just if the people were faithless in their relationship. In other words, persons and deeds were only just in the context of the relationship (Ps 18:21-31).[1]

The covenant relationship between Israel and God focused not on just individuals, but on justice as a quality of life in common. Whereas contemporary persons might ask, "What must I do to be just?" Israel's question was rather, "What does a just community look like?" Given the lived situation of the Hebrew people some three thousand years ago, the survival of individuals depended on the survival of the community. The just community structured around patterns of right relationships meant life for all its members (Isa 32:15-20).

This concrete experience perhaps gave rise to a theology which recognized that God was the Creator God who made all persons in God's own image and likeness. Since all persons were created in God's own image, the acceptance of God's ways of relating meant life in the Garden of Eden, while the refusal to acknowledge God's plan of relationships resulted in disharmony with the land and rupture with one another (Psalm 106).

The story of the Exodus and formation of the nation Israel repeats the faith conviction that God graciously intervened on Israel's behalf (Psalm 103), judged the Egyptian relationships with this same people as unjust, and restored them to the land promised to their ancestors

---

[1] This understanding of justice is operational to some degree in a current understanding of justice as fulfilling the terms of a legal contract between persons or between corporate bodies. However, the contract constitutes a legal relationship and is the source of the duties and obligations which justice requires. If a relationship is understood as a source of obligations and responsibilities, the fulfillment of these duties is not viewed as justice. Indeed there is a movement to specify the obligations of relationships in legal terms as in pre-nuptial agreements.

(Psalm 111). Hence the Hebrew understanding of justice was social and communal at its heart.

The response to the question "What does the just community look like?" also touched on the whole of life. Faithful adherence to God in the whole of living encompassed patterns in economic, political, and social relationships, as well as ritual expression (Isa 11:1-9; Psalm 72). Economic, political, social, and religious patterns were just when they reflected the community's adherence to God as creator and liberator. The practical denial of this relationship with their creator and liberator was community injustice: rituals without relationship, economic exploitation of the poor, political intrigue, and social abandonment of the widow or orphan (Amos 8:4-6). The prophets proclaimed that these unjust practices destroyed relational patterns reflected in the harmony of Eden's garden and in liberation from Egypt's bondage.[2]

In the covenant context of the Hebrew Scriptures, then, justice is best described as the faithful fulfillment of the demands and obligations flowing from the covenant relationship. Both God and Israel had duties in justice. Since God initiated the covenant, the justice of God entailed gracious intervention on behalf of those who were denied justice, right judgment toward those who perpetuated injustice, and restoration of a just community. Since Israel did not initiate, but confirmed or denied the covenant relationship, the justice of Israel required a faithful adherence to the relationship with their God. Thus justice in the Hebrew Scriptures refers to faithfulness in relationships, the majority of which were not voluntarily or freely chosen. We will look at the justice of God and of Israel in more detail.

First, God's justice shows itself in constant commitment to these covenant relationships. This faithful commitment entails gracious intervention on behalf of Israel and on behalf of the widow, the orphan, the poor, and the stranger whose life situations threatened right relationships. When the Hebrew people were enslaved in Egypt, God's gracious intervention liberated them from slavery for just relationships with each other and with God (Exod 20:2; Deut 5:15). Similarly God

---

[2] This essentially social and communal understanding of justice is echoed in the work of persons like Michael Walzer, *Spheres of Justice: A Defense of Pluralism and Equality* (New York: Basic Books, 1983). Walzer holds that membership in the human community is the greatest social good available; thus justice is concerned with who sits at the table of humanity in order to distribute the remaining social resources. Catholic social thought on social justice also seeks to retrieve the richness of the Hebrew scriptural sense of justice with some success. In addition, feminist, womanist, and other liberation ethics are developing the essentially social framework for justice. All of these efforts recognize that an articulation of justice as social requires a communitarian understanding of the human person.

graciously intervened to right the community's neglect of the widow, abandonment of the orphan, exploitation of the poor (Isa 10:1-5), and exclusion of the stranger. God's justice thus takes the form of gracious intervention to right relationships gone wrong (Zech 8:4-8). God's gracious intervention liberates those who are wronged.[3]

Second, God's justice also stands as a measuring standard against which to measure the faithfulness and deeds of Israel (Amos 7:7-8) as well as the nations (Isa 28:17). God's just judgment marks faithfulness to the relationship as well as unfaithful deviation from the standard of right relationship. The prophets insist that Israel was judged and found lacking because the demands of the covenant relationship were ignored and guidelines of the Law were violated. But the nations who oppress and overrun Israel are also judged justly and their departure from right relationship punished (Ps 9:8-10). The Hebrew Scriptures stress the correctness of God's judging justice: the innocent will be judged as innocent and only those who deviate from right relationships will be punished (Isa 11:4). Hence God's just judgment provides a sense of comfort and trust that justice will be served (Isa 26:8-10). God's judging justice is often described in legal or forensic images of lawsuits, courts, and city gates.[4]

Finally, when Israel rejected the covenant and showed itself unfaithful to its relationship, God entered into a new covenant (Isa 59:16–60:22). The eschatological and messianic descriptions of this new covenant are in terms of justice and right relationships in economic, political, and social patterns. The new Jerusalem will have justice at the city gates, food, rich wine, and long, peace-filled lives (Zech 8:4-14). The reign of the Messiah will be a reign of justice, peace, and abundant harvest (Isa 9:1-6; Psalm 72). Jubilee years will restore the Hebrew servant to a proper freedom, the land to its rightful owner, and distribute the fruits of the earth, so that all people have a share (Leviticus 25). Thus even when

---

[3] This notion of God's saving justice is probably the root of preferential option for the poor as described in the documents of the Latin American bishops' conferences and recent social encyclicals. A similar concern may be reflected in the work of John Rawls when he argues for the terms of justice prior to knowledge of one's social situation, so that the marginated are not penalized or ignored in the description of justice. Possibly the recognition that situations of injustice cry out for God's just intervention has been taken over by liberation ethics in claiming the experience of injustice as the beginning of an understanding of justice.

[4] These images, along with the predominant Greek understanding of justice in situations of civil and divine law, account for many of the current concepts of justice. In addition, God's judging justice appears to be linked to contemporary efforts to understand justice as universal (the rulers of the earth are subject to God's judging justice) as well as beyond human whim and vested interest.

injustice prevails, God's justice re-creates, restores, redeems, and reconciles injustice into right relationships.

The dreams of restoration and re-creation of right relationships suggest two additional dimensions of justice in the Hebrew Scriptures. Since the images are primarily drawn from sociopolitical and economic living, justice cannot be separated from the possibility of a restructured social order. These images also stress the importance and role of a vision of justice to set the direction, to inspire, and to empower for the realization of the vision.

The justice of Israel, in turn, rested on God's choice and establishment of the covenant relationship with creation and with Israel. God's initiative invited and required the Hebrew people to affirm this covenant relationship. Hence the justice of Israel was essentially faithfulness to the relationship with God and with one another. The demands of justice extended not only to God and the people Israel, but also to relationships among the people Israel. God's creation covenant established relationships with the world and all peoples with resulting obligations and duties in justice. Thus justice included Israel's treatment of the stranger in their midst and the Sabbath rest given to the land.

Whether Israel accepted the relationship, rebelled against it, or disregarded it, the covenant relationship remained a given, a contour of community living. What this faithfulness looked like in daily living came over time to be articulated in the Torah. When they were faithful to their relationships with God and the community, Israel kept the Law. Observance of the Torah did not create the covenant relationship nor did it necessarily express the covenant relationship. It was possible to keep the Law and be unfaithful to the relationship.

For the Hebrew people, life was one profound unity. Thus when the people were in right relationship, justice was present in all concrete daily lived realities including legal claims, cultic rituals, care of the land, treatment of widows, sociopolitical alliances, economic weights and measures (Amos 2:6-8). In Wisdom literature, the just were those whose lives were marked by moral character (e.g., Proverbs 10), which included not only specific deeds of justice, but a quality of relational faithfulness.[5]

These introductory comments began with the statement that the Hebrew Scriptures use more than one word to convey the content of what

---

[5] Justice came to be included in Catholic Social Teachings predominantly due to economic and political crises—the emergence of the modern nation state and distribution of the economic goods in the aftermath of the Industrial Revolution. Catholic Social Teachings on justice remain linked to social, economic, and political realities of modern living.

we call "justice" today. Justice typically translates any one of four words: ṣĕdāqâ, mišpāṭ, ḥesed, and ʾĕmēt. Ṣĕdāqâ refers to justice or rightness in covenant relationships as has been described in the preceding paragraphs. Mišpāṭ carries the nuance of legal claims or judgments emerging from the Torah. As has been noted, however, true fulfillment of the Law in the Hebrew Scriptures can be accomplished only in right relationships. Thus mišpāṭ and ṣĕdāqâ are often paired together in a twinning characteristic of poetic speech or emphatic statement.[6] While ḥesed is often translated as loving kindness, in fact, the word connotes a commitment to loving service arising within social relationships which are constituted by covenant or tribal bonds. Ḥesed thus is less an attitude or feeling, but rather an appropriate response to claims of a relational commitment which parallels legal obligations or responsibilities. The gracious intervention of God on behalf of a covenanted people is God's ḥesed, that is, God's saving justice or covenant faithfulness. The word ʾĕmēt refers to God's covenant fidelity, which means that God's justice does not end when human persons are unfaithful in the relationship.

This survey on justice in the Hebrew Scriptures highlights the relational covenant context of justice. In addition, we see that this covenant relationship requires that (1) God intervene on behalf of persons who are oppressed, (2) God judge those who oppress others, and (3) God establish a new city characterized by justice. God's practices of justice set up the contours of Israel's practices of justice.

JUSTICE IN PAUL AND IN THE SYNOPTIC GOSPELS

Jesus of Nazareth was a Galilean Jew whose ministry extended into Judea and Jerusalem. The disciples and first Christians were Jewish people who gathered together into communities in these same areas. Thus it is no surprise that the understanding of justice from the Hebrew Scriptures carried over into the Christian Scriptures. The language of the Christian Scriptures, however, was Greek, which accounts for a Greek influence on the Christian Scriptures alongside the Jewish influence.

When the early Christian authors wrote the Scriptures, they used dikaiosynê, the Greek term for justice. This is the term which the Greek translation of the Hebrew Scriptures had used to render ṣĕdāqâ. The New Testament usage of this term reflects the influence of Judaism, of

---

[6] Isa 9:6; 10:4-5; Pss 1:5; 17:2; 48:11-12; 50:6; 58:12; 72:1-4; 94:15; 96:14; 97:2; 98:9; Job 36:17.

the Greco-Roman world, and the specific Christian understanding of God's action in Jesus on behalf of the believers and the world. It is a matter of dispute among the specialists whether the Hebrew or the Greek influence prevails in a particular occurrence of *dikaiosynê*.[7]

Justice in the Greco-Roman world was first of all a legal term connected with the law and its obligations. Justice also carried a more general sense of the right, the fitting and proper, or even custom and tradition. The just fulfilled their obligations to the laws and customs. Individual fulfillment of these obligations according to one's roles and status brought inner harmony and a life of virtue. Virtuous actions reflected what was proper for each given the laws, customs and traditions.[8] Justice in the Greek worldview did carry a sense of individual virtue, which departed sharply from the relational worldview of the Hebrew Scriptures where it "connotes the right conduct of God and of humans . . . within the perspective of the concrete life relationships of partners to each other . . . [*dikaiosynê* is a] characteristic of God in his conduct toward his people . . . in conformity with his covenant."[9] In recent years scholars agree that by and large the New Testament usage of *dikaiosynê* is closer to the Hebrew than to the Greek concept.

Jesus of Nazareth embodied both the justice of God and of the believers.[10] Jesus was the incarnate gracious intervention of God on behalf of the poor, the *anawim*, those faithful ones whose trust in God set them at the fringes of the social order. Jesus brought good news to the poor, proclaimed release to the captives, recovery of sight to the blind, and set the oppressed free (Luke 4:18). Jesus proclaimed God's own reign to the poor, the meek, the merciful, the pure in heart, the peacemakers, to those who mourn, who hunger and thirst for justice, and who are persecuted (see Matt 5:3-10). The message of Jesus coupled

---

[7] The distinction between Hebrew and Greek usage is found, for instance, in Karl Kertelge, *"dikaiosynê,"* EDNT 1 (1990) 325–30, esp. 326. The validity of a clear distinction between Hebrew and Greek cultures at the time of the New Testament writers is much disputed. Besides running the risk of being too simplistic, it also ignores the fact that Judaism (even in Palestine including Jerusalem) was under the influence of Hellenism at the time.

[8] Cf. ibid.: *dikaiosynê* is a human virtue and refers to legality, honesty, equality. It is human conduct "within a view of an ideal norm of what is right."

[9] Ibid.

[10] Since the earliest written sources we have about Jesus date from about a generation after Jesus' death, it is a challenging task for historical scholarship to try to reconstruct the earthly Jesus in distinction from a specific gospel's portrayal of Jesus. Since we cannot enter into this discussion here, we will present some elements which are generally accepted in modern scholarship. For the historical Jesus debate see, among others, John Meier, *A Marginal Jew: Rethinking the Historical Jesus,* 2 vols. (New York: Doubleday, 1991–94).

care for the hungry, the thirsty, the ill, the homeless, and imprisoned with the inheritance of God's reign (Matt 25:31-46).[11] Through Jesus God offers and extends justice to tax collectors and sinners, that is, to those whom the establishment considered irredeemably unjust. In Jesus there is no opposition, but agreement between mercy and justice. The evangelists described the ministry of Jesus as the gracious intervention of God in the flesh for the establishment of justice.

For Paul, the earliest Christian writer, justice is essentially christological, but also soteriological. Although *dikaiosynê* in Paul is sometimes translated "righteousness," the term "justification" may better reflect its roots in the Hebrew concept of justice. Justification is about the believers' relationship with God in Jesus. The Pauline understanding of justification posits a new relationship with God in Jesus based on God's grace and our faith.

God entered into relationship with the Gentiles and the world in the covenant of creation. When the initial covenant of creation was ignored, God renewed that covenant at Sinai and in connection with the Babylonian Exile, when the people again disregarded the covenant relationships and its expression in the Law. Paul recognized that the people had failed the covenant relationship inaugurated by God and were guilty before God. However, God graciously intervened again in Jesus to establish a new covenant relationship; thus God's justice made Jews and Gentiles just and restored the relationship. As such, God's justice and not human works or efforts reestablished the covenant relationship and brought about a new creation (see 2 Cor 5:17). In Jesus God's gracious intervention reestablished the covenant relationship with all persons, symbolized for Paul by Jew and Greek, slave and free, male and female (Gal 3:28). God's justice was effective. It truly re-created a covenant community. Finally, the historical and incarnational center of God's justice was Jesus, the one whom the Christian Scriptures understand as the incarnation of God's gracious intervention, the enfleshment of God's judgment, and the presence of the re-created and restored community of the endtimes.

After Paul we need to examine the gospel witness to justice. Concerning terminology we note that, out of the 302 New Testament occur-

---

[11] See also John R. Donahue, "Biblical Perspectives on Justice," *Faith That Does Justice: Examining the Christian Sources for Social Change*, ed. John C. Haughey, Woodstock Studies 2 (New York: Paulist Press, 1977) 68–112, esp. 87: "Yahweh's rule and the establishment of justice are closely joined (Pss. 97:1-2; 96:10). In the apocalyptic literature the coming of the time of the Messiah will inaugurate the victory of God's justice and his mercy. By identifying the advent of God's Kingdom with his ministry and teaching, Jesus proclaims the advent of God's justice." In this section on "Justice in the Christian Scriptures" we are indebted to Donahue's study.

rences of *dikaiosynê* and its cognates, only 2 are found in Mark and 6 in John. Therefore, most of the attention has been focused on Matthew and Luke. In Matthew Jesus is presented as the new Moses, the teacher of *dikaiosynê*. John R. Donahue points us to two striking examples. The parable of the unmerciful servant (Matt 18:23-34) is an invitation to understand the close bond between justice and mercy.[12] For Matthew true justice is justice qualified by mercy. Having experienced mercy, just persons are those who extend mercy to others. The parable of the final judgment (Matt 25:31-46) is a reminder that it is not enough to know *what* just action consists of, but also *where* we are confronted with the demands of justice in concrete situations.[13]

Luke is recognized as the evangelist with the most explicit concern for social issues and consequently for justice. He presents Jesus as a prophet in line with the great prophets of the Hebrew Scriptures. As the programmatic scene in Nazareth at the beginning of Jesus' public ministry shows (Luke 4:16-30), Luke presents Jesus' role in the words of Isa 61:1-2. "The Lukan Jesus speaks to his Church with the same prophetic voice for justice with which the Old Testament prophets spoke."[14] True to the prophetic tradition, the Gospel of Luke contains a stern critique of wealth and possessions in general.

We conclude that Paul and the Synoptics essentially follow the meaning of justice in the Hebrew Scriptures as human conduct in conformity with a concrete life relationship. Paul, Matthew, and Luke see God's intervention on behalf of the oppressed realized in the historical person, Jesus of Nazareth. These New Testament authors are convinced that this intervention had lasting effects despite its apparent failure in Jesus' execution on the cross. They express the lasting effects with the concepts of new creation and reign of God. Paul stresses the universality of God's intervention in Jesus in pointing out that no one is excluded from it. Matthew is concerned about the acceptance of mercy as part of justice and tries to enable his readers to recognize where justice needs to be practiced under concrete circumstances. Luke reminds us that there can be no justice unless the concrete historical social structures foster justice. Therefore he stresses the need for social change.

Our treatment of justice in Paul's letters and in the Synoptics was not intended to be an in-depth analysis, but rather to provide a context for the following detailed analysis of the justice dimensions in the Gospel of John.

[12] Ibid., 104.
[13] Cf. the question, "Who is my neighbor?" in the Lukan parable of the Good Samaritan (Luke 10:29-37).
[14] Donahue, "Biblical Perspectives," 106.

JUSTICE IN THE GOSPEL OF JOHN

In the remainder of this chapter we focus on this question: What can the Gospel of John teach us about justice? The Gospel is often viewed as the least likely candidate in the search for a scriptural teacher of justice. Justice belongs to concrete historical reality, while the Fourth Gospel has often been called a "spiritual" or "mystical" gospel. Already more than thirty years ago Wayne A. Meeks called this an "outdated notion."[15] Many studies of the second half of the twentieth century have demonstrated John's firm foundation in a historical setting[16] and vivid interest in concrete historical reality. David Rensberger expects a new era in the theological understanding of John because "we are now in a position to ask about the social implications of Johannine thought and in the case of the 'spiritual gospel,' this, I believe, may rightly be considered revolutionary."[17]

The view of the Gospel of John as a spiritual gospel considered ethics almost completely absent. If one restricts ethics to moral rules and individual responses to the question "What should I do?" then the Fourth Gospel has indeed very little to contribute.[18] The only moral rule which scholars found in the Gospel is "love one another." This commandment was commonly interpreted as restricting love to those in the Johannine community. From such a perspective, John has little to offer to the understanding of social justice.

But a number of the above-mentioned assumptions have recently been challenged. Some scholars have broadened the above approach to ethics as a set of rules for the individual to include "stories, symbols, social structures and practices that shape the community's ethos."[19] Johannes Nissen sees John's story as "laden with ethical implications

---

[15] Wayne A. Meeks, *The Prophet-King: Moses Traditions and the Johannine Christology,* NTSuppl 14 (Leiden: Brill, 1967) 64, n. 1.

[16] J. Louis Martyn, *History and Theology in the Fourth Gospel* (Nashville: Abingdon, 1979).

[17] David Rensberger, *Johannine Faith and Liberating Community* (Philadelphia: Westminster Press, 1988) 25. See also Wes Howard-Brook, *Becoming Children of God: John's Gospel and Radical Discipleship* (Maryknoll, N.Y.: Orbis Books, 1994).

[18] See also Wayne A. Meeks, "The Ethics of the Fourth Gospel," *Exploring the Gospel of John: Essays in Honor of Dwight Moody Smith,* ed. R. Alan Culpepper and C. Clifton Black (Louisville: Westminster/John Knox, 1996) 317–26; 320, who summarizes the first part of his investigation: "We have seen so far that the Fourth Gospel meets none of our expectations about the way ethics should be constructed."

[19] Johannes Nissen, "Community and Ethics in the Gospel of John," *New Readings in John: Literary and Theological Perspectives: Essays from the Scandinavian Conference on the Fourth Gospel, Arhus 1997,* JSNTSS 182, ed. Johannes Nissen and Sigfried Pedersen (Sheffield: Academic Press, 1999) 194–212, esp. 199.

for the community that accepts the message and finds itself rejected by the world."[20] Wayne A. Meeks has pointed out that the moral lessons or the ethical challenge of the Fourth Gospel can only be perceived if we "first submit to its own idiom and the coercive voices of its narrator and its protagonist."[21]

These narrative, pragmatic, and community-oriented approaches have shown convincingly that, despite its inward-looking focus, the Johannine community is committed to giving testimony to those outside, "that the world may believe" (17:21). These approaches have also brought to light the countercultural stance of the Johannine community and its egalitarian[22] and political[23] consequences. In this perspective it will be clear that the Gospel of John has much to offer ethics, albeit in unexpected and perhaps more indirect ways. We are convinced that its narrative world and its theological vision have important implications for justice. In what follows we first focus our attention on the way the Gospel of John presents God and the human person because we are convinced that every concept of justice is shaped by its implicit image of God and the human person (see Chapter 2).

A Theological Framework for Justice

The central character of the Fourth Gospel is Jesus. In and through Jesus, the evangelist puts the reader in contact with God and with the Spirit. While John does not have a developed Trinitarian doctrine in the line of the later dogmatic development, the theological framework of the Fourth Gospel clearly includes God, Jesus, and the Spirit.

God

We identified three areas in John's presentation of God which have important justice implications: God's immanence and transcendence, the relational character of God, and the abundance of God.

We meet God's immanence and transcendence in John's characterization of God. While God is the horizon of reality, the characterization

---

[20] Ibid.

[21] Meeks, "Ethics," 120.

[22] Nissen, "Community," 211–2.

[23] See Meeks, "Ethics," 323–4, and Nissen, "Community," 208–10. Cf. Reimund Bieringer, "'My Kingship Is Not of This World' (John 18,36). The Kingship of Jesus and Politics," *The Myriad Christ: Plurality and the Quest for Unity in Contemporary Christology*, BETL 152, ed. Terrance Merrigan and Jacques Haers (Leuven: University Press and Peeters, 2000) 159–75.

of God is consistently indirect. God's actions are either implied, assumed, or indirectly communicated through the actions of Jesus.[24] We never see God act, we are only told about God's actions ("No one has ever seen God," 1:18; people have never seen God's form, 5:37). Moreover, people have never heard God's voice (5:37).

The indirect characterization of God suggests a fundamental tension in the Gospel, namely the tension between God's transcendence and immanence. God is thoroughly involved in the world: Through the Word, God made all things (1:3). God gave the law through Moses (1:17). God gave the manna to the Israelites in the desert (cf. 6:31, 49). The Johannine God is the God who called Abraham (cf. 8:31-59), who favored Jacob (cf. 4:12), and who sent the prophets (esp. Isaiah, cf. 1:23; 12:38, 39, 41). "God so loved the world that he gave his only Son, so that everyone who believes in him may not perish but have eternal life" (3:16). The Fourth Gospel also expresses this idea by saying that God sent Jesus into the world (3:17) and that God gave all things into Jesus' hands (3:35; 13:3). God's prerogatives of giving life and judgment are given to Jesus (5:21-22, 26-27). God is immanent to such a degree that whoever has seen Jesus has seen the Father (14:9).

Despite this stress on the immanence, the Johannine God remains transcendent. This is expressed in the statement "God is spirit" (4:24), which means that God belongs to the mysterious heavenly sphere which is beyond human control. In his parting words, Jesus tells the disciples that the Father is greater than he (cf. 14:28). We take this to mean that the revelation of God's eschatological fullness in the earthly Jesus has not revealed God exhaustively. Thus God's transcendence is not a remoteness or an aloofness with regard to people in the world and to their destiny. God's transcendence does not cancel out God's immanence, but brings about a creative tension which shows that the Johannine God is *deus semper maior* ("God is always greater").

The immanence and transcendence of the Johannine God has important justice implications. As we already saw in Chapter 2, justice presupposes a God who is involved in the world and who is active in history. At the same time, God's transcendence is an important foundation for ideology-critical assessment of theories and actions inasmuch as God's transcendence calls into question human institutions which

---

[24] See Marianne M. Thompson, "'God's Voice You Have Never Heard, God's Form You Have Never Seen': The Characterization of God in the Gospel of John," *Semeia* 63 (1993) 177–205, esp. 189. See also 188: "According to the Gospel, their only access to God is through Jesus, the incarnate Word of God, who speaks so that God is heard and in whom they see the Father. God is known primarily through the agency of Jesus. And the reader encounters God in the pages of the Gospel only as mediated by the character of Jesus."

usurp the place of God or claims which make out unjust situations to be unchangeable.

The second area we will discuss is the relationality of God. John's Gospel differs from the other Gospels, the Hebrew Scriptures, and Jewish literature insofar as it uses comparatively few descriptive statements about God. Only four adjectives (one, holy, just, and living) are used to characterize God. John almost exclusively refers to God with *theos* (God) or *patêr* (Father). In the Fourth Gospel the word "Father" is a relational term.[25] God is presented as a father who intimately loves his son and who so loves the world that he gives his only son (3:16). God is also seen as a mother through whom the believers are born to new life (1:12-13; 3:3, 8). The Gospel uses the father image to characterize the relationship between God and Jesus as a Father-Son relationship.[26]

With regard to the genitive phrases John prefers "of God" to "God of"; for instance, Son of God, Lamb of God, gift of God, bread of God. This way the evangelist expresses the relationship which things or human beings (in particular Jesus) have with God instead of trying to define who God is.[27] Whatever the Fourth Gospel tells us about God, is about how God relates to Jesus or to the world. The Johannine God is a relational God. The purpose of Jesus' mission is to draw believers into this God relationship.[28] Through Jesus, God calls the disciples (believers) to be friends, that is, God invites them into a reciprocal and mutually engaging relationship.

As we saw in Chapter 2, justice practitioners saw doing justice as a dimension of their intimate relationship with God. Our investigation of the relational character of the Johannine God demonstrates that the Fourth Gospel offers believers such a love relationship with God. Moreover the universal scope of God's love thwarts any attempt to

---

[25] See Gail R. O'Day, "John," *The Women's Bible Commentary*, ed. Carol A. Newsom and Sharon H. Ringe (Louisville: Westminster/John Knox, 1992) 293–304, esp. 304: "Father language in John is essentially relational. . . . This language . . . is not primarily the language of patriarchy but instead the language of intimacy, relationship, and family." Even though we agree with O'Day's assessment, one may not overlook that the prevalence of father terminology in John and its specific application to the God-Jesus relationship is nonetheless characterized by the patriarchy of the evangelist's world. Cf. Bianca Lataire and Reimund Bieringer, "God the Father: An Exegetical Study of a Johannine Metaphor," *Gender: Tradition and Renewal, Religions and Discourse*, ed. Robert Platzner (Frankfurt: Peter Lang, forthcoming).

[26] The few instances where God appears explicitly or implicitly as shepherd (1:29-36) or vinedresser (15:1) are also focused on relationship.

[27] Thompson, "God's Voice," 196.

[28] Ibid., 197.

favor some groups and exclude others from the sources of human flourishing.

The third aspect is the abundance of God's action in the world. According to the Fourth Gospel, the incarnation is characterized by generous extravagance. God gives the Spirit to Jesus beyond measure (3:34). Through Jesus Christ the fullness of God's grace and truth came into the world (1:14) and from his fullness we all received "grace upon grace" (1:16), in other words, immeasurable amounts of grace and love. What God offers through Jesus is nothing short of a new birth. Inasmuch as they believe, God gives birth to children (1:12-13; cf. 3:3-8). God's generous extravagance is further exemplified in Jesus providing an abundance of wine at the wedding feast at Cana (2:1-11) and an abundance of bread for five thousand hungry people. Both times the provision far surpasses the need.

In the healing of the sick person (John 5) and more explicitly in the healing of the blind person (John 9), there is evidence that the work of God is to liberate people from suffering. "The 'work of God,' it turns out, is not punishing sinners with suffering but overcoming the suffering."[29] God's action toward human persons (especially believers) is also characterized as giving bread from heaven, sanctifying them in truth, honoring them, teaching them, and drawing all to God. Through Jesus, God calls the disciples (believers) to be friends. These are all activities in which God's abundant love exceeds human dreams and expectations. God accepts them as partners in an equal-to-equal relationship. But there is also the other side: Inasmuch as they refuse to believe, "God's wrath"[30] rests on the unbelievers (3:36). This demonstrates the two prerogatives of God: to give life (e.g., God raises the dead and gives life) and to judge.[31]

God's extravagant gifts for humanity in John's Gospel constitute a new element for our elaboration of the meaning of justice which we did not yet meet in the survey of the justice practitioners. The Gospel suggests that human dignity requires an abundance of resources and that the people can experience the motivation to practice justice in recognition of an abundance of gifts received, not merely as duty or obligation.

---

[29] Ibid., 193.

[30] Commentators are quick to point out that the term "God's wrath" in John 3:36, which is unique in the gospel but frequent in the Hebrew Scriptures, refers to God's eschatological judgment which, according to the evangelist, is already effective in the present. See, e.g., Rudolf Schnackenburg, *The Gospel According to St. John*, vol. 1 (New York: Crossroad, 1968) 391.

[31] See below, 74 where we suggest that "to judge" in John may have the connotation of "to bring to justice" or "to intervene on behalf of the oppressed."

Jesus

As we saw above, the indirect characterization of God in the Fourth Gospel points to Jesus. While the Johannine stress on God's transcendence illustrates that we may not reduce God to Jesus, much of what John has to say about God is found in his presentation of Jesus. We will focus our attention on three dimensions and their justice implications: The Word became flesh, Jesus' relationality, and the completion of his mission in nonviolent resistance.

The Johannine Jesus has typically been perceived by many as a thoroughly divine and transcendent figure. He is in control of whatever happens and has miraculous foreknowledge. His signs are exceedingly impressive. He has descended from heaven and is ascending into heaven. Nevertheless scholars have recently rediscovered the humanity of Jesus in the Gospel of John.[32] The surprising frequency of the occurrence of the name Jesus in the Gospel in comparison with Christ, Jesus Christ, or Lord points in this direction. Jesus is presented as someone whom people perceive as having human parents (1:45; 6:42). Jesus gets tired (4:6) and is at times overcome with emotion (11:33, 38). We hear about his special friends (Martha, Mary, and Lazarus in 11:5). Jesus lives a very active life, tries to evade the persecution of his opponents, and is finally executed on a cross where he dies a real death.

The strong equivalent emphasis on both divinity and humanity of Jesus is present from the very beginning of the Gospel. The Word that was with God, the Word that was God became flesh (1:1-2, 14). Here divinity and humanity truly meet in a most radical way. One cannot be reduced to the other. In 1:14 we do not read: *The Word came into the flesh.* This would mean that the Word only changed location, but did not really change. Nor does 1:14 read: *The Word turned into flesh,* as if the Word changed to the point of ceasing to be the Word. In the former case the human dimension is not really taken seriously; in the latter case the divine dimension is not really taken seriously. The way 1:14 expresses the idea, namely, *The Word became flesh,* avoids both pitfalls. The Word truly changes to become something it was not before, but it does not cease to be the Word, that is, it does not just turn into flesh. Both the divine aspect (Word) and the human aspect (flesh) are fully present. They are not canceling each other out, nor are they in competition with each other. This emphasis on the divinity and the humanity of Jesus is the most basic characteristic of John's presentation of Jesus throughout the Gospel. For example, in the encounter with the first disciples the two

---

[32] Marianne M. Thompson, *The Humanity of Jesus in the Fourth Gospel* (Philadelphia: Fortress Press, 1988).

dimensions are present in the fact that Jesus is called "son of Joseph" and "Son of God" (1:45, 49).

There are three important justice implications in John's understanding of the incarnation which are closely related to the word "flesh." First, "flesh" implies frailty, finitude, and mortality. The incarnation thus witnesses to God's solidarity with the human condition. Second, the Word could only become flesh because the flesh was *"capax Dei."* This illustrates the dignity of every human person despite the frailty of human existence. Whoever oppresses or violates flesh, violates flesh that is *capax Dei.* Third, the use of the word "flesh" also emphasizes universality and inclusiveness. It is essential that the Word became a human person, that is, that the Word took on what is common to all human persons of any time and place. The incarnation thus witnesses to God's identification and solidarity with all human beings without exception.

The major focus of the Gospel of John is the person of Jesus and how he relates to both God and human beings. In order to characterize these relationships, John uses a wide variety of images: father/son/brother, bridegroom/bride/friend of the bridegroom, friend/friend, teacher/disciple, (healer)/healed, sender/messenger, king/(subject),[33] lord/servant/slave, shepherd/sheep/lamb, vine grower/vine/branches. The images are from the spheres of family life, friendship, politics, the economy, religion, health care, and agriculture.

When analyzing these models of relationship which the fourth evangelist uses, we noticed that the relationships in the Gospel are consistently located on three levels: God/Jesus, Jesus/believers, believers/believers.[34] What is even more striking is that these three sets of relationships are frequently described in very similar or even identical images and terminology. In short, Jesus offers human beings a share in a relationship characterized by the same qualities which are true of Jesus' relationship with God. After Jesus' return to the Father, the believers are to share among each other a relationship similar to the one Jesus shared with them.

We note a movement from the God/Jesus relationship via the Jesus/believers relationship to the believer/believer relationship. Neither the God/Jesus nor the Jesus/believer relationship exists for its own sake. Each in its own way becomes the source and the model of another relationship which one of the partners of the first relationship initiates with

---

[33] The words in parentheses are not found in John, but are implied by the use of the related terminology.

[34] We use the word "believer" with the assumption that those who believe in Jesus and remain in his word are "disciples" (see 8:31).

a new party. This inner, albeit implicit dynamic of the relationships in John can therefore not come to its end in the believer/believer relationship. We rather see in it a challenge to invite people outside the believing community to share in the believer/believer relationship. The question whether this was the intention of the original author can remain open in our context.[35] We take it as a valid implication of the text of which the author may or may not have been aware. The inclusivity of the word "flesh" in 1:14,[36] the insistence on God's love for "the world" (see 3:16), and the universalist elements in the Gospel on which we shall focus below[37] are sufficient evidence that such a (re)reading is not in contradiction with important dimensions of the Gospel.

The clearest expression of the tripartite relationship[38] is found in John 15:9, 12 (cf. 13:34): "As the Father has loved me, so I have loved you" and "This is my commandment, that you love one another as I have loved you." The love of the Father for the Son is the model of love the Son has for the believers, and the Son's love is to be the model for the love the believers are to have for one another. The love relationship between Father and Son is neither self-sufficient nor closed. Rather it is open to include others. This is realized in the way that the Son shares with the believers the love relationship which unites him with the Father. But the movement of love does not end there. This love relationship between Jesus and the believers is not an end in itself. It becomes the source and the model of the relationship which the believers have within the community. In light of what we said above about the inner dynamic of the three levels of relationships in the Fourth Gospel, the Johannine love commandment implicitly points beyond the believing community to include those outside.

The tripartite relational structure of the Fourth Gospel, in which Jesus plays the role of mediator and enabler, illustrates the constitutive role of relationality in John's symbolic universe. If justice means participation in the life of the human community, then the centrality in John's relationship makes a significant contribution to the justice

---

[35] In Johannine research there is a long-standing discussion whether the gospel has a pastoral or a missionary purpose. See, for instance, Teresa Okure, *The Johannine Approach to Mission: A Contextual Study of John 4:1-42*, WUNT 2:31 (Tübingen: J.C.B. Mohr, 1988). The debate is also connected with the interpretation of 20:30-31. See D. A. Carson, "The Purpose of the Fourth Gospel: John 20:31 Reconsidered," JBL 106 (1987) 639–51.

[36] See above, 55.

[37] See below, 76–78.

[38] There are many other examples in the gospel. See Reimund Bieringer, "The Paraclete and the Community of Disciples," a paper presented during the 1999 Society of Biblical Literature Meeting in Boston.

debate. In Johannine perspective, ethical demands made on the believers are not appeals to the good intentions of individuals, but are expected to be fulfilled as participation in the divine life with the support of a believing community.

After incarnation and relationality we turn our focus to the Johannine presentation of Jesus as the nonviolent Messiah-King. From the Hebrew Scriptures we learned that God intervenes on behalf of an oppressed people. The Messiah is announced in the prophetic tradition as God's agent for this same intervention. It is therefore to be expected that the Johannine concept of Jesus as Messiah will highlight the same dimension.

The hope for a Davidic king, who would rule the people with justice and establish peace with the neighbors, played a role in Jewish eschatology since the prophets. Many scholars agree that both in the first half of the first century and at the beginning of the second century a movement in Judaism strongly expected a nationalistic-political messiah, one who would drive out the Roman occupation forces. This is the background with which the Johannine passion narrative must be read. The question of Jesus' messiahship plays an important role in John 1–12 in the perception of the disciples (cf. 1:41, 49), in the dialogue with the Samaritan woman (4:25, 29), and in the controversies with "the Jews" (cf. 9:22; 10:22-30). However, the title "Messiah" can only be applied to Jesus after it has undergone radical transformation. For instance, the Jewish tradition did not expect the Messiah to be the Son of God.

In the passion narrative (John 18–19), the concept of messiahship also plays a prominent role. But now the term is "king," rather than Messiah or Christ. Here also John shows that Jesus is a different type of king in comparison with the kings one knows from experience. In 18:36 Jesus states, "My kingship is not of this world" (RSV). In 8:23 the evangelist tells us that Jesus is in the world, but he is not of the world. This means that both Jesus and his kingship have their origin in God, not in the world. The consequences are clear from what follows in 18:36 (RSV): "if my kingship were of this world, my servants would fight, that I might not be handed over to the Jews." The term used for "fighting" is the same one that is found in 2 Macc 8:16 and 13:14 for the violent military fighting of soldiers under the leadership of Judas Maccabeus. Unlike Judas Maccabeus or other worldly rulers, Jesus does not have soldiers to fight for him. Jesus is a Messiah who dies for his followers, instead of asking them to die for him. The divine origin of Jesus' kingship implies nonviolence.

Since Jesus' kingship consists in "bearing witness to the truth" (18:37), nonviolence may not be mistaken for passive condoning of evil. Jesus does not passively accept his sentence. He rather bears witness to the truth before Pilate. If Pilate was of the truth, he would hear Jesus' voice and would not hand him over to be crucified. Many scholars agree that "bearing witness to the truth" in John means "bearing witness to the divine reality."[39] In the Fourth Gospel the accusation of Jesus before Pilate is formulated both in political and in religious terms. Asking Jesus whether he is the king of the Jews (cf. 18:33), Pilate begins with the political charges, but Jesus tries to lead him to the religious dimension by talking about truth. This religious dimension has been present in the Gospel since 5:18 and 10:33 and is taken up again in 19:7. In the trial before Pilate (18:28–19:16a) John connects the religious dimension of messiahship with the political one. He does not disclaim a political dimension in Jesus' kingship altogether; rather he shows that, because of the love relationship between Jesus and God, Jesus can only be king in a nonviolent way.

The justice implications of this dimension of Johannine christology are obvious. The evangelist tells us unmistakably that active nonviolent resistance is a real option for Christians. Jesus' option for nonviolence seems to lead to a failure of his divine intervention for the sake of justice and to the triumph of injustice. But the evangelist testifies to the faith conviction that in Jesus' passion, death, and resurrection the forces of injustice are defeated and messianic peace is established (see 14:27; 20:19, 21, 26).

The Spirit

The Spirit plays an important role in the Fourth Gospel, both during Jesus' earthly ministry and in the post-Easter period. In view of its justice implications we will discuss the Spirit as an agent of mystery, as an agent of life, as an agent of newness.

The spirit *(pneuma)* appears in the Fourth Gospel as a reality that is compared to a dove (1:32), wind (3:8), and breath (20:22; cf. 19:30b). These metaphors locate the Spirit in the realm of the divine and mysterious which is beyond human control. John uses *pneuma* in reference to God, Jesus, and the believers. *Pneuma* characterizes God as mysterious and beyond human control in the statement, "God is spirit" (4:24). *Pneuma* also describes the way Jesus is equipped for his ministry in the world. The Spirit descends upon him and stays upon him (1:32, 33). God gives the Spirit to Jesus beyond measure (3:34). *Pneuma* also plays a role in the way the evangelist refers to Jesus' interactions with people.

---

[39] See Rudolf Bultmann, *"alêtheia,"* *TDNT* 1 (1935) 232–51, esp. 246.

Jesus baptizes with the Holy Spirit (1:33), gives life as the Spirit does (cf. 5:21 with 6:63; cf. 7:39), and speaks words which are spirit and life (6:63). Finally, *pneuma* is used to describe the new birth (3:5, 6, 8), the baptism (1:33), the new life (6:63; cf. 7:39),[40] and the new worship (4:23) of the post-Easter believers, as well as the way the disciples are equipped for their mission in the world (20:22).

As the metaphors illustrate, the Spirit represents the dimension of transcendence which we already addressed in the context of God.[41] That is why the Spirit is connected with the new life *(zôê)* of the believer, which is the Johannine equivalent to the kingdom of God in the Synoptics and new creation in the Pauline letters. This has important implications for justice. Justice is ultimately a gift from God which is beyond human control. The goal of justice is that all may share in the new life which the Spirit gives through Jesus.

In the farewell discourse the names for the Spirit are Holy Spirit (14:26), Spirit of truth (14:17; 15:26; 16:13), and Paraclete *(paraklêtos)* (14:16, 26; 15:26; 16:7). The Paraclete sayings address the presence and activity of the Spirit in the post-Easter community. The role of the Paraclete is to guarantee the continuity with Jesus and to lead the community into the future, even in the face of adversity from the world. The focus now is not how they came to be believers, but rather how the life and message of Jesus can continue to shape their lives and how they can meet new challenges which were not yet a reality in Jesus' life.

The name "Paraclete" which the Fourth Gospel gives to the Spirit in the context of the farewell discourse is not found elsewhere in the Bible. Using "Paraclete" and thus not translating the Greek word, we acknowledge the broad spectrum of possible meanings and the difficulty of settling for one. The juridical meaning reflected in the translation "Advocate" (see NRSV) seems too narrow. A broader understanding is found in the book of Isaiah, to which the Fourth Gospel as a whole is greatly indebted. In Isaiah the verb *parakaleô* is used in connection with the return from the Exile to refer to the comforting of those who mourn, the tender encouragement by the shepherd, the nursing and nourishing of the mother, the protection provided by a leader, the building up of ruins, the repair of cities, and the restoration of the deserts to fruitful land (cf. Isa 40:1-2; 49:8-13; 51:1-6; 61:1-7). In John "Paraclete" is used in

[40] Raymond E. Brown, *The Gospel According to John (i-xii): Introduction, Translation and Notes,* Anchor Bible 29 (New York: Doubleday, 1966) 324: "The Spirit was not a reality as far as man was concerned until the glorified Jesus would communicate the Spirit to men (xx 22). Then the Spirit would operate in a new creation in a way not hitherto possible."

[41] See above, 52.

contexts which allude to persecution and thus conjure up images of fear, hatred, and death. Calling the Spirit "Paraclete," the fourth evangelist probably intended to transfer to the Spirit some of the connotations found in Isaiah.

Repeating Jesus' words of the past is not enough for the future life of the community. In 14:25 Jesus prefaces the second Paraclete saying by the words, "I have said these things to you while I am still with you." On the contrary the Spirit of truth, who will be with them "forever" (14:16), will teach them everything.[42] Because of his specific social location, the earthly Jesus cannot tell the disciples everything. This limitation is also expressed in 14:28 ("The Father is greater than I," i.e., the earthly Jesus)[43] and in 16:7 ("it is to your advantage that I go away, for if I do not go away, the Advocate [Paraclete] will not come to you"). Concerning the disciples Jesus says in 16:12, "I still have many things to say to you, but you cannot bear them now." The Paraclete rather "will guide you into all the truth" and "will declare to you the things that are to come" (16.13).

Interpreters have been puzzled with the question what these "things that are to come" are. They can hardly be the crucifixion of Jesus because at the moment when the Spirit will be given, the crucifixion of Jesus will be past, not future. Nor is it likely that they are the persecution of the believers, since in the immediately preceding context (15:18-25; 16:1-4a) Jesus predicted to the disciples in no uncertain terms the hatred and persecution that they would have to face. In the context it is also difficult to accept that the Spirit should be limited to adapting the message of Jesus to a new situation[44] or to bringing out its implications for the future.[45] What Jesus cannot tell the disciples because of their limitations, the Paraclete will tell them by "guiding you into all the truth." The earthly Jesus told the world what he had heard from the one who sent him (8:26). A little further in 8:40 he calls himself a human person "who has told you the truth that I heard from God." But it is only the Paraclete who can tell the full truth and he does so without deviating from the truth of the Father and the Son. The newness in the work of the Paraclete is therefore very similar to the greater works that

---

[42] Against many interpreters we assume that "that I have said to you" in 14:26 only belongs to "he will remind you of everything," not to "he will teach you everything." The NRSV translation seems to reflect the same interpretation.

[43] See above, 52.

[44] See Udo Schnelle, "Johannes als Geisttheologe," *NovT* 40 (1998) 17–31, esp. 21.

[45] See D. A. Carson, *The Gospel According to John* (Leicester/Grand Rapids, Mich.: Inter-Varsity/Eerdmans, 1991) 541: "he is doing little more than fleshing out the implications." Cf. also Francis J. Moloney, *The Gospel of John,* Sacra Pagina 4 (Collegeville: The Liturgical Press, 1998) 440–1.

will be done by those who believe in Jesus (14:12). Neither the new work of the Paraclete nor the greater works of the believers are achieved in separation from the Father and the Son, but in and through them.

At the end of our investigation we need to consider one last question: How does the Paraclete achieve all the things we talked about above? The Paraclete is not incarnate in one historically limited human being, but takes on flesh in the believers and in the community. The Paraclete is in the believers and works through them. When the farewell discourse says that the Paraclete does certain things, we may not overlook the fact that disciples do these things and the Paraclete does them through the disciples. This is evident in 15:26-27 where giving testimony is said of the Paraclete and of the disciples.[46] In 2:22 and 16:4 (cf. 12:16) we see that the disciples remember the words of Jesus and in 14:26 the Paraclete reminds them of Jesus' words. The teaching, the guiding in the truth, the announcing of the things to come, the witnessing as well as the proving wrong are all activities which the Paraclete does in and through human beings who believe in Jesus.

In the Gospel of John, then, the Spirit functions as the agent of God's new creation, which is envisioned and realized in the community of the disciples. Gifted with the Spirit, the disciples receive the task to continue the mission of Jesus (20:22). The Spirit-Paraclete enables them to do for one another what the earthly Jesus had done for them. Loving, washing feet, teaching, tending sheep, being a spring of living water, being one, intervening for the sake of justice would all be asking too much of disciples to do on their own, but become possible inasmuch as the Paraclete does these things in and through them. This is the only way that Jesus' works and even greater works can continue after his death. Jesus' works also included a justice dimension, which is essential for the way the disciples do his works and even greater ones.

Looking back at the end of this investigation of the theological framework for justice, we see that the Johannine presentation of God, whom we meet in the Gospel as Father, Son, and Paraclete, contains many elements which are constitutive for justice. The Johannine God is involved in the world and yet transcendent; constituted by intimate intradivine relations and at the same time sharing that relationship with the world via Jesus and the Paraclete; in solidarity with all human

---

[46] Schnackenburg, *The Gospel According to St. John*, 117–8: "The Paraclete cannot, however, speak to the world directly, but has to make use of the disciples to do this. This means that v. 27 is indispensable, providing clarification and the context in which the disciples are addressed. The witness borne by the Paraclete and that borne by the disciples are expressed in two separate sentences placed side by side, but they come together to form a single witness."

beings without exception, nonviolently, but actively resisting evil and guiding people on their journey into the future to meet new challenges. All this illustrates that the Johannine God is about what justice is and what justice implies. John's presentation of God favors a relational concept of justice focused on participation.

An Anthropological Framework for Justice

Justice concepts are not only shaped by images of God, but also by understandings of the human person. In this section we will therefore investigate the Johannine anthropology for its contribution to justice. We will submit the Gospel to an analysis according to five aspects used in contemporary theological anthropology: embodiment, relationality, social location, difference, and accountable agency.[47]

Embodiment

Out of the six anthropological terms used by John, three (flesh, body, and belly/womb) are relating to the dimension of the human person which is accessible to sense perception. The other three—spirit, heart, and *psychê*—represent that dimension which is inaccessible to sense perception. Flesh, body, and belly/womb on the one hand, and spirit, heart, and *psychê* on the other, are the two inseparable dimensions of embodiment. In fact, each one of them refers to the whole person but from a unique perspective. John shows no signs of any negative attitude toward the body or the belly/womb. As Luise Schottroff has pointed out, John shows no signs of identifying bodily realities with evil.[48]

The Fourth Gospel clearly recognizes a duality of flesh and spirit, but it does not conceive of them as mutually exclusive. John knows the limits of the flesh (see 6:63), but does not judge it as intrinsically evil. Flesh points to the finitude, not to the sinfulness of the world. It is, of course, possible that sin takes charge of the flesh. But eternal life can also shape the flesh. The spirit does not abolish or replace the flesh, but penetrates and transforms it.

The place of the flesh is most clearly evident from the statement in John 1:14: "The Word [*logos*] became flesh [*sarx*]." John's understanding of the incarnation implies an unprecedented appreciation of the flesh,

---

[47] See below, 146–9.

[48] Luise Schottroff, "The Samaritan Woman and the Notion of Sexuality in the Fourth Gospel," *"What Is John,"* vol. 2: *Literary and Social Readings of the Fourth Gospel,* SBL Symposium Series 7, ed. Fernando F. Segovia (Atlanta: Scholars Press, 1998) 157–81, cf. esp. 176–7.

not only from the christological but also the anthropological perspective. Becoming human was only possible for the *logos* because the *sarx* was *"capax Dei."* In distinction from Phil 2:7 ("but emptied himself, taking the form of a slave, being born in human likeness"), there are no indications in John that becoming flesh was a humiliation for the *logos*. To the contrary, the flesh in its finitude and fragility was capable of providing what was needed, so that the invisible could be seen, the inaudible could be heard, and the untouchable could be touched. Flesh is a term with such a general application that it applies to any human being regardless of gender, ethnicity, or class. Moreover, flesh is characteristic of human persons no matter where or when they live. This incarnational reality throws light on John's understanding of the human person. Incarnation reveals the dignity of the human flesh (embodiment) and establishes the human flesh as a dwelling place of God.

John's positive evaluation of the body and non-dualist anthropology is also reflected in the sign stories.[49] They demonstrate clearly that the Johannine Jesus is not treating people as disembodied spirits, but rather as embodied persons whose bodily ailments he cures (see the royal official's son in ch. 4, the sick person in ch. 5, and the blind person in ch. 9). Jesus is also frequently shown as someone who provides for bodily needs. This is not only illustrated in signs (see the wine in ch. 2, the bread in ch. 6, and the fish in ch. 21), but also in some "I am" sayings ("I am the bread of life" in ch. 6; "I am the light of the world" in 8:12; 9:5). Still both sign stories and "I am" sayings address human needs of food or health in more than a material way; that is, "bread" means more than material food. The blending of material and spiritual needs happens in John on the basis of an awareness and an appreciation of the material needs.[50]

Our findings with regard to embodiment lead us to the conclusion that for John embodiment is a constitutive part of what it means to be human. John's incarnational perspective implies that so-called material and spiritual human needs cannot be separated from one another. By presenting Jesus as providing for basic human needs and by connecting the faith-dimension of Jesus' ministry closely with the so-called

[49] H. von Lips, "Anthropologie und Wunder im Johannesevangelium. Die Wunder Jesu im Johannesevangelium im Unterschied zu den synoptischen Evangelien auf dem Hintergrund johanneischen Menschenverständnisses," *EvTh* 50 (1990) 296–311.

[50] We see proof of this in John's understanding of the incarnation (see above) as well as in John's use of the word *sêmeion* for Jesus' miracles. See Thompson, *The Humanity of Jesus;* and Gilbert Van Belle, *The Signs Source in the Fourth Gospel: Historical Survey and Critical Evaluation of the Semeia Hypothesis,* BETL 116 (Leuven: University Press and Peeters, 1994).

material dimension of life, the Fourth Gospel lays the foundation for an integrated concept of justice. This concept demands that respect for human dignity includes provision for basic human needs. If bodies matter, justice has to be concerned about concrete, tangible realities.

Relationality

When we enter the world of the Fourth Gospel, we encounter people who are characterized by the network of relationships to which they belong. We see that in John the primary relationships are family relationships (siblings, spouses) and status or function within the community.

Jesus is presented as deeply involved in relationships with people around him. Jesus calls Lazarus "our friend" (11:11) and the evangelist tells us that Jesus "loved Martha and her sister and Lazarus" (11:5). Jesus also calls his disciples friends (15:14-15) and he reminds them of his love for them (13:34; 15:9). From the very beginning we see Jesus inviting people to be with him (cf. "come and you shall see" in 1:39). He creates a new community which can be described under the images of a new family,[51] new school (cf. teacher and disciples), or as a new circle of friends. After Jesus' death this new community of Jesus is realized in the Johannine community that sees itself as a direct continuation of the community of disciples around the earthly Jesus.

Many qualities of the bond that unites God and Jesus[52] are not reserved for their relationship, but are shared by Jesus with the believers. The Johannine Jesus does not jealously guard his relationship with the Father, but he shares important aspects of this relationship with those who believe in him and invites them to participate in this relationship. The Gospel begins by stating that "the Word was with God" (1:1) and in 16:32 Jesus tells his disciples that the Father is with him. Similarly Jesus is presented frequently as being with people. The disciples have been with Jesus from the beginning (15:27; cf. 14:9). This togetherness is interrupted by the death of Jesus, since the disciples cannot accompany Jesus where he is going. But in the Paraclete whom Jesus sends, a new togetherness is made possible (14:17). Jesus also promises to prepare a dwelling place for the disciples and that he will come back to get them "so that where I am, there you may be also" (14:3; cf. 17:24). In addition

---

[51] O'Day, "John," 304: "The promise . . . that a new family will be born, a family that is determined by faith, not by flesh and blood relationships." Even when Jesus is about to die he promises a new home (14:1-3). See also 14:18: "I will not leave you orphaned."

[52] See above, 56.

to the "being with," John also speaks about "being in" and "dwelling/abiding in." Jesus says, "I am in the Father and the Father is in me" (14:10). The parallel with the disciples is established in 17:21: "As you, Father, are in me and I am in you, may they also be in us" (cf. 17:23, 26). Jesus abides in the Father's love (15:10). Jesus and the believer mutually abide in each other (15:5; cf. 15:4, 7, 9; 6:56; 8:31).

The mutual indwelling of God and Jesus and of Jesus and the disciples is also the basis of a number of activities. Just as Jesus has kept his Father's commandments, the disciples are invited to keep Jesus' commandments (15:10). As Jesus does the works of the Father (4:34; 5:36; cf. 14:10), the believers do the works that Jesus does (14:12). The Father gives glory to the Son and the Son gives glory to the disciples (17:22). Jesus testifies to what he has seen (God in 3:11; cf. 5:37; 8:18), and the eyewitness of the piercing of Jesus' side testifies to what he has seen (19:35; cf. 21:24).

The mission of Jesus and his disciples is also strikingly similar. During the farewell discourse Jesus says, "As you have sent me into the world, so I have sent them into the world" (17:18). The risen Christ commissions his disciples with the words: "As the Father has sent me, so I send you" (20:21). As the Father sanctified the Son for his mission into the world (10:36), so the Son asks the Father to sanctify the disciples for their mission into the world (17:17; cf. 17:19).

Our observations have brought to the fore that being in relationship is central to the Fourth Gospel. The relationship between God and Jesus (including the Spirit-Paraclete) is the model and space within which people's relationships with Jesus and God, as well as their relationships among each other, are made possible. The intra-divine relationships are foundational for human community. Inclusiveness and participation have firm roots here. These will provide a firm foundation for an understanding of justice as participation.

Social Location

The fourth evangelist has a variety of ways in which he addresses the issue of his characters' social locations. Frequently John points to the city or region where people are from. In close connection with these geographic specifications, John identifies them ethnically and/or religiously as Galileans, Jews, Samaritans, or Greeks.

In 4:44 the evangelist implicitly identifies Galilee as Jesus' "fatherland,"[53] as opposed to Judea where Jesus goes for the feasts, where he

---

[53] Gilbert Van Belle, "The Faith of the Galileans: The Parenthesis in Jn 4,44," *ETL* 74 (1998) 27–44.

enters into disputes with his opponents in the Temple, and where his trial, execution, burial, and resurrection take place. While there were characteristic differences between Galileans and Judeans, the Galilean Jews fully shared in the national and religious identity of Judaism.[54] Unlike the Samaritans they recognized Jerusalem as the center of worship and went there on pilgrimage for the major feasts. Nevertheless in comparison to the Judeans, the Galileans were clearly the underdogs. In the eyes of some of his contemporaries, Jesus' social location in Galilee makes his religious claims even more unlikely. Some call into question that he is the Messiah when they ask, "Surely the Messiah does not come from Galilee, does he?" (7:41). The Pharisees say to Nicodemus: "Surely you are not also from Galilee, are you? Search and you will see that no prophet is to arise from Galilee" (7:52).

As we have seen, the Gospel of John presents Jesus as embedded in a social location, but he is not a prisoner of his social location. He is a Galilean Jew from Nazareth, but he is not accepted in his hometown. The focal point of his ministry is Judea, Jerusalem in particular. He is a member of a family, but his brothers reject him. Jesus is presented as a Jew and his Jewishness is not called into question. Nevertheless on occasion he distances himself from some of "the Jews" whom he encounters in his ministry. In these ways the Johannine narrative presents Jesus as fully embedded in a social location,[55] and yet as someone who does not allow himself to be imprisoned by his social location. The Johannine Jesus is remarkably free in assessing and critiquing the constraints imposed upon him by his social location (cf. his homeland, his family, his gender, even his religion) in light of his close relationship with God and the vision that flows from it.

In John the people who are interacting with Jesus are from a variety of social locations. There are Galileans, Judeans, Samaritans, Greeks, and Romans. There are leading and influential people like Nicodemus, Annas, Caiaphas, and Pilate, as well as marginated persons like those who are lame or blind or from Samaria. The first disciples are identified as Galileans—Peter, Andrew, and Philip being from Bethsaida (1:44), and Nathanael from Cana (21:2). While in the Synoptics they are fishermen, nothing is said about their occupation in John (except perhaps 21:3). In the Fourth Gospel we also meet Annas and Caiaphas, the high

[54] Meier, *A Marginal Jew,* 1:207–8, speaks of a "vigorous Jewish presence" and a "reawakening of Jewish national and religious identity" in Galilee after the victories of the Maccabees.

[55] The description of the Johannine Christ as "striding on earth" ("über die Erle Schreitend") (cf. Ernst Käsemann, *The Testament of Jesus: A Study of the Gospel of John in the Light of Chapter 17,* trans. Gerhard Krodel [Philadelphia: Fortress Press, 1968] 9) is highly questionable.

priest, as well as Nicodemus, a Pharisee and a leader of the Jews, i.e., a member of the Sanhedrin, the highest Jewish council in religious and civil matters (3:1 and 7:50-51). When Jesus talks to Nicodemus about the need of being born from above (3:3) and of being born of water and Spirit (3:5), his words imply that, as a disciple, Nicodemus would have to give up his privileged social location and start anew. This illustrates in an exemplary way a common experience of early Christians, namely, that following Christ had far-reaching implications for their social location. In the Gospel this is expressed in the phrase "fear of the Jews," which keeps so-called crypto-Christian Jews (like Joseph of Arimathea and perhaps Nicodemus) from becoming disciples openly. The fear is concretized in the prospect of being excluded from the synagogue (9:22; 12:42; 16:2) and in the threat of being killed (16:2).[56]

In socioeconomic perspective, the Gospel of John presupposes a social location that is closer to the well-to-do than to the poor and destitute, even though in general the level is not more than what we would call lower middle class today.[57] The scathing remarks against the rich in Luke's Gospel are conspicuously absent in John. The few times that the poor are mentioned they are the "other" who need to be helped (cf. 12:5 and 13:29). The expression "rich" is not used at all, even though there are a few people who are very rich. Nicodemus is able to bring a mixture of myrrh and aloes of about a hundred pounds (19:39), which must have cost a fortune. Mary of Bethany can afford "a pound of costly perfume made of pure nard" (12:3), which Judas claims could have been sold for three hundred denarii (12:5), while two hundred denarii would not have been enough to buy bread for one meal for five thousand men. Interestingly enough the Fourth Gospel lacks information about the trade of Jesus or his father. We have to wait until 21:2-3 to get the slightest hint of the prominent male disciples' trade. Even then can we conclude that they were fishermen from the fact that they went fishing?

By way of conclusion we note that John uses town of origin, status, or function within the community and, perhaps most prominently, ethnic/religious background as coordinates to sketch the social loca-

---

[56] U. C. von Wahlde, "The Johannine 'Jews': A Critical Survey," *NTS* 28 (1982) 33–60, is convinced that all the references to hostile Jews in the original layer of the Gospel of John are pointing to the Jerusalem authorities. Others admit that the group of Jews hostile to Jesus sometimes includes common people.

[57] We disagree on this point with G. D. Kilpatrick, "What John Tells Us About John," *Studies in John Presented to Professor Dr. J. N. Sevenster on the Occasion of His Seventieth Birthday,* NTSuppl 24 (Leiden: Brill, 1970) 73–87, esp. 77, who claims that John's world is the world "of the Palestinian peasant, a poor man in a poor province."

tion of his characters.[58] John is well aware of the importance of social location for people's well-being. He takes seriously the implications which social location has for people's lives. There are several instances where those disadvantaged by their social location—as for instance Galileans, Samaritans, women, patients with long-term illnesses—are given pride of place. On the other hand, people with a privileged social location—for example, Nicodemus or Pilate—are challenged to let go of their privileges.

Difference

Difference is closely connected with originality and uniqueness. In this section we will deal with questions such as: Does the Gospel present a wide range of unique human beings? Is their originality respected in the way they are treated? Does the Gospel tend toward stereotypes and generalizations?

The Gospel in its canonical form begins and ends by recognizing difference. In 1:35-51 we are introduced to four disciples. They are mentioned by name and city of origin. Simon even receives a new name from Jesus (1:42), and Nathanael is called "an Israelite in whom there is no deceit" (1:47). Jesus invites the disciples to come and see, to remain with him (1:39), and to see greater things (1:51). Jesus has special knowledge of Simon and Nathanael. It seems that Jesus approaches each one in the way best suited for him. John 21:22 points out that the destiny of different disciples may vary ("If it is my will that he remain until I come, what is that to you?"), but that each should only be concerned about their own call to follow Jesus. While John does not talk explicitly about creation of humans, the uniqueness of each person's call and destiny before God is evident.

Similarly the Gospel respects each disciple's unique way of coming to believe in the resurrection. The Beloved Disciple witnesses the empty tomb, the linen wrappings, and, as the Gospel tells us, "saw and believed" (20:8). Mary Magdalene has a very intimate encounter with the risen Christ at the tomb. She touches him and receives a message for the brothers and sisters from him (20:17). The disciples without Thomas see the risen Christ while hiding behind locked doors, and Thomas is even invited, in a following appearance, to touch the marks of the nails (20:27).

---

[58] Cf. R. Alan Culpepper, *Anatomy of the Fourth Gospel: A Study in Literary Design* (Philadelphia: Fortress Press, 1983) 145: "John's characterization is also peculiar in that it does not give the age or physical characteristics of any character. Only the barest outline of their past is ever related. . . . Instead, the characters are individualized by their position in society and their interaction with Jesus."

The Fourth Gospel confronts its readers with a wide variety of people or groups from different genders, geographic or ethnic background, religious affiliation, social-political background, and health condition. In the Gospel we meet men and women; Judeans, Galileans, Samaritans, Greeks, and Romans; a beggar and a member of the leading class; as well as people with and without serious illnesses. Nevertheless, in keeping with Johannine dualism, certain groups are privileged while others are reduced to the status of "the other." The disciples (or believers, community members) are the norm and unbelievers (mostly called "the Jews" and "the world") are "the other." Similarly the poor are perceived as "the other" in comparison to the disciples.[59] In these cases the evangelist strongly identifies with one group (believers, middle class), while others are pushed to the margins and their perspective is lost.

Another danger for difference is stereotyping. John uses the term "the Jews" more than seventy times. In many cases "the Jews" refers to people who are hostile to Jesus. Some authors have tried to demonstrate that virtually all the hostile occurrences point to the Jerusalem authorities and not to the common people.[60] Even if this were correct, the use of a generalizing term would produce a stereotyping effect implicating all Jewish people. In contrast to the diversity of Jewish groups reflected in the Synoptics (Pharisees, scribes, Sadducees, high priests, Herodians, Zealots etc.), John mostly speaks of "the Jews." The question is whether, as Raymond Brown claims, the destruction of the Temple or whether the evangelist himself "had simplified Judaism."[61] Even though it is too simplistic to assume that the Pharisees were the only group that survived the destruction of the Temple, Brown may have a point. Nevertheless, the Gospel's dualism which divides the world into believers and unbelievers apart from any other consideration simplified and stereotyped Judaism in the expression "the Jews." In so doing, John violates the value of difference. The Fourth Gospel also uses the terms "the Samaritans" (4:39, 40; 8:48), "the Galileans" (4:45; cf. 7:52), and "the Greeks" (12:20) in a generalizing manner, albeit to a much lesser degree. "Samaritan" in 8:48 and "Galilee" as references to origin in 7:52 are used with negative connotations.

We conclude that the Fourth Gospel respects diversity and difference as constitutive dimensions of what it means to be human. In some areas, however, the Gospel's respect for difference reaches its limit. The Gospel's presentation of "the Jews" and unbelievers in general has a stereotyping effect. Stereotyping, generalizing, and reducing people or

---

[59] See 12:8, "You always have the poor with you," and 13:29, "that he should give something to the poor."

[60] Von Wahlde, "The Johannine 'Jews,'" 33–60.

[61] Brown, *John,* lxxii.

groups to the status of "the other" violate the value of difference and are serious dangers for justice.

Accountable Agency

The fifth and last dimension of the anthropological framework to be considered is accountable agency. This dimension is about self-determination and accountability in interdependence. Johannine christology has crucial implications for Johannine anthropology. We will start our investigation of accountable agency with Jesus.[62]

The relationship between the Johannine Jesus and God is characterized by love, mutual indwelling, and oneness. Jesus says of himself that he does the will and fulfills the commandment of the Father. The Johannine Jesus repeatedly stresses that he did not come of his own accord (7:28; 8:42), that he does not do anything of his own accord (8:28) or speak of his own accord (7:17; 12:49). Jesus emphasizes that he does not do his own will, but the will of the one who sent him (5:30; 6:38). Jesus repeatedly underlines that he keeps the Father's commandments (10:18; 12:49; 15:10). But these statements are not speaking of humility or obedience. Rather, their function is to point out Jesus' origin in the Father, his unity with the Father, and the authority that flows from this. Not dependence and self-effacement, but accountable agency, freedom, and self-determination characterize the Johannine Jesus.

Next to the symmetrical love relationship, John also describes the Father-Son relationship in terms of an asymmetrical working relationship. The central asymmetrical concept is sending or mission. The Father sends the Son, not vice versa. The Father gives everything into the hands of the Son (3:35; 13:3) and shows to the Son everything he does (5:20). But even here the Gospel does not use sending terminology to undermine Jesus' agency. Rather, in keeping with the Jewish understanding, Jesus as the messenger shares in the agency of the one who sent him.[63] In the case of Jesus, this is even more true than with any other messenger, because Jesus is not just any kind of a messenger, but the Son, one who shares in the Father's life.

The agency of Jesus is demonstrated in the fact that Jesus has life in himself, something that can only be said of God. The fact that for Jesus having life in himself is a gift from God (5:26) does not diminish Jesus' agency, for what Jesus received as a gift from God is truly his and does not create dependency. God also gives authority to Jesus: authority to

---

[62] For more background on what follows see Lataire and Bieringer, *God the Father*.

[63] Cf. Peder Borgen, "God's Agent in the Fourth Gospel," *The Interpretation of John*, Issues in Religion and Theology 9, ed. John Ashton (Philadelphia: Fortress Press, 1986) 67–78, esp. 68.

bring to justice (5:27), "those who have done good, to the resurrection of life, and those who have done evil, to the resurrection of condemnation" (5:29), authority to lay down his life and take it up again (10:18), and authority over all flesh to give them eternal life (17:2). The most important precondition for agency is life. The fact that Jesus has life in himself qualifies him as the ultimate accountable agent. He uses his freedom and authority to share his life with human persons in order to make them accountable agents too. The Son gives life to whomever he wishes (cf. 5:21).

Human agency has its foundation in the gift of life from Jesus and through him from God. The characteristic stress which the fourth evangelist puts on life gives ample evidence to the primary importance which he gives to agency. This is why believing in Jesus gives the believers the authority or power to become children of God, i.e., to be born out of God (1:12-13 and 3:3, 5). The image of a new birth is the most radical expression of receiving the gift of life and thus the potential for agency. Since sin enslaved human persons (cf. 8:34), they can only be truly set free (cf. 8:32) by a radical new beginning.

The Gospel states repeatedly that the gift of life which the believers receive is an abundant gift. The receivers have it to share with others and they have it forever.[64] By receiving the knowledge of what Jesus has heard from God and seen in God, the disciples are transformed from being slaves to being friends (cf. 15:15).[65] They are accepted into an equal to equal relationship and their agency is enhanced.[66]

---

[64] Cf. 4:14, "The water that I will give will become in them a spring of water gushing up to eternal life," and 6:51, "Whoever eats of this bread will live forever."

[65] We note that the social reality of slavery or servanthood is not actively opposed despite Jesus' calling the believers to become friends. The royal official as well as the high priest have slaves (4:51; 18:10, 18, 26). In 8:35; 13:16; and 15:20 the social reality of slavery is used to illustrate a theological point. The fourth evangelist does not seem to see a contradiction between these places and 15:15. The seed is present, however, for later generations of Christians to realize that the social reality of slavery or servanthood cannot be reconciled with the call to friendship that Jesus extends to the believers.

[66] The way people are invited to believe also speaks of accountable agency and freedom. Believing in Jesus is not forced on anyone. People are invited to "come and see" (1:39, 46). In other places, however, threats are issued to those who do not believe (3:36) and the demonization of the opponents of Jesus (cf. 8:44) fails to respect accountable agency. Even though the disciples are in a privileged position they miss the point most of the time, including in the farewell discourse (14:6-14) and when Jesus is arrested (18:10-11). Among the Twelve who are chosen by Jesus there is one who betrays him and one who denies him. In the company of Jesus they have neither undergone brainwashing nor has their intellectual freedom been impaired in any other way. They continue to decide for themselves, even if it is to the disadvantage of Jesus, others, or themselves.

We conclude that the concept of accountable agency is present in the Fourth Gospel as a dimension of full personal flourishing. The foundation of human agency is the gift of life, the promise of being born anew out of God. In John the resultant authority and agency of Jesus as God's messenger as well as accountability to God underscore an anthropology which urges action on behalf of justice.

John's Contribution to a Theological Ethics of Justice

In the previous sections we saw that the Gospel of John contains understandings of God and the human person which have important implications for a theological understanding of justice. In a final section we will investigate whether we can also gain more direct insights with regard to the theory and practice of justice in the Fourth Gospel. We will first concentrate on the terminology and then on building blocks of justice.

Justice Terminology

As we saw above,[67] in the Hebrew Scriptures there are four words which cover the meaning of justice: *ṣĕdāqâ* (right relationship), *mišpāṭ* (just judgment), *ḥesed* (loving kindness), and *ʾĕmēt* (covenant fidelity). The Greek translation tends to translate them as *dikaiosynê, krisis, eleos,* and *alêtheia* respectively. Except for *eleos*, these words are found in the Fourth Gospel. In general exegetical discussion, however, none of these terms is connected with justice. *Alêtheia* is interpreted as meaning truth in the perspective of revelation theology. *Krisis* is understood as meaning the judgment of the unbeliever. *Dikaiosynê* is often taken to mean moral uprightness, holiness, or obedience to the will of God.

The fact that justice is first and foremost a quality of God has a faint echo in Jesus' addressing God as "just Father" in his farewell prayer (17:25). Here John uses the adjective *dikaios* for "just." In the context, Jesus refers to the love with which God loved him before the foundation of the world (17:24) and to his sharing of that love with the disciples (17:26). At the beginning of the farewell prayer Jesus had already referred to God as *alêthinos*, true, faithful (17:3; cf. 3:33; 7:28 and 8:26).[68] God's justice and fidelity are revealed in his sending Jesus.

---

[67] See above, 46.

[68] The close relationship between *dikaiosynê* and *alêtheia* in John is evident in 3:21 where the expression "to do *alêtheia*" is used. Josef Blank, *Krisis: Untersuchungen zur johanneischen Christologie und Eschatologie* (Freiburg: Lambertus, 1964) 106, affirms that "to do *alêtheia*" should be read in line with the Hebrew Scriptures as almost synonymous with "to do *dikaiosynê*," i.e., "to act justly."

Since John transfers divine qualities to Jesus, it is not surprising that *dikaios* and *alêthinos* are also associated with him. When applied to Jesus, justice refers to the way he conducts the judgment which God has given into his hands. In the context of 5:25-30, Jesus is speaking about the last judgment when those who have done good will come to the resurrection of life, those who have done evil to the resurrection of condemnation. Jesus judges the deeds of people as good or evil and in 5:30 he underlines that his judgment *(krisis)* is just. The Johannine Jesus does not claim justice in the sense that his judgment is in keeping with the requirements of an ideal norm, namely, that the good people must be rewarded and the evil punished. Rather, the evangelist strongly emphasizes that Jesus did not come to judge/condemn the world, but rather to save it. Jesus' coming gives everyone a last chance to change their evil ways. The reason why those who do not heed this call to conversion will be judged is not to please an ideal norm. Rather, God is faithful to his love relationship with the world. As in the Hebrew Scriptures, judgment is associated with God's intervention on behalf of those oppressed by evildoers. Calling evildoers to conversion is a necessary part of bringing justice to the victims of their evil deeds. Not intervening against those who persist in their evil deeds would be an injustice toward those who suffer from their oppression.

After the Sabbath healing of John 5:1-9, questions were raised about Jesus' attitude toward the law. In the eyes of his opponents, Jesus' treatment of the law amounts to injustice; for Jesus it is justice. It seems that the opponents treat the law as an ideal norm and only those can be just who fulfill the requirements of this norm. Jesus, however, in his healing the sick person, does precisely what his and God's fidelity to the love relationship with the world requires. For Jesus justice amounts to a concern for the whole person and it was this concern that moved him to the Sabbath healing (7:23).

We conclude that in John as in the Hebrew Scriptures justice is in the first place a quality of God. Through the incarnation, God's justice, i.e., *dikaiosynê, alêtheia,* and *krisis,* is realized in the world. Jesus' deeds are presented as just, because they take into consideration the entire picture and not just isolated facts. They apply the law in view of God's faithful love relationship with people instead of making the law into an ideal norm that needs to be followed at all cost.

Building Blocks for a Theological Ethic of Justice

We are not looking for a ready-made ethic of justice in the Fourth Gospel. Our focus is rather on the ethical vision of the Johannine community as expressed in the Gospel. This vision is present in the stories and symbols of this Gospel as well as in its underlying theology. The Gospel is primarily concerned about faith in Jesus as the Christ, the Son of God (20:30-31). But it is impossible to talk about faith without talking about love. Concerning this issue, Johannine studies have too long been under the influence of Rudolf Bultmann, who gives priority to being over doing. We rather agree with Johannes Nissen when he states: "The basic moral stance is not just a consequence of faith; it is a constitutive part of Christian existence. Faith and love are one. Our being shapes our doing."[69] In the following it is our concern to demonstrate that in the Gospel of John not only love, but also justice is a constitutive part of what the Fourth Gospel means by faith.

Abundance: An abiding justice issue since Aristotle has been the scarcity of resources and the concomitant need for fair distribution. In response to this approach, the Gospel puts before us an alternative world of abundance, thus challenging the starting point of most justice theories. In the Johannine symbolic universe, God provides an abundance of the basic goods of life for everyone who believes through the eschatological messenger, Jesus the Christ. These goods are given the names "grace and truth" (1:14), the Spirit who is given beyond measure (3:34), "abundant gift" (4:10), "life" (10:10b), and are concretized in the extravagant gift of choice wine at the wedding feast of Cana (2:6-10), in the gift of living water that is so abundant that one does not have to come back to draw from the well (4:10, 14), in the overflowing measure (twelve baskets) of bread left over after five thousand are fed with five barley loaves (6:13). These are not the scraps from the table of the rich for the poor, but the poor and marginated receive choice gifts in abundant measure. People like the Cana wedding party, who were too poor to provide enough wine for their guests to make merry and for whom quality wine was out of reach, are restored in their dignity by receiving the fare of royalty. People like the Samaritan woman, for whom getting water daily was a chore, are set free to become messengers of the Gospel. And a crowd of people struggling to provide the bare minimum for their survival, whom Jesus would have had every right to dismiss at the end of a long day, are freed from the task of finding food to be able to listen to God's word.

These abundant gifts have a symbolic meaning in the framework of John's realized eschatology. But this is no excuse to ignore the realistic

[69] Nissen, "Community," 200. See also José P. Miranda, *Being and the Messiah: The Message of St. John* (Maryknoll, N.Y.: Orbis Books, 1977) 36–45, 73–86, 137–48; and David Rensberger, "Love for One Another and Love for Enemies in the Gospel of John," *The Love of Enemy and Non-Retaliation in the New Testament,* ed. W. M. Swartley (Louisville: Westminster/John Knox, 1992) 297–313, esp. 303.

overtones of quantity and quality which are found throughout the Gospel. The Fourth Gospel's realism is a reminder that its theology is incarnational and rejects disembodied spiritualism. A theological ethic of justice can learn from John that guaranteeing minimum levels of resources is not enough, but that the Christian worldview requires that all persons have a share in God's abundant gifts, which include water, bread, and light.

Inclusive Community: A related and equally central building block of an ethic of justice is inclusive community. While talking about abundance, we already noted a move away from the individualist concern of distributive justice expressed in the formula "to each his own." In the horizon of abundance, justice evolves as a constitutively social reality. The Gospel of John has a universalist perspective and models inclusive community despite a number of exclusivist traits. As is clear from 20:30-31, the primary concern of the Gospel is the faith of its addressees. In the prologue we encounter the purpose of the Gospel as personified in the purpose of John's testimony, "so that all might believe through him" (1:7). Throughout the Gospel the invitation to believe that Jesus is the Christ, the Son of God, is extended to people without any limitation.

Those who approach or encounter Jesus as candidates for faith include Galileans (cf., for instance, Andrew, Simon, Philip, Nathanael), Judeans (cf. Nicodemus, Mary and Martha of Bethany), Samaritans (cf. the unnamed woman of Samaria and the people of Sychar), Greeks, and Romans (cf. Pilate). Universalist tendencies are also found in 10:16 ("other sheep that do not belong to this fold"), 11:51-52 ("to gather into one the dispersed children of God"), and 12:32 ("I . . . will draw all people to myself").

The call to accept Jesus as the Christ is equally addressed to men and women in the Fourth Gospel. Next to male disciples like Andrew, Peter, Philip, and Nathanael, a number of women have prevalent places in the Gospel. In 4:25-26 Jesus reveals himself to the Samaritan woman as the Messiah (cf. Andrew's confession in 1:41). In 11:27 Martha is presented as having arrived at the full faith in Jesus which the author of the Gospel desires of all the addressees (see 20:30-31). Martha confesses: "I believe that you are the Messiah, the Son of God, the one coming into the world." Her confession closely parallels that of Simon Peter in Matt 16:16 (cf. Mark 8:29).

Social or class distinctions do not have any bearing on whether people are invited to believe in Jesus or not. Even though in John the rich versus poor antithesis is not explicitly present, the potential believers include a leader of the Jews (3:1, cf. 12:42), a royal official (4:46), a woman who can afford "a pound of costly perfume of pure nard" (12:3) worth three hundred denarii, i.e., nearly a year's wages for a day laborer (see 12:5),[70] and the Roman procurator of Judea (18:37). On the other hand social outcasts like a Samaritan woman who is living with a man out of wedlock (4:17-18), a person "who had been ill for thirty-eight years" (5:5), a blind beggar, i.e., a person who had been born blind and who was considered as having been born in sin (9:34), are also invited.

In the Fourth Gospel, the invitation to believe in Jesus is extended to people independent of their ethnicity, gender, social status, marital status, or health condition. The call to faith in John is universal without any restrictions. Believers are born of God (1:12-13), born from above (3:3), or born of water and Spirit (3:5). Among other things this also means that those who believe in Jesus form a community of equals where socially generated inequalities are abolished.

John's universal perspective, however, reaches its limit in the confrontation with people who do not believe in Jesus (3:18, 36) or who do evil (5:29). They are called to conversion and, if they reject this opportunity, they have to face condemnation and God's wrath, i.e., they have to undergo ultimate exclusion from the community. John's universalism is called into question by the way he presents a group of Jews whom he describes as hostile to Jesus and to whom he refers stereotypically as "the Jews."

This raises the question whether the ideal of an inclusive community is unconditional acceptance or whether certain conditions must be postulated. Since inclusive community built on unconditional acceptance runs the risk of leading to chaos, the limits of inclusiveness are reached where people use their liberty to harm others. To believe in Jesus is presented in John as a necessary condition for inclusion into the community. John tries to convince his readers of this by closely associating unbelief with darkness,[71] sin,[72] murder, and lies.[73]

This identification of the religious with the ethical dimensions of human existence is unacceptable. To associate people with immorality solely because they are refusing to believe that Jesus is the Christ, the Son of God, not only disregards fundamental ethical principles but also

---

[70] See Bruce J. Malina and Richard L. Rohrbaugh, *Social-Science Commentary on the Gospel of John* (Minneapolis: Fortress Press, 1998) 205. Cf. Matt 20:2.

[71] See 8:12: "I am the light of the world. Whoever follows me will never walk in darkness."

[72] See 8:24: "for you will die in your sins unless you believe that I am he."

[73] See 8:44: "You are from your father the devil, and you choose to do your father's desires. He was a murderer from the beginning and does not stand in the truth, because there is no truth in him."

calls into question John's own theology of creation (1:3) and God's universal love for the world (3:16). Consequently we reject John's use of faith in Jesus as a criterion for inclusion in the community of morally good people. We do not dispute the legitimacy of postulating the condition of believing in Jesus for membership in the Johannine community. But this may not be combined with claiming the community of Jesus' disciples as the only community that is morally upright.

We note by way of conclusion that the Fourth Gospel has a strong desire that everyone should receive God's abundant gift of salvation through Jesus the Christ. No one is excluded from the community of disciples on extrinsic reasons. This inclusiveness which is present in the Fourth Gospel is a central building block for a theological ethic of justice. Exclusion happens in John on the basis of an intrinsic reason (not believing in Jesus). But combining the exclusion from the community of believers with the exclusion from the community of all moral persons, i.e., blurring the boundaries of theological and ethical evaluation, is itself an injustice and inconsistent with John's overall stance.

An Eschatological Vision of Justice

In this section our focus is not on the Gospel's explicit eschatology. Our interest is rather in implicit dimensions of the text which can inspire Christian communities today to participate in building the eschatological community. We will ask in which way the Gospel text invites us to go beyond it, in which way it liberates and empowers us to move into the eschatological future. In doing so we express our conviction that texts are living realities, a symbolic medium which invite dialogue, which challenge and point beyond themselves. The power of literary texts lies in the fact that they contain the seeds of a future world which presents itself as an alternative to the world in which the readers live. The vision of this alternative world is frequently present in the text as an invitation to participate in its fuller realization.

In John, we meet at least one explicit reference to the eschatological future of the last judgment (5:28-29). John presents most aspects of salvation as already realized in the earthly Jesus, albeit in paradoxical statements like "the hour is coming and is now here" (4:23; 5:25; cf. 2:4; 7:6, 8, 10). Other salvific actions of Jesus remain reserved for the time after his death and resurrection[74] or for the last day.[75] In 14:3 the Johan-

---

[74] See 12:32: "And I, when I am lifted up from the earth, will draw all people to myself."

[75] See 6:39: "And this is the will of him who sent me, that I should lose nothing of all that he has given me, but raise it up on the last day" (cf. 5:28-29).

nine Jesus announces his future Second Coming and the salvific actions connected with it.[76]

John does not absolutize Christ even though he is presented as greater than the patriarchs. The implicit dynamic of the Gospel toward the future does not come to a halt in Jesus. The Gospel achieves this by means of two statements found in the farewell discourse. The first statement (14:28) compares the earthly Jesus with God. The Gospel thus avoids absolutizing Jesus by reminding its readers that the mystery of God cannot be exhausted in the life of a human person who is limited in time, place, ethnicity and culture. While this statement is not taking anything back of what the Gospel says and believes about Jesus' being the Son of God, God remains always greater. Similarly God's revelation, that is, God's ongoing communion of love with human persons and communities, continues even after Jesus' death in a living and ever new way (cf. 16:7). Jesus is not the revelation of God in the sense that everything has already been said and all future generations can merely repeat past revelation. Rather, the dialogue continues and new things can still be expected.

Jesus' second statement in 14:12[77] expands this point to include the works. The greater works are, of course, not done by the disciples on their own accord, but through the exalted Christ and the Paraclete whom he sends. It would therefore be a misunderstanding to see here a competition between the disciples and Jesus. Finally, in 16:13, "The journey into 'all the truth' . . . has not yet been completed, even though Jesus has been with the disciples as 'the way and the truth and the life.'"[78] The Paraclete is the one who guides the disciples in doing the works of Jesus and even greater ones.

The healthy recognition of the limits of the earthly Jesus in relationship with God and with the future disciples demonstrates that the Gospel is open toward the future. The intention of the author of this Gospel therefore cannot have been to write a text which statically binds its readers or even all future generations. Rather, the Gospel sees itself already as part of the process of moving into the future of the "greater works." The surprising editorial freedom which this Gospel betrays with regard to the sources and in comparison with the Synoptics is ample evidence to this fact. By so doing the Gospel invites future believers to do the same.

---

[76] "And if I go and prepare a place for you, I will come again and will take you to myself, so that where I am, there you may be also" (14:3).

[77] "Very truly, I tell you, the one who believes in me will also do the works that I do and, in fact, will do greater works than these, because I am going to the Father."

[78] Moloney, *The Gospel of John,* 441.

The alternative world which the Gospel of John envisions is one that has as its origin the loving relationship between God and Jesus (and the Spirit). As is characteristic of love, God and Jesus want to share the fullness of their love (cf. 1:14 "grace and truth") with others. This (and not human sin) is the reason for the incarnation (1:14, 16). Human community takes as its model the intra-divine communion of love. The most fundamental vision expressed in the Gospel is therefore inclusive community, the invitation to share in God's love and to extend it to every human person without exception. In this perspective the refusal to share in the intra-divine love relationship is particularly tragic. But even in this situation the reaction to this rejection may in no way go against the fundamental vision of inclusivity. As we saw above, the Gospel fails most painfully in this regard, since in its effort to include those who oppose the invitation, it sometimes seems to lose sight of its own vision.

Although the Gospel of John does portray an endtimes community, this section focused rather on the implicit dimensions of the Gospel. The fourth evangelist presents Jesus as the concrete embodiment of God's intervention, judgment, and new life, but not the absolute and only embodiment. Such an approach cries out for ever-new embodiments of the endtimes vision in concrete communities of justice and inclusion.

Conclusion

Chapter Three studied justice in the Gospel of John within the context of the Hebrew and Christian Scriptures. The gospel approach reflects traces of the Hebrew Scriptures' covenant understanding of God's practice of justice as intervention in oppression, judgment of oppressors, and the establishment of a new life. The gospel portrayal of the divine persons stresses intimate relationality between God, Jesus, the disciples, and the world. This stress on relationality and the relational context of justice in the Hebrew Scriptures provides a strong theological foundation for a relational dimension to justice. The Johannine understanding of the human person picks up this emphasis on relationality and suggests an awareness of human particularity and difference. In addition, the persons in John's Gospel are accountable agents. The specific exploration of justice within the gospel showed first that justice is a quality of God. Second, the stress on abundance suggests that scarcity of resources may not be the only, or best, starting point for a discussion of justice. Third, the inclusion of diverse persons in discipleship and the Johannine community point to inclusion as a dimension of justice. Finally, the gospel portrayal of Jesus as the embodiment of God's intervention, judgment, and new life urges us to understand that justice is not a static reality, but seeks ever-new concrete embodiments.

4

Justice in Catholic Social Teachings

In addition to experience and the Scriptures, ministers and practitioners of justice have access to Catholic Social Teachings[1] as a resource for a just response to the dilemmas which they encounter in their daily living. This chapter explores the concepts of justice present in Catholic Social Teachings within their theological framework, namely, the images of God and the understanding of the human person.

A Theological Framework for Justice

The God-language in the documents of Catholic Social Teachings[2] relies on images of the Spirit of God, Jesus the Christ, and God. Since the focus of the documents is a Catholic social ethical response to issues of economic, political, and social wrongs, the images and understandings of God are rarely developed. Rather, references to God occur as an

---

[1] The documents of Catholic Social Teachings are primarily papal encyclicals which deal with sociopolitical and socioeconomic issues, although some other magisterial documents from Vatican Council II and the United States Catholic Conference are also included.

[2] All references to Catholic Social Teachings are taken from Michael Walsh and Brian Davies, eds., *Proclaiming Justice and Peace: Papal Documents from* Rerum Novarum *through* Centesimus Annus (Mystic, Conn.: Twenty-Third Publications, 1991). The numbers in parentheses refer to the numbered paragraphs in this edition of the documents.

assumed framework within which the social concerns of the respective documents are addressed. With this in mind, this section examines how God is imaged and presented.

Spirit of God

Seventy-five percent of the approximately sixty references to the Spirit occur in documents issued between 1965 and 1971, that is, the immediate Vatican Council II era of renewal and reform. One-half of the references comes from *Gaudium et spes*, nos. 1–45 and 91–3, with an additional 25 percent in *Populorum progressio, Octagesimo adveniens,* and Justice in the World. Mention of the Spirit typically occurs in connection with the endtimes reign of God (GS 38–40; PP 42). The Spirit is the first fruits and pledge of full inheritance which is the renewal of humanity already begun in Jesus. Through the action of Christians (OA 51), the Spirit is at work transforming this world into the city of God by nurturing the values of dignity, community, freedom, justice, and peace (GS 39). In the power of the Spirit, Christian initiative in the service of humanity testifies to "those things which are decisive for the existence and future of humanity" (JW 38). In the Spirit, human work and the earthly goods embody and proclaim the city of God (SRS 48) and advance the work of Christ (GS 3, 11, 43). These passages describe a Spirit who leads, pulls, and attracts humanity into the future which is the Spirit's home.

The documents of Catholic Social Teachings written before and after the Vatican II era refer to the Spirit infrequently (about fifteen times). When the Spirit is mentioned, an alternative image of the Spirit emerges. The single mention of the Spirit prior to *Gaudium et spes* associates the Spirit with magisterial rule (QA 138). Later documents, *Laborem exercens* (27) and *Sollicitudo rei socialis* (1), link the Spirit with the institutional Church and the inspiration of official magisterial texts of Vatican II and Catholic Social Teachings in general. This "Spirit" is not encountered in human longings and transforming activities, but rather stands apart from earthly realities. The "Spirit" is used to qualify human dignity, work, bread, and wine explicitly as holy or Christian (LE 27; SRS 47–8). Although this ecclesial and institutionalized perspective on the Spirit is not completely absent from *Gaudium et spes*, it is the prevalent perspective of the few mentions of the Spirit in the documents of the last twenty years of the twentieth century.

In our analysis we encountered two theologies of the Spirit in the documents of Catholic Social Teachings. The first theology presents an image of the Spirit which inspires believers to take up the transformation of the world into the city of God. The other theology links the Spirit with the institutional Church and the works of sanctification. While the latter frustrates, the former encourages the practice of justice.

Jesus Christ

The documents of Catholic Social Teachings contain approximately six times as many references to Jesus Christ (351) as to the Spirit. A wide variety of names is attributed to Jesus Christ, but the expression "Lord Jesus Christ" predominates as a name. The documents do not present a developed christology, but rather discuss the role and function of Jesus Christ as conclusions to anthropological statements (GS 22, 32, 43–4) or as concluding exhortations to Christian action (MM 255–9; LE 24–7). By exception, Justice in the World 30–4 situates Jesus Christ within God's salvific and liberating plan for the world.

Just as two theologies of the Spirit are present in the documents of Catholic Social Teachings, two distinct christologies can also be detected: a christology of imitation and a christology of discipleship. The christology of imitation predominates in the documents before and after the era of Vatican Council II, while the christology of discipleship predominates in the conciliar period (see the four documents issued between 1965 and 1971). Often, particularly in the documents of John Paul II, the two christologies coexist.

The christology of imitation proposes that Jesus Christ came from God, redeemed believers once and for all, and returned to God when his work was completed. In this approach, God's reign has already been established by Jesus Christ, but will fully come in the next world; therefore, suffering (RN 18) and poverty (RN 15) are part of the human condition and must be accepted as "the way things are." Work takes its meaning from Christ's work as a carpenter (LE 26); hence, human work is toilsome just as Christ's work of salvation entailed suffering and death (LE 27). The material world, which will pass away, is an obstacle to eternal salvation; but until that time materiality must be controlled and dominated (LE 9; CA 31).

The christology of discipleship submits that God's salvific activity reached a high point in Jesus Christ, but must be continued in the body of Christ today. Work is one continuation of God's ongoing creative and redeeming activity in this world (MM 259; JW 35–6). Suffering, however, is the result of evil (GS 32). As such, suffering is often inflicted on those who work for justice and transformation by persons and groups who have something to lose if the system changes (GS 38). Since God intervened on behalf of those who are poor or oppressed and since all, including the poor, are created in the image of God, poverty must be resisted (PP 21). Because God is the creator of all things, materiality is the locus of God's action and presence (PT 3; GS 38–9; CA 37). Thus material things are to be stewarded, not dominated (OA 21; CA 38). Sacraments reveal God's presence and continue God's liberating activity (MM 6).

Catholic Social Teachings do present a christology of discipleship which inspires believers to take up the transformation of the world into the city of God as a continuation of God's redemptive action in Jesus Christ; however, this is not the only image of Jesus Christ. Consequently, the works of justice are both potentially encouraged and frustrated by the operative christologies in Catholic Social Teachings.

God

The documents of Catholic Social Teachings refer to God approximately twice as often as they do to Jesus Christ; however, two-thirds of these approximately 650 references occur in four documents, namely, *Gaudium et spes* and the encyclicals of John Paul II. Two points shed some light on this usage. First, the relative absence of references to God in the majority of the documents points to their reliance on philosophical reasoning, which sought to be understandable to all rational persons. Second, many of the references to God are generic references to divinity in contrast to humanity. As a term, God reflects a somewhat ambiguous history. In early Christianity, "God" meant the first person of the Trinity; however, as a result of the controversies surrounding Jesus Christ's divinity, "God" came to be used in reference to the shared divinity or the unity of the three diverse persons. The documents of Catholic Social Teachings use the word "God" in both these senses.

The words "Lord" and "Judge" are almost never used in reference to the first person of the Trinity or to God, the divine unity. In addition, "God" is used in some expressions such as the Family or People *of God*, which only occur in the documents of the Vatican II era, namely, *Gaudium et spes, Populorum progressio,* and Justice in the World.

As was the case with language about the Spirit and Jesus Christ, two constellations of understandings about God occur in the documents of Catholic Social Teachings. These two constellations take shape along the lines suggested in the works of Kathryn Tanner, Marie Augusta Neal, and Andrew Greeley which were presented in Chapter 2, namely, God as non-relational and distant as well as God as relational and engaged in this world.

The non-relational and distant constellation of images includes references to God as Source of Authority (QA 118; MM 249; CA 45) or the Source of Laws such as the Ten Commandments (RN 42; MM 253; SRS 36), natural law (RN 37; PT 6), Church laws (QA 41; CA 54), human laws (PT 50–1), and moral laws. God was specifically mentioned as the source of the laws, e.g., increase and multiply (MM 196; PP 37), subdue the earth (LE 16), as well as laws concerning the permanence of marriage (GS 48), the condemnation of discrimination (GS 29), and universal access to goods of the earth (RN 57; GS 69; PP 22). Other non-relational and distant images for God include Author of Nature (QA 43; LE 16), First Cause of Creation (MM 215), Source of the Purpose of all things (RN 58), and Final Destiny of all persons (RN 24; CA 41). These images of God are linked to God's plan, design, providence, or will to which all persons are expected to conform (PT 165; CA 26, 37). This constellation of images of a distant and non-relational God predominates in documents prior to Vatican II. They are, however, also prevalent in the documents of John Paul II. They occur less frequently, but are not completely absent from them.

The relational and engaged images of God picture God as Father of all (RN 24; PT 6; GS 92),[3] as a Friend or Intimate (GS 48) whom believers love in loving their neighbor (RN 26; JW 31–4; SRS 33). This relational God invites believers to take up the tasks of building the human community with bonds of solidarity and friendship (MM 256; PT 164). God is portrayed as One who invites persons into a relationship with a future (GS 18–19, 21, 41; PP 42). The human response to this invitation is rooted in an innate attraction to God, but the decision to enter into relationship is adult and free (GS 17). One-third (30) of the images of God as Creator reveal an Engaged Creator with whom human persons collaborate as co-creators (GS 33, 47, 50; LE 12) in the transformation of this world into the city of God (GS 21; PP 17). The image of God as Liberator (JW 30) uncovers a God engaged in releasing human persons from oppression and poverty. While such images of a relational and engaged God are absent from pre–Vatican II documents, they predominate in the documents of the Vatican II era, but are not completely absent from the documents of John Paul II.

Gaudium et spes (92) and *Sollicitudo rei socialis* (40, 47) specifically image God as Trinity of divine persons. While *Gaudium et spes* noted that Trinitarian unity was reflected in unity among all peoples, the

---

[3] Father or parent is the most frequent relational image of God. It occurs some fifty times. Fatherhood as an image for God can be problematic when this image is used to stress patriarchy or familial relationships as normative for the believing community.

ethical implications were explored twenty-five years later in *Sollicitudo rei socialis.* Therein the Trinity provides a model for solidarity, that is, the Christian virtue which embraces and delights in the human reality of interdependence. The "common fatherhood of God," the "brotherhood of all in Christ," as well as the "presence and life-giving action of the Holy Spirit" provide both a vision and new criteria with which to measure the progress of the human communities toward the city of God. Forgiveness, reconciliation, the possibility of dignified lives, and love of enemy are listed as these new criteria. Both *Gaudium et spes* and *Sollicitudo rei socialis,* however, accent Trinitarian unity rather than fundamental equality and relationships constituted in diversity.

This analysis of the understandings of God in the documents of Catholic Social Teachings reveals two quite different approaches. In one approach, God is distant and unengaged in this world, Christ has already accomplished redemption which will be made apparent at the end of time, and the Spirit is absent or restricted to institutional roles. In the other approach, God is relational and engaged in this world. God's saving activity reached a high point in Jesus and continues through the body of Christ. The Spirit arouses, animates, empowers the body of Christ for transformation of this world into the city of God.

Catholic Social Teachings reveal a theological framework which can promote action on behalf of justice, transformation of the world into the endtimes city of God, as well as the self-understanding of believers as Spirit-animated participants in the creative and saving activities of God in Jesus. This theological framework, however, is not the only framework. To the extent that a distant and unengaged God predominates in Catholic Social Teachings, as well as in liturgical ritual, preaching and teaching, the practice of justice is pushed to the margins in the Catholic ethos, and faith-based understandings of justice are obstructed. On the other hand, the very existence of two approaches to God both legitimates diversity and opens the door to still other understandings of God.

AN ANTHROPOLOGICAL FRAMEWORK FOR JUSTICE

The understandings of the human person which surface in the documents of Catholic Social Teachings also reveal diverse approaches.[4]

---

[4] Charles Curran, "The Changing Anthropological Bases of Catholic Social Ethics," *Directions in Catholic Social Ethics* (Notre Dame, Ind.: University of Notre Dame Press, 1985) 5–42, discusses the shifts in the personal and social dimensions of the human person in Catholic Social Teachings. He includes an initial reading of the anthropology of John Paul II.

Since the focus of the documents is a Catholic social ethical response to issues of economic, political, and social wrongs, theological anthropologies tend to be in service of the issues rather than a systematic presentation in their own right. The first part of *Gaudium et spes*, however, presents a well-outlined anthropology. With this in mind, this section examines three approaches to theological anthropology advanced in the documents of Catholic Social Teachings.

Dualistic Anthropology

The first understanding of the human person has its roots in dualism. This approach gives priority to the spiritual world, especially after death; thus the material conditions of this world are of little consequence (RN 5). As a result, social inequalities and hierarchy define the God-ordained human reality which benefits both the individual and society (RN 15). Such a social order entails certain duties and obligations, namely, the wealthy and elite of the social order ought to care for the poor masses (RN 21); workers must accept their suffering and pain in this world (RN 15) and rejoice in their blessedness (RN 23). Equality and modern liberties are suspect efforts from an impossible socialist illusion (RN 3–4). Yet within this dualistic approach, a limited sense of personal and Christian dignity dawns within a context of the obligations of contractual justice (RN 17). In general, human dignity is connected to the soul (RN 41), to redemption in Christ (RN 24), or to virtue (RN 23). Thus oppression of workers and degrading working conditions violate human dignity, because worker and employer alike are redeemed by Christ and bear the image of God in their souls.

Personalist Anthropology

A personalist anthropology takes center stage in *Gaudium et spes* 12–34. These paragraphs represent the most developed anthropological statement in Catholic Social Teachings. According to the personalist anthropology of *Gaudium et spes*, the autonomous agent is a free (GS 17), rational (GS 15) person created in the image and likeness of God. This personalist anthropology differs in two regards from the previous anthropology. First, creation, rather than faith or redemption, is the source of human dignity (GS 12) and enables human persons to encounter God in their consciences (GS 17). Human dignity is renewed, but not established, through the incarnation and redemption of Christ Jesus (GS 22). Second, *Gaudium et spes* stresses the social nature of the human person as a reflection of the Trinitarian God (GS 24). The historical realities of interdependence provide ways for the development of full human potential (GS 25) and require access to the fulfillment of basic human needs (GS 26).

This approach has shifted from an oppositional attitude toward spirit and matter which characterized earlier documents. Materiality takes on a new value, because it contributes to full humanness. Still, the autonomous agent has a body (GS 14) which is good and not to be despised. The human person, however, is superior to bodily concerns. In other words, the human person has a body, but the embodiment is not constitutive of the human person.

Relationality (GS 24–5) and culture (GS 44) are consequences of personal agency as well as means to human fulfillment. Finally, all human persons must be accorded dignity, rights, and humane conditions of living (GS 29) because in spite of their differences they are all created in the image of God, redeemed by Christ, and head toward the same final destiny. At the same time, *Gaudium et spes* recognizes that the Church must attend to the signs of the times (GS 4) and human experience (GS 46) as well as the gospel. This new value of materiality occasions two shifts. First, culture, bodiliness, and difference provide contours for human living which must be included in assessments of anthropology and ethics. Second, the material dimension of the human person receives new recognition, even though it remains inferior and non-constitutive of humanness.

Thomistic Personalist Anthropology

The social encyclicals of John Paul II present yet another anthropology which he has termed Thomistic personalism.[5] In short, this anthropology seeks a synthesis of the first two anthropologies. The foundation for transcendental dignity of the human person rests in creation as a "visible image of the invisible God" (CA 44). On this foundation Thomistic personalism builds dominion and transcendental subjectivity: the human person "has to subdue the earth and dominate it, because as an 'image of God,' he is a person, that is to say a subjec-

[5] See Ronald E. Modras, "Karl Rahner and John Paul II: Anthropological Implications for Economics and the Social Order," *Religion and Economic Ethics*, The Annual Publication of the College Theology Society 31, ed. Joseph F. Gower (Lanham, Md.: University Press of America, 1990) 123–50. See also Ronald E. Modras, "The Thomistic Personalism of Pope John Paul II," *The Modern Schoolman* 59 (1982) 117–27; and John Hellman, "John Paul II and the Personalist Movement," *Cross Currents* (Winter 1980–81) 409–19.

tive being capable of acting in a planned rational way, capable of deciding about himself and with a tendency to self-realization" (LE 6).

In his work on the Thomistic personalism of John Paul II, Ronald E. Modras points out three levels in the human person: the physical sphere, the emotional sphere, and the transcendental sphere. The higher spheres are charged with subduing the lower spheres (SRS 29). Hence will, domination, self-discipline, and suspicion of the body are recurring themes in the Thomistic personalism of John Paul II (LE 4–6; SRS 29; CA 36). The will governs corporeal actions. The capacity for self-reflection expedites domination. Human transcendence is the principle of unity which enables persons to rule over their bodies.[6]

Human transcendence grounds the claims for human rights, for participation in social life (LE 22; CA 44), and for shared responsibility (CA 46). Although Thomistic personalism stresses the individual, John Paul II's encyclicals maintain a social dimension to the human person (CA 13) and grant a certain agency to society (CA 13, 46) and nations (SRS 15). Thus, totalitarianism is condemned (SRS 15) and claims to democratic governance and structures of participation are grounded (CA 44).

In summary, then, Thomistic personalism's emphasis on human transcendence is coupled with ahistorical consciousness and hierarchical domination. This understanding of the human person resembles the autonomous agent of *Gaudium et spes,* while adding an emphasis on the universal and ahistorical transcendence that was less apparent in *Gaudium et spes.* Transcendence can be conceptualized as a dimension of history, culture, and embodiment,[7] for example, a sacramentality of the world or an incarnate divinity. Thomistic personalism, however, holds that the emphasis on ahistorical and universal transcendence is a necessary grounding for objective moral norms, because a historically conscious approach cannot sufficiently ground an ethic of absolute norms.

All the above mentioned approaches to anthropology in the documents of Catholic Social Teachings identify subjectivity or agency as the constitutive dimension of the human person. All other dimensions of the human person are less significant (Dualism), develop full humanism (Personalism), or require domination (Thomistic Personalism). Within this context the theological anthropologies in Catholic Social Teachings call attention to human dignity, relatedness or sociality, human rights, participation, agency, equality, option for the poor, and provision for basic human needs.

[6] Modras, "Karl Rahner and John Paul II," 139–40.

[7] Ibid., 127–31 and 148 discusses Rahner's transcendental humanism in which transcendence is a depth dimension of the human person and culture.

JUSTICE IN CATHOLIC SOCIAL TEACHINGS

The understanding of justice in Catholic Social Teachings is rooted in the late-nineteenth-century interpretation of Thomas Aquinas' presentation of justice in the *Summa theologiae*. Consequently, this section begins with a brief treatment of justice according to Thomas Aquinas before tracing the development of that understanding in the social encyclicals of the last one hundred years. Thomas Aquinas defines justice as "a habit whereby a person renders to each one his due by a constant and perpetual will" (ST II-II, q. 58, a. 1).[8] Since it is described as a constant habit, justice is seen as a virtue. Unlike the other cardinal virtues treated in this section of the *Summa theologiae*, the virtue of justice is dependent not only on the intention of the actor, but also on relationships.[9] Thus one cannot merely intend to do justice; external actions and things must actually render to another what is concretely due the other according to relationships of proportionate equality.

Thomas Aquinas divided justice into general (legal) and particular justice. Particular justice is further divided into commutative (contractual) justice and distributive justice. General justice directs one's relationships with all other members of a community in general, that is, it seeks the common good. Because laws have the task of specifying what the common good requires, general justice can be termed legal justice (q. 58, a. 6). Commutative justice regulates mutual dealings between two private individuals as in contracts. Distributive justice allots common goods proportionately (q. 61, a. 1).

The basis of a claim to justice is human relationality, for in the words of Thomas Aquinas "justice is concerned only about our dealings with others" (q. 58, a. 2). For Thomas, however, relationality did not convey personal intimacy, but one's place in the social order or one's social role. These social roles were a dimension of the Provident God's divinely established order or eternal law. In addition to the rather hierarchical and role-based description of the human person, Thomas understood the human person as composed of dual elements, body and soul. Because the soul includes reason (intellect) and will (freedom) which enables persons to participate in God's eternal law, it is the higher power which regulated the lower bodily element.

---

[8] The quotations from the *Summa* are taken from Thomas Aquinas, *Summa theologiae*, Latin text and English translation, introduction, notes, appendices, and glossaries (London: Blackfriars, 1964–76).

[9] *ST* II-II, q. 57, a. 1: "Because a man's work is said to be just when it is related to some other by way of some kind of equality, for instance the payment of the wage due for a service rendered."

According to Thomas, God's right provident order was justice. Therefore, human actions ought to conform to this order through natural law made manifest in Church and civil laws. Without recourse to God as this absolute source of justice through eternal law and divine providence, Thomas' framework for justice cannot be maintained.

The goal of justice is "the right" (q. 57, a. 1). "The right" was an exterior object or action which actualized what was due another in a relationship of equity, that is, proportionate equality. Some of the mediating principles on which Thomas relied to specify the right included civil laws, juridical sentences, the human art of knowing what is right, the human faithful practice of making moral decisions and rightful living, and the "principle of objective mean," which he described as a certain proportionality between the just act and the one receiving justice. Even though Thomas Aquinas speaks of general (legal) justice which regulated the common good, social structures and institutions besides laws have a minor place in his overall approach. Justice essentially directs individuals capable of action in their relations with others.

Thomas used a deductive methodology. God's providence and eternal law are the absolutes. Through human reason and life, persons participate in God's providence. On the basis of that participation persons deduce mediating principles to guide the practice of justice. To the extent that human reason contributed to the determination of just actions, interpretations of Thomas Aquinas reflect the possibility of corrections and self-criticism. To the extent, however, that justice was God's provident order, interpretations of Thomas Aquinas reflect limited possibilities for correction and self-criticism.

The late-nineteenth-century interpretation of Thomas Aquinas stressed human reason as part of its Enlightenment heritage. In addition, the situation of the worker in the aftermath of the Industrial Revolution inaugurated and the mechanization of production in England in the 1820s occasioned a radically changed social context. In 1891 Pope Leo XIII responded to this context in the form of the encyclical letter *Rerum novarum,* signaling the beginning of what has come to be called "Catholic Social Teachings."[10]

---

[10] Other authors have traced the developing understandings of justice in the eras between the close of the canon of the Christian Scriptures and the first social encyclical. Interested readers can consult William J. Walsh and John P. Langan, "Patristic Social Consciousness: The Church and the Poor," and John P. Langan, "What Jerusalem Says to Athens." Both studies are published in *Faith That Does Justice: Examining the Christian Sources for Social Change,* ed. John C. Haughey, Woodstock Studies 2 (New York: Paulist Press, 1977) 113–50 and 152–80. See also Geoffry Robinson, "Do We Know What Justice Is?" *Origins* 23 (November 25, 1993) 423–30.

Rerum novarum *(1891)*

Since *Rerum novarum* was written in response to the plight of the industrial worker, the discussion of justice revolves around issues of private property, wages, and state intervention. Leo XIII was influenced by the Neo-Scholastic philosophy[11] of his day; hence his fundamental understanding of justice was "what is due" to another (9, 44). This notion dimly reflected the relational notion of justice, so prominent in the Scriptures. As it was used in *Rerum novarum,* "what was due" was less an obligation stemming from a faith or creation relationship and more a duty coming from a contract, law, the common good, prior natural rights, or basic bodily needs.

Rerum novarum maintained that not all contracts and laws were just. Rather, in addition to fulfilling the terms of the contract completely and faithfully, justice obliges the worker to avoid damage to employers' property or person (Cf. 39), to refrain from force, and to avoid socialism (17). In turn, justice obliges the employer to treat workers as persons of human and Christian dignity, to keep the religious needs of workers in mind, to shield workers from corruption and sin, to promote family life and the wise use of wages to require only those tasks in keeping with workers' strengths and to give to each what is just (17). The wage contract was not considered just because it was agreed upon. A wage was just when it was "sufficient for the bodily needs of a temperate and well-behaved worker" (45), that is, provision for basic bodily needs determined justice, not the contract alone. Furthermore, justice prevented employers from force, fraud, or usury in payment of wages as well as from exploiting worker poverty, since poverty did not equip persons to claim justice with regard to wages and working conditions. Hence justice imposed more obligations than the contract; these obligations emerged from basic human needs, Christian dignity, and the natural right to private property.

In *Rerum novarum* distributive justice required that the state impartially care for each and every class of citizens, especially for the lives and well-being of those without property (34). Laws, policies, and processes which uphold natural rights, the common good, and freedom of action (37) were given as examples of state care. Since laws were not automatic sources of obligations in justice, *Rerum novarum* cited two examples of unjust laws, namely, excessive taxation (47) and state seizure of Church property (52) on the basis of the natural right to private property.

---

[11] Neo-Scholastic philosophy was a nineteenth-century interpretation of Thomas Aquinas. See above, 93.

Rerum novarum noted that laws and contracts were not the only sources of justice; in fact, justice was not even sufficient, but required charity as well (18). The description of charity concluded that persons were required to give alms after one's needs, the needs of one's family and social status were met. Almsgiving was a matter of justice only in extreme cases (21). This approach links the abolition of poverty to charity and not justice.

In summary, justice in *Rerum novarum* focused on an understanding of justice as obligation, but as an obligation rooted in sources other than contractual terms and state laws. Thus *Rerum novarum* looked to common good, Christian dignity, natural rights, and basic human needs as the sources for obligations in justice.

Quadragesimo anno *(1931)*

Forty years after *Rerum novarum,* Pius XI responded to the economic crisis of the Great Depression with an appeal to contractual justice and to social justice. Relations between capital and labor (owners and workers) were to be regulated by contractual justice, charity, and public authorities (110). Contractual justice required respect for the existence, distribution, and use of private property as an obligation of the natural right of private property. The necessities of social living, however, obliged owners either in the right itself or in its exercise to use their property correctly. This duty was neither regulated by justice nor was it legally enforceable. Thus justice gave rise to duties of non-interference with the right of private property, while other virtues urged a use of private property in keeping with social necessities. This position reflects the bias and fear of socialist understanding of property.

Pius XI also introduced the expression "social justice" into Catholic Social Teachings, but the concept of social justice had already appeared in Catholic social thought for nearly one hundred years.[12] Twentieth-century Catholic social thought has identified social justice with general justice, distributive justice, and with contractual justice depending on the perspective of the author. An analysis of the use of social justice in the encyclicals of Pius XI revealed elements similar to each of the Thomistic divisions of justice, but precluded identification with any one.

---

[12] Social justice first appeared in Taparelli d'Azeglio, *Saggio teoritici di diritto naturale,* Palermo, 1840, nos. 353–4. The concept also appeared in works of Heinrich Pesch in the latter half of the nineteenth century.

Social justice was a foundational principle for the socioeconomic order. Pius XI identified social justice with the norms of the common good (58), such that public institutions would embody social justice and facilitate the good of all (110). In this way, social justice focused on public and structural dimensions of the social and legal order (88), while contractual justice concerned itself with contracts and individual rights. Within this socioeconomic context, social justice forbade one social class to exclude another class from the benefits of society (57); it decried the gap between wealthy property owners and the property-less poor (58). Social justice demanded a just wage as determined by the resources necessary to support a family (71), by the conditions of the business (72), and by the requirements of the common good (74). These criteria highlighted the social dimension of work (69) by concluding that "social justice demands that wages and salaries be managed, . . . so as to offer the greatest number the opportunity of getting work" (74).

This concept of social justice in *Quadragesimo anno* concerned itself with all the institutions, structures, and policies which promote the good of the whole. Social justice does not focus on the relationship of the whole to the individual (distributive justice), on the relationship of the individual to the whole (contributive justice), or on the relationships between individuals (contractual justice). In *Quadragesimo anno*, Pius XI used the term "social justice" to refer to a justice which regulated a common good in which both human persons and organizational structures figured prominently.

Social justice was not sufficient to resolve all the economic issues brought on by the Great Depression. Social justice needed to be yoked with social charity, as form and shape were yoked to spirit and soul (88). Social justice removed obstacles, while social charity perfected the unity of the human family. Social justice was about structures, while social charity was about the motivation and life-giving animation (137).

Such an embodiment of charity as the soul of social justice compelled restructuring in economic institutions and the whole social order. Pius XI suggested a restructuring of the industrial economic model into corporatism (91–8). Although corporatism as a new socioeconomic structure never came to prominence, at least in part given its links with Italian, Austrian, and Portuguese totalitarian regimes, the link between social justice and alternative social and economic structures remained.

Pius XI and *Quadragesimo anno* have left a legacy of social justice, as distinct from earlier Thomistic divisions of justice, which concerns itself with the institutions that structure and facilitate the good of the whole social order. When such institutions fail to promote the common good, social justice calls for change and restructuring which enhanced both the good of human persons and the common good.

Mater et magistra *(1961)*

Similar to *Rerum novarum* and *Quadragesimo anno,* John XXIII's inaugural encyclical *Mater et magistra* also used justice to address the economic issues, including wages, ownership, conditions of work, the economic system, taxes, insurance, social security, imbalance, and the distribution of wealth. The encyclical did not continue to use Pius XI's term "social justice," although *Mater et magistra* did extend justice to international and global economic systems. In addition to a broad and undeveloped scattering of the word "justice" throughout the encyclical, *Mater et magistra* elaborates on justice as distributive and contributive.

Distributive justice entails sharing of wealth (168), of consumer goods (161), and of social benefits connected with work (136). *Mater et magistra* also includes worker participation in ownership (77) and in other business activities as a dimension of distributive justice. For John XXIII, distributive justice has its roots in the human nature of the worker (91). The links between participation, justice, and human nature will be developed in later documents.

In a section which addresses a just wage and the various considerations in determining a just wage, *Mater et magistra* includes among those considerations the contributions of workers to the financial enterprise (71) and to the good of the community (70). When the document turns to the subject of worker participation, *Mater et magistra* insists that the structures and organizations of an economic system must enhance human dignity, responsibility, and personal initiative. In short, if an economic system does not allow workers enough opportunities[13] to contribute to the good of the human community as well as to the business enterprise, then that system is unjust. This is the clearest articulation of the demands of contributive justice in Catholic Social Teachings in this century.

The encyclical *Mater et magistra* makes two contributions to the evolving understanding of justice. First, a seminal connection between

---

[13] See David Hollenbach, "Unemployment and Jobs: A Social, Theological and Ethical Analysis," *Justice, Peace and Human Rights: American Catholic Social Ethics in a Pluralistic Context* (New York: Crossroad, 1988) 52–70 for a more recent treatment of contributive justice and work, even though Hollenbach suggests that contributive justice and social justice are equivalent terms.

participation, justice, and the human person is noted. Second, contributive justice now includes the organization of systems so that persons have opportunities to be responsible and to contribute to the whole human community. Although the international and global dimensions of economic justice are being recognized, the perspective and resolution of the issues remains Eurocentric.

Pacem in terris *(1963)*

Shortly before his death in 1963, John XXIII appealed to a world caught up in the throes of the Cold War to work toward an international political world order. Although justice took a back seat to the primary concept of human rights and duties, *Pacem in terris* did examine justice in a political context, rather than the economic context of previous documents. In general, justice in the political context is undeveloped and remains a rather abstract principle or virtue made concrete in rights and in the juridical systems of states. With this background, justice is specifically called upon to regulate relationships between political entities, treatment of ethnic minorities, de-escalation of the arms race, and development of a universal common good.

Gaudium et spes *(1965)*

The contribution of Vatican II to Catholic Social Teachings in the Constitution on the Church in the Modern World confirms a number of earlier dimensions of justice. Immense economic and social disparity is a violation of distributive justice which regulates the use of the goods of the earth. Social justice reappears, albeit infrequently.

Previous seminal ideas are fleshed out. The linkage between dignity and justice now holds that the human dignity of persons demands just living conditions (29). The obligations of justice as contributive are met only when each person can contribute to the common good in keeping with their abilities, with the needs of other persons, and in such a way that the institutions of public life promote a better human life (30). This document does recognize that certain living conditions, namely, poverty and indulgence, make it difficult to recognize and act on the demands of contributive justice (31). This statement insists that the needs of the social order help determine the concrete expression of justice.

Other ideas are brought together into a new synthesis. The international perspective from *Mater et magistra,* the political context of justice in *Pacem in terris,* together with *Rerum novarum*'s insistence on state intervention on behalf of justice, become building blocks for *Gaudium et spes'* position that an international authority must regulate economic relationships according to the norms of justice (86). Likewise, the appeal to political justice to end the arms race in *Pacem in terris* becomes a building block for the description of peace as an enterprise of justice and the result of a social order built on justice (77–8).

Gaudium et spes offers two new perspectives on justice which will be developed in subsequent documents. First, chapter two, "On the Human Community," links justice both to the dignity of the human person and to the essentially social nature of humanity, that is, the foundations of justice in Catholic Social Teachings have shifted from natural law to the human person. Second, justice is relocated in a Christian and ecclesial context alongside its traditional place in Neo-Scholastic philosophical tradition. To be sure, *Gaudium et spes* does not present a biblical foundation for economic, political, and social justice. However, *Gaudium et spes* does recall that working for justice often results in having to take up the cross (38). In addition, the Church needs agencies to promote justice for the poor (90). Furthermore, Christians engaged in the struggle for justice and faithful to the gospel contribute to the peace and prosperity of the world (72). Indicative of the balance sought, the document proclaims that the Church "in light of the gospel has worked out the principles of justice and equity demanded by right reason" (63).[14] These two perspectives will be advanced in Justice in the World and *Centesimus annus*.

Populorum progressio *(1967)*

As the title suggests, this encyclical by Paul VI focuses primarily on the economic development of nations, which is the context for its discussion of justice. Within this context *Populorum progressio* makes three contributions to the evolving understanding of justice in Catholic Social Teachings. The introduction of the document describes the purpose

---

[14] If *Gaudium et spes* sought to ground economic teachings in the Scriptures, instead of reason and natural law traditions as had been the custom in Catholic Social Teachings, the council fathers obviously were unfamiliar with the scriptural justice tradition. The recurring linkage of justice with equity could have been a response to contemporary definitions of justice as fairness. However, John Rawls' *A Theory of Justice* was not published until 1971 (see our treatment of Rawls in Chapter 5). Furthermore, the twelve or more principles evoked in GS 67–71 mention justice only in connection with strikes and the common use of the goods of the earth, although several principles are radical departures from a so-called market economy. Perhaps a newly emerging emphasis connecting justice with the essentially social nature of humanity and the scriptural traditions provides the most fruitful explanation for this obvious shift.

of the recently formed Pontifical Commission on Justice and Peace as "to awaken in the People of God full awareness of their mission today." This mission is immediately spelled out in terms of development, social justice, and self-actualization of poorer nations (5). Thus social justice is described as a dimension of the mission of the People of God.[15]

Second, *Populorum progressio* addresses justice in relationships of structured inequality, that is, relationships which are set up to privilege the strong and powerful at the expense of the weak and vulnerable. Although the focus is trade relationships between nations, justice is also called for in work relationships between persons of differing status (70). In its discussion of the relationship between rich and poor nations, *Populorum progressio* includes social justice as one of three obligations of wealthy nations. In this context, social justice is described as "the rectification of trade relations between strong and weak nations" (44). The rectification includes movement toward a certain equality of opportunity in the trading relationships so that competition can operate justly and fairly (61). *Populorum progressio* recognizes that so-called free trade agreements work when the partners are relatively equal economically (58). However, when trading partners are unequal, social justice ought to regulate not merely adherence to the agreement, but the terms of the agreement itself to ensure fairness to all parties (59, 70).[16] *Populorum progressio* mentions higher import prices, higher taxes for public development assistance, direct support of development projects, and personal assistance in developing nations (47) as examples of structured justice in trade relations. In this document, then, social justice seeks to build a free and equal human community of nations through change in policies and re-structuring trade relationships because the current unequal relationships must be made equitable or fair.

Finally, *Populorum progressio* addresses nationalism and racism (62–3) as obstacles to just social orders and world solidarity. Again the document focuses on patterned behaviors and attitudes which privilege some members of the society at the expense of others. Social justice requires that these patterns be transformed into equity and fairness. Since social justice is a specification of the mission of the People of God, this structural transformation of unjust structures into just policies and agreements is an integral task of Christian communities.

[15] This document also continues the effort of GS to ground justice in the scriptural traditions. For example, Genesis 1 is used as the basis of distributive justice in PP 22, albeit in a problematic way.

[16] *Quadragesimo anno* and *Rerum novarum* made similar points with regard to wage contracts.

Octagesimo adveniens *(1971)*

Paul VI's letter to Maurice Cardinal Roy *(Octagesimo adveniens)*, then head of the Pontifical Commission on Justice and Peace, marked the eightieth anniversary of *Rerum novarum* and anticipated the upcoming Synod of Bishops which would address justice in the world. *Octagesimo adveniens* continued to refer to social justice (1, 5, 12), to distributive justice (43), and the structures which promote justice (15, 45). Three other dimensions of justice are also noteworthy contributions to the evolving understandings of justice.

First, *Octagesimo adveniens* shifts from a static to a dynamic notion of justice. Paul VI frequently speaks of "more" and "greater" justice or the process of justice, almost as if justice were a goal to which the human community was progressing in tentative and varying degrees. Second and related to this dynamic notion of justice, justice is described as the object of human thirst (48), striving (31), and yearning (2). *Octagesimo adveniens* presents the vision of the city of God characterized by justice (among other qualities) as an attractive call from the endtimes which draws men and women to seek after this vision and to build up the city of God here and now (12, 31, 37). Justice appears as a desire placed in the human heart which moves Christians to establish the city of God.

Third and not disconnected from the first two dimensions, *Octagesimo adveniens* highlights justice as relational. For example, the letter notes that in the arena of work, progress has been made in introducing greater justice (and sharing of responsibilities) in human relationships (15), although the need remains for structural changes. Solidarity among all persons is called "an indispensable basis for authentic justice" (17). Justice as relational cannot be created by laws (23) or by force (43). Rather, the vision of the city of God, the Spirit, and Christian faith provide hope in resolving the difficulties of living together in justice. Thus *Octagesimo adveniens* offers a dynamic, relational vision of justice which calls persons, especially Christians, to create structures and patterns of living together which ever more approximate the justice of the city of God.

Justice in the World (1971)

The synodal statement Justice in the World, which Paul VI anticipated as he wrote *Octagesimo adveniens,* provides a biblical and theological grounding for Christian action on behalf of justice which had not before been attempted in Catholic Social Teachings. Because the God of the Jewish and Christian traditions is a God of justice who liberates the oppressed and defends the poor, conversion to God requires action on behalf of justice (30). In Jesus' identification with persons who are oppressed, love of God and love of neighbor were inextricably bound together, such that Jesus Christ proclaimed the intervention of God's justice toward the oppressed and toward all believers (31). The Church of Christ then continues to be the intervention of God's justice and stands under the judgment of this same justice. In fact, justice, liberation, and salvation are the mission of the People of God.

Hence Justice in the World challenges the People of God to dedicate themselves to the liberation of persons in their existing situations (35), to do the justice required by love of neighbor (34–5), and to give credibility to the gospel message by their loving, just actions (35). While recognizing that justice does not only oblige Christians, Justice in the World maintains that justice is a specific responsibility of the Church identified with its very mission of evangelization (36).

This theo-ethical foundation for action on behalf of justice, rooted as it is in the mission of Jesus, unites human activity and faith. Every sector of human activity and every aspect of daily living become expressions of faith and the locus of action on behalf of justice. Christians work out their salvation by deeds of justice (56). The whole human person and the whole world stand in need of redemption, salvation, liberation, and justice/justification.

Consequently Justice in the World can remark that "action on behalf of justice and participation in the transformation of the world fully appear to us as a constitutive dimension of the preaching of the gospel, or, in other words, of the Church's mission for the redemption of the human race and its liberation from every oppressive situation" (6). Subsequent discussion has asked whether "constitutive," as it is used here, means "an important or integral expression" of preaching the gospel or an "essential requirement" without which the gospel is not preached and the Church has failed its mission.[17] Although other passages in Justice in the World reflect both interpretations, the theo-ethical foundation in the God of justice, in the incarnation, and in the redemption of Christ give important credence to justice as an essential requirement of the Church's mission.

Justice in the World, however, is acutely aware that action on behalf of justice and participation in the transformation of the world are shaped and given flesh according to the concrete historical situations.

---

[17] See, for example, Charles M. Murphy, "Action for Justice as Constitutive of Preaching the Gospel: What Did the 1971 Synod Mean?" *Theological Studies* 44 (1983) 298–311; Seamus Murphy, *The Many Ways of Justice*, Studies in the Spirituality of Jesuits 26 (St. Louis: The Seminar on Jesuit Spirituality, 1994) esp. 3–5.

Hence justice in developed communities may well entail renunciation of that which does not promote justice, while justice in developing nations entails consciousness-raising, self-liberation, and taking responsibility for their own destiny (51). Unless local churches give flesh to justice, this document will be ineffective (72).

The clear contribution of Justice in the World to the evolving understanding of justice in Catholic Social Teachings is the theo-ethical foundation built on the Jewish and Christian God of justice and on the central tenets of Christian belief, namely, the incarnation and redemption of Jesus Christ. These foundations place action on behalf of justice at the heart of Christian practice.

Laborem exercens *(1981)*

Pope John Paul II promulgated *Laborem exercens* as a treatise on work to commemorate the ninetieth anniversary of *Rerum novarum*. As a result, work and economic realities provide the context for the treatment of justice. The encyclical explicitly depicts systemic economic injustices (8), including inequitable distribution of wealth (2), absence of legal protections (21), unacceptable patterns of unemployment (8) and of ownership (21). The systemic and international (2) scope of economic injustice places the burden of social justice[18] practices on nations acting alone or collaboratively (18). Their address of injustice ought to include diagnosis, overall planning, organization, coordination so as to preserve individual and local initiative and effective implementation (18).

The demands for justice are linked with universal access to the goods of the earth (19) and with the "just good" (20) which seems to be another expression for the common good (20). Distributive justice is traditionally associated with universal access to the goods of the earth and contributive justice with the common good. In *Laborem exercens,* however, the focus returns to the policies, structures, patterns, and systems by which resources are distributed and life in common is fostered.

Universal access and the just good provide a lens from which to address specific issues, including unemployment (18), wages (19), unions (20), agricultural work (21), persons who are disabled (22), and emigration (23). Just wages are called "the concrete means of verifying the justice of the whole socio-economic system" (19). Unions function to

---

[18] *Laborem exercens* generally uses the noun "justice," although "social justice" does occur in 2, 8, and 20. Still the contexts for the use of justice throughout the document are social and structural, as will be demonstrated. Widespread use of the adjectival form "just" may suggest that a given structure can be just or unjust. The meaning of "just" in this widespread use lacks precise definition.

secure the just rights of workers and the just good of the whole society (20). Because work is a fundamental right of all persons, work ought to minimize unjust differences in standards of living for workers around the world (18). Persons who are disabled ought to receive just wages and be included as workers (22). Just legislation is needed to protect persons who emigrate (23).

This pervasive international and systemic framework within which to approach justice is a significant contribution of *Laborem exercens.* Just policies, structures, patterns, and systems facilitate just practices.

Sollicitudo rei socialis *(1987)*

Since *Sollicitudo rei socialis* commemorates the twentieth anniversary of *Populorum progressio,* the international dimensions of access to the earth's resources (10) and of development (22, 26, 28) receive expected and appropriate focus. The encyclical notes that an "effective political will" is needed to replace the misguided political and economic mechanisms which thwart development. *Sollicitudo rei socialis* concludes that the effective political will to establish new, just structures in service of the common good of humanity (35) is lacking.

After this stinging evaluation, the encyclical, nonetheless, leaves the structural realm and immediately turns to what it calls the moral dimensions of these obstacles, namely, sin (36–7), which can be transformed through conversion (38), and the moral virtue of solidarity (39). Even though "structures of sin" are addressed, *Sollicitudo rei socialis* recalls that all sin is rooted in "the concrete acts of individuals who introduce these structures, consolidate them and make them difficult to remove" (36). The encyclical urges conversion to solidarity among persons who feel personally affected by the injustices afflicted on others (38). Structural and political obstacles apparently are overcome by personal change of hearts.

Centesimus annus *(1991)*

John Paul II commemorated the one hundredth anniversary of *Rerum novarum* with the encyclical *Centesimus annus* eighteen months after the collapse of the Eastern Block. Within that economic context, the document offers two significant contributions to Catholic Social Teachings on justice. First, justice requires that persons and countries who are economically disadvantaged have access to resources and contribute to the good of the whole by their work (28). This principle rests on a shift in the understanding of the causes of poverty, namely, that persons who are poor are not "irksome intruders trying to consume what others have produced." Rather, poverty results from "tragic historical events which were violently imposed on them and which prevented them from following the path of economic and social development." If poverty is structurally imposed injustice and not individual free choice, then an appropriate response must address unjust structures.

Second, justice requires that fundamental human needs and inclusion in the human community be accorded to all persons because of their dignity as persons:

> It is a strict duty of justice and truth not to allow fundamental human needs to remain unsatisfied and not to allow those burdened by such needs to perish. It is also necessary to help these needy people to acquire expertise, to enter the circle of exchange and to develop their skills in order to make the best use of their capacities and resources. Even prior to the logic of a fair exchange of goods and the forms of justice appropriate to it, there exists something which is due to the person because he is a person, by reason of his lofty dignity. Inseparable from that required "something" is the possibility to survive and, at the same time, to make an active contribution to the common good of humanity (34).

Human dignity becomes the foundation of ethical imperatives. Therefore trade unions and workers' associations defend workers' rights to basic human needs as well as enable workers to participate in and contribute to the society (35). Similarly, the issue of debt repayment to the International Monetary Fund should be regulated by the same considerations of justice, namely, the repayment of debt ought not to compromise basic human needs of citizens and ought to facilitate inclusion in the community of nations (35). Consequently, charitable giving from surplus goods does not meet the requirements of justice. Rather, justice requires actions which enable entire peoples "presently excluded or marginated to enter the sphere of economic and human development." Such inclusion entails lifestyle changes, the transformation of production and consumption patterns, the modification of governance and power structures, as well as global perspectives in social organization (58). These universal and structural changes are necessary so that basic human needs and inclusion in the human family can be met as required by justice.

Centesimus annus thus confirms the foundation of justice in the dignity of human persons, whose survival requires access to basic human resources and whose essential relationality requires participation in the human community. In addition, the challenge to understand poverty as a result of historical forces and structural coercion asserts that justice, too, must deal with historical realities and social structures.

Conclusion

This examination of justice in the documents of Catholic Social Teachings provides some insights into an understanding of justice. First, justice is utilized to respond to concrete situations, that is, the meaning or understanding of justice is shaped by the specific eras and events to which it is responding. Thus this survey of justice illustrates that Catholic Social Teachings emerge from a process which begins in experience, moves to expression, and proceeds to theological thinking, before magisterial recognition. The initial Thomistic definition of justice as "giving to another what is due in relationships of equity" has not served as an all-encompassing definition from which secondary principles and applications have been deduced. Rather, beginning with *Rerum novarum*, changing historical situations have stretched that assumed concept of justice and caused its evolution. As we read through the social encyclicals, we encounter justice as obligation (*Rerum novarum*), as distribution of resources (*Quadragesimo anno*), as equity (*Mater et magistra*), as access to basic human needs (*Gaudium et spes*), as structural facilitation of fairness (*Laborem exercens*), and as contributing to the common good (*Centesimus annus*).

Second, in the documents justice primarily addresses economic issues, albeit with an evolving social awareness. *Pacem in terris, Gaudium et spes*, and Justice in the World, by way of exception, focus on political or other issues. As a result, justice is not developed in the documents of Catholic Social Teachings with regard to ecological concerns, ecclesial matters, domestic injustices, or social issues. For example, issues of race and gender are rarely mentioned in conjunction with justice,[19] even though discrimination is condemned on the basis of dignity, rights, and equality. Thus the contribution of Catholic Social Teachings to a more comprehensive understanding of justice focuses on those

---

[19] There are three instances in which justice is mentioned in conjunction with mothers and ethnic minorities. PT 97 recognizes that the principles of justice urge civil authorities to improve the lot of ethnic minorities. GS 66 holds that justice and equity require an end to discrimination against ethnic and agricultural workers. LE 19 calls "family allowances or grants to mothers devoting themselves exclusively to their families" an example of just remuneration. In addition, in the description of the current situation, CA 8 notes some employment contracts of women and children ignore "the most elementary justice," and OA 16 lists persons experiencing discrimination as "victims of situations of injustice."

dimensions of justice articulated in an economic context which have potential to foster a just and inclusive community as an embodiment of the endtimes city of God.

Third, virtually from the beginning Catholic Social Teachings maintain that the human person is social. Growing interdependence among persons and nations points to sociality as an obvious dimension of human living. Social relationships are necessary for full human development and are rooted in human dignity and freedom. Participatory and mutual relationships enhance political, social, and economic life. Human interdependence provides a foundation for an understanding of justice as participation, even though this approach to justice is not explicated until Economic Justice for All (1986) and *Centesimus annus* (1991).

Fourth, the concrete economic issues addressed, the adoption of a social anthropology, as well as a growing awareness of the global and structural nature of injustice over time have transformed justice into social justice. Social justice differs from the Neo-Scholastic conception of justice in three ways: (1) social justice concerns itself with the structures, patterns, policies, and laws which facilitate or hinder the practice of just deeds. Over time the documents increased attention to structures of employment, to reordering the socioeconomic orders, to patterns of unequal trade relationships, and to systemic injustices. (2) Social justice attends not only to "what is due" in relationships, but to the creation of circumstances so that it is possible for persons and nations to contribute what is due. (3) Social justice is interested in the whole socioeconomic order as an interlocking system, rather than in its parts. In other words, social justice concerns itself with the functioning of the whole order in its interacting parts, rather than with the various relationships between the parts.

This transformation of justice into social justice originated in *Rerum novarum.* For example, Leo XIII stretched the Neo-Scholastic concept of contractual justice to include not only the fulfillment of a contract, but also the terms of the agreement itself, that is, the structure of the contract. With regard to contributive justice, *Mater et magistra* held that an economic system must provide opportunities for workers to contribute to the business enterprise and to the common good. Later, *Centesimus annus* explicated the demands of contributive justice to include the development of expertise and skills as well as changes in consumption and production patterns as demands of contributive justice.

Distributive justice also shifted in meaning. Initially *Rerum novarum* called upon the state to care for those without property as a directive of distributive justice. Both *Laborem exercens* and *Centesimus annus* called for a restructuring of economic systems in order that persons are able to satisfy their basic human needs through their participation in that system.

In each of these instances what began as a concept of justice within the Neo-Scholastic tradition of contributive, distributive, and contractual justice has been transformed into social justice with the corresponding focus on the structures, the environment, and the socioeconomic order as a whole. The adoption of a social anthropology provided an understanding of the human person in which participation in a society was "what is due." Such a foundation certainly facilitated the shift from specific kinds of justice (contributive, distributive, and contractual) to social justice. This foundation also facilitated a shift from charity to justice as an appropriate response to poverty.

Fifth, the documents of the Vatican II era (1965–71) took up the task of providing a biblical and theological foundation for action on behalf of justice. This departure from the previous philosophical approach to justice has not yielded a fully developed theological framework,[20] but has drawn attention to God's history of intervention on behalf of the oppressed and to Jesus' identification with the marginated. *Populorum progressio* and Justice in the World identify the mission of the body of Christ as the continuation of God's mission of justice and liberation in Jesus Christ. *Octagesimo adveniens* presents justice as a dimension of the vision of the city of God, which calls the People of God to embody that endtimes city in each new era. Thus justice is connected with God's action in this world and in Jesus Christ as well as with the eschatological fulfillment of the reign of God.

In other words, in the midst of the historically situated statements of justice directed primarily to the economic order, there are flashes of insight which open the way to the existence and a future for the human community. Even in the rhetorical laments against socialist unions and state controlled production, there are glimmers of the future city of God where justice, peace, and love provide the guiding principles. Even in ideologies of hierarchy, patriarchy, and Eurocentrism there are moments where the dream of a just and inclusive community is envisioned (participation, social anthropology). These insights, glimmers, and moments indicate the in-breaking of a future which provides norms for the establishment of a just and inclusive community today.

---

[20] The concept "God" was not absent from the earlier treatments of justice in the documents of Catholic Social Teachings. The presentations emphasized "God" as first cause and final destiny of humanity, the source of authority, and the purpose of all things. This understanding of God can be linked to the understanding of justice as duty and obligation which will be examined in Chapter 5.

5

Classic Contemporary Theories of Justice

The interpretation of justice from Catholic Social Teachings, the Scriptures, and human experience takes place in the contemporary context with its own practical and theoretical understandings of justice. Chapter 5 will examine a number of these articulations of justice, in hopes of contextualizing and clarifying comments read in the newspapers and heard over coffee. Just as casual conversations about justice surface opposing understandings, the positions described will at times conflict with each other. Perhaps most importantly, most of the positions articulated in casual conversation have their roots in contemporary theories of justice. In order to compare these understandings, the same questions will be posed to each of these articulations of justice. These are:

- What is the basis of the claim to justice?

- What are the implicit absolutes in this theory?

- What is the understanding of the human person (the anthropology)?

- Who decides what justice is?

- What is the goal of justice?

- What are some of the mediating principles of justice, that is, how would one recognize a just society?

- What attention is given to structures in the understanding of justice?

- What is the relationship between specific just actions and justice?

- What is the method?
- What is the place of self-critical mechanisms in this understanding of justice?

JUSTICE AS DUTY AND OBLIGATION
(CATHOLIC SOCIAL TEACHINGS)

The previous chapter on justice in Catholic Social Teachings has set forth the evolving understandings of justice in magisterial teachings since 1891. One recurring thread in the encyclical tradition describes justice as mutually binding obligations with attention to the special claims of those in need. This description reflects Thomistic roots in its stress on obligations and a scriptural influence in its stress on the special claims of those in need. Without denying the multiple understandings of justice uncovered in Catholic Social Teachings, this section will focus on justice as duty through the lens of the ten comparative points mentioned in the introduction.

Basis of the claim: Justice as obligation arises both from the dignity of human persons and from relationships. Human dignity obliges reciprocally, that is, dignity imposes a corresponding duty to recognize and enhance human dignity in others. In the social encyclical tradition, inviolable human dignity is reinforced by its anthropology as well as three faith convictions. First, human persons are created in the image and likeness of God. Second, believers are called to love one another as they have been loved. Third, the treatment of the widow, the orphan, and the poor is the concrete measure of the believer's love of God.

Obligations of justice also arise from voluntary and involuntary relationships. Initially Catholic Social Teachings stressed the obligations which arose from so-called voluntary wage contracts. Later documents recognized the obligations rooted in involuntary relationships such as membership in a family, in the human family, and in the community of believers. These obligations of justice are not primarily external obligations, but rather are internal obligations emerging from identity and membership in the human community and in the community of believers. God's creation covenant with all creatures which was renewed with all believers establishes a community in which equitable treatment of other persons becomes a mutually binding obligation.

Inherent absolutes: God and God's justice provide an inherent absolute. The Creator God has a divine plan which is expressed in eternal and natural law as well as in reciprocal loving covenants. These laws and covenants remain constant and faithful throughout the course of human history and the unjust practices of believers and nations. God's justice as expressed in law and covenant invites a response to God in faithful love and to neighbor in just love.

Anthropology: The essentially social nature of the human person provides an anthropological foundation for the mutually binding nature of justice as obligation. This essential socialness gives rise to equal rights, reciprocal claims, and duties, while the inherent dignity of each person as person occasions the duty to recognize the worth and value of each. This social anthropology was anticipated in Thomas Aquinas' insistence on the relational nature of justice and reaches its pinnacle in an understanding of justice as membership in the human community. If persons are social by nature, a corresponding obligation arises to create those conditions of social life by which persons can survive and thrive through a network of relationships.

Who decides what justice is: The determination of justice is complex. On one hand God's eternal and natural law has determined what is due to others in relationships of equity. Human persons come to understand their obligations from their human dignity, from laws, from God's covenant with them, and from their discipleship. On the other hand, justice as reciprocally binding obligations with attention to the special claims of persons in need points to a certain dialogical nature in decisions around the meaning of justice. In point of fact, the special claims of those in need have moved persons to justice action and the Roman Catholic magisterium to pronouncements. In addition, relationships of equity were a keystone in the definition of justice advanced by Thomas Aquinas. Hierarchy, non-participation, and appeals to divine legitimization, however, characterized the historical processes which selected, promulgated, and interpreted this approach to justice. As a result, persons in academic and ecclesiastical positions of power in practice exercised disproportionate influence in the determination of justice.

Goal of justice: In the language of philosophy the goal of justice as obligation is the good of human persons as a whole (common good) as well as individuals. The faith expression for this goal is the reign or city of God. Both the common good and the city of God are inherently relational. As such both require and provide a framework for justice as mutually binding obligations which make achievement of a common good possible. Both the method and the inherent absolute point to an identification of the common good with God's eternal plan.

Mediating principles: Over the past century the documents of Catholic Social Teachings have elaborated various principles which mediate or make concrete some demands of justice as duty. These include participation in political and economic life, protection of social and political rights, protection of the disadvantaged or preferential option for the poor, provision of humane living conditions necessary for human dignity, universal access to the goods of the earth, equitable trade relations, and non-discriminatory practices and legislation.

Attention to the structures of justice: Already *Rerum novarum* and *Quadragesimo anno* called for attention to the terms of wage contracts in the determination of a just wage, while stressing the individual obligations in justice for workers and employers. More recent documents have shifted the stress from individuals to the structures in the social, political, and economic spheres. Attention has focused on institutions, policies, organizational patterns, terms of agreements, and cultural conditions of living.

The relationship between specific just actions and justice: Just actions are the concrete embodiment and expression of God's justice and eternal plan. This description suggests an incarnational and sacramental approach. Since persons are created in the image and likeness of God, specific actions can incorporate or give a body to the justice of God in this world.

Method: The method generally used in the documents of Catholic Social Teachings deduces principles for action from reason, eternal law, and God's revelation. It is not clear that justice as obligation in itself requires a deductive approach. As it is located in Catholic Social Teachings, however, with the Thomistic presuppositions that God's eternal law has already determined what is right, the requirements of justice are understood officially as deductions from revelation and reason, particularly in its legal expressions. Chapter 4 has documented that in practice, obligations to do justice emerged from historical economic, political, and social injustices to which the encyclicals responded. Beginning with *Mater et magistra,* the social encyclical tradition also recognized a more inductive methodology of "see, judge, and act." In this methodology the demands of justice may be deduced from one's identity as a believer, while the determination of specific just actions may rely on an inductive methodology.

Self-critical mechanism: To the extent that God's eternal plan is viewed as unchangeable and completely revealed, this approach provides little room for self-critical mechanisms. To the extent that identity as a disciple and member of the human community provides the ground of obligation, the dynamism inherent in personal development and faith provides fertile ground for self-critical mechanisms.

This approach to justice as obligation stresses the link between justice and beliefs about God, as well as convictions about the human person. The theological framework accentuates God as a creator of all persons in God's own image and as the establisher of a covenant people. In Catholic Social Teachings the requirements of justice emerge from this constitutive dignity and relationality of the human-person-in-community. Since God is Creator God, these requirements are God-given demands.

Justice as Law

On July 17, 1998, the 159 member states of the United Nations approved a treaty creating the International Criminal Court. In the words of Aryeh Neier, one of its chief architects: "For the first time in human history, those committing war crimes, crimes against humanity or the ultimate crime, genocide, have to reckon seriously with the possibility that they will be brought before the international bar to face truth, be held accountable and serve justice." In other words, the legal structures of the newly established International Criminal Court will bring about justice.

Widespread popular opinion equates justice with legal structures including laws and the court system. For example, some persons hold that anything is just unless it is prohibited by law. Those who disagree with legal decisions or their application to specific cases conclude that "there is no justice!" Two intertwined conceptions of justice as law lurk in these popular comments. Sometimes legal justice emphasizes procedures,[1] that is, the equitable and consistent application of laws under which society operates and disputes are adjudicated. Other times legal justice emphasizes the substance of justice, that is, the ideal just society. In acknowledging the lack of agreement on what constitutes a just society, Ronald Dworkin speaks of three approaches to substantive legal justice:[2] conventionalism, naturalism, and instrumentalism. Conventionalism looks to legal precedent for the substance of justice. Instrumentalism seeks to make community as just as possible without regard to legal precedents; the substance of justice then is the external and internal ideal of justice. Naturalism looks to past legal decisions interpreted in as broad a context as possible and to current conceptions of a just society for the substance of justice.

Basis of the claim: The basis of the claim for justice as law is membership in the particular social order regulated by specific laws. This membership entails the creation and acceptance of social roles, including

---

[1] Tom R. Tyler and Kathleen M. McGraw, "Ideology and the Interpretation of Personal Experience: Procedural Justice and Political Quiescence," *Journal of Social Issues* 42:2 (1986) 115–28.

[2] Ronald A. Dworkin, "'Natural Law' Revisited," *University of Florida Law Review* 34:2 (1982) 165–88; Ronald A. Dworkin, "Law as Interpretation," *Critical Inquiry* 9 (September 1982) 179–200; and Linell E. Cady, "Hermeneutics and Tradition: The Role of the Past in Jurisprudence and Theology," *Harvard Theological Review* 79:4 (1986) 439–63.

legal roles, as well as processes for the establishment of legislation and for the resolution of competing claims under the law. In a procedural approach, the legal system maintains and makes possible a social order which emerged from a historical process of conflicting interests. This understanding of the social order certainly highlights the conflictual, participatory, and historical dimensions of the social order, along with a possible stress on the voluntary nature of membership reflected in statements like, "If you don't like it, then leave it." In a substantive approach, some shared understanding of the ideal just society among the members gives rise to legislation and legal decisions accountable to ideal justice.

Inherent absolutes: Substantive legal justice sees the ideal just society as its inherent absolute. Procedural legal justice looks to equitable and consistent application of laws as its inherent absolute. Generally speaking these absolutes are dynamic and changeable. Politico-religious appeal to specific laws as God-given or divine in origin, however, can function as an absolutization of both the substance and the application of specific laws. Appeals to divine legitimization enable persons in positions of social power to maintain that power by discouraging the participation of others in the legislative and juridical processes typically associated with ever changing legal justice.

Anthropology: Human persons are viewed of as free and equal agents capable of influence and participation in the process of creating society through legislative, judicial, and executive action. Although it is not inherent to the understanding of justice as law, human persons are further described as driven by self-interest and protection of interests. Such self-interest can collide with a recognition of others' participatory self-agency. As a result the participatory dimensions of human persons can be obscured and undermined.

Who decides what justice is: Members of the social group determine the substance of justice through dialogical and broad-based participatory processes either around a shared understanding of a transcendent justice or around the laws which create a just society. Lawyers, defendants, witnesses, prosecutors, experts, police, citizens, and legislators all influence these ongoing processes through voice, decision, or interpretation. In practice, however, access to influence is weighted disproportionately to persons who control human, political, legal, and economic resources.[3]

---

[3] For example, welfare regulations are decided with minimal voting and voice participation by those most affected by the regulations. Tyler and McGraw, "Ideology and the Interpretation of Personal Experience," 115, conclude that citizens focus on opportunities to speak rather than on actual control over decisions as evidence of

Goal of justice: The goal of justice is a more just society. When an anthropology of self-interest is stressed, then protection of private goods is a central characteristic of the just society. When procedural justice is stressed, then equitable application of laws determines the just society. When substantive justice is stressed, then a shared understanding of justice becomes central to the just society, while laws become structures to facilitate just action. In both substantive and procedural legal justice, the goal of a more just society provides a standard to discriminate between "good laws" and "bad laws."

Mediating principles: When justice is identified as law, the following mediating principles surface. First, citizens are urged to develop the skills and practice of public discourse to influence legislative and juridical process. Second, all laws can be reformed and changed. Third, all persons ought to have the opportunity for participation (voice, vote, influence, and decision-making) in the development of procedural or substantive justice in their given society.

Attention to the structures of justice: Legal justice highlights the place of structures of justice. Whether laws are understood as changing structures to facilitate just practice or as the constitutive elements of procedural justice, the power of structures to promote or to establish justice is recognized.

The relationship between specific just actions and justice: To the extent that procedural justice identifies just acts (fair application of laws) with justice, the relationship of just acts to justice is univocal. In the case of substantive legal justice, the law is not justice itself, but rather legal structures summarize those conclusions about justice which are developing throughout history and civilization. From this perspective, civil rights legislation did not bring about racial justice, but reflected a social change in attitudes toward racial justice. Laws legitimate or ratify a change in the shared understanding of justice which social and historical changes have already accomplished. According to Dworkin, the ideal of justice or a more just society provides a transforming power disclosed within specific actions or laws.[4]

---

fairness in procedures. See ibid., 126 for their assessment of the dysfunctional nature of this focus, which emerges from cultural socialization into dominant values. In this way, one can see the disproportionate influence of the existing social structures and those who hold positions of influence in that system.

[4] Dworkin's work focuses on the interpretation of legal precedents in new decisions. Whether one approaches substantive justice as conventional, naturalist, or instrumental, the rule of decision seeks to promote the just society in the way in which the presiding judge understands it. Rigid reliance on legal precedents still contains the potential for transforming rules of decision.

Method: The beginning point of the description of justice as law is the communal experience of disorder, disorganization, or lawlessness. Disorder urges a social group to come together in an effort to establish a social order which either brings about justice or reflects the communal understanding of justice. The initial social order is open to reform through an ongoing process of influencing policy changes and resolving competing interests. This method relies on praxis-based access to and participation in the legislative or community organizing processes. Such a dialogical method can be thwarted by individualistic anthropologies or the absolutization of laws.

Self-critical mechanism: Justice as law has inherent self-critical mechanisms both in the historical nature of the evolving human community and in its methodological processes for influencing the legislative and judicial structures. Politico-religious legitimization of laws and denial of access to the influence process can impede these self-critical mechanisms. In addition, criticism of the legal system on the basis of perspectives outside that system have little or any influence.

Legal justice includes both an emphasis on consistency in application of laws (procedural) and progress toward an ideal just society (substantive). Both of these emphases, however, highlight a participatory and a structural dimension to justice. Legal justice must attend to those legal processes which provide consistent, equitable application of the law as well as legislative and interpretative potential to make society more just. Judicial, legislative, executive, and interpretative processes involve a broad range of citizen participation.

JUSTICE AS RESTRAINT OF SELF-INTEREST
(REINHOLD NIEBUHR)

All this talk about justice has no place in the church. Churches and ministers are to help us become loving and holy like God. Priests should preach about loving our neighbor the way Jesus did. It's okay if they offer us opportunities to give money or do service. We shouldn't have to hear or think about politics and economics in church. We deal enough with racism and joblessness Monday through Friday. Religion, church services, and Jesus are the places where we are comforted and strengthened to do God's will so we can get to heaven.

Although Reinhold Niebuhr did not write the above statement, he does assign justice to the spheres of political, economic, and social institutions, while religion and personal relationships are assigned to the selfless love of Jesus.[5] For Niebuhr, the meaning of justice is dependent

---

[5] Reinhold Niebuhr, *Love and Justice: Selections from the Shorter Writings of Reinhold Niebuhr*, ed. D. B. Robertson (Louisville: Westminster/John Knox, 1957) 25.

on love and the concrete social situation. While Niebuhr holds that the only true definition of justice is perfect love, he maintains that love apart from justice arrives at naive solutions to social problems.[6] Niebuhr also holds that self-giving love to which Jesus invited disciples remains an impossible practice in a world characterized by self-interest, domination, and power. Consequently, justice is an "approximation of brotherhood under conditions of sin."[7]

The sphere of justice is the place of the struggle, an intermediary sphere, between the ideal of love and the reality of sin and selfishness. Justice has a certain pragmatic and relative character, given a world of contingencies and social locations. In Niebuhr's words, justice belongs to the "realm of tragic choices."[8] Justice restrains self-interest so that the weak are protected against the strong. Justice discerns between competing claims in complex social, economic, and political worlds. Because justice focuses on the balance of powers as well as the ordering of competing obligations in the collective arena,[9] justice concerns itself with the total organization of human living, not only the distribution of resources.

Basis of the claim: The impossibility of fulfilling the love commandment of Jesus provides the basis of the claim to justice. The love command functions as an individual call to perfection, hence it is neither social nor attainable.[10] The persistence and universality of human sin in concrete historical realities makes Jesus' ideal of voluntary, disinterested love an impossible possibility on which to found a social order. A social order, however, can be founded on justice, that is, the approximation of the Christian ideal of love in the social and sinful world of coercion, self-interest, and competing power claims. Consequently, any definition of justice must presuppose sin, which Niebuhr describes as a failure to value the claims of the other or a failure to see another's claims as equal, instead of inferior, to one's own claims.[11] Justice restrains self-interest and balances competing claims so that the ideal of disinterested love can turn into the city of God at the end of time.

Inherent absolutes: According to Niebuhr the ultimate criteria for justice are outside of history in the city of God, namely, the unattainable ideal of Christian love and human possibility. Although human history can reveal ultimate norms, justice in this world is ever reshaped by the impossible ideal of love, by the contingent situation, and by ever greater

---

[6] Ibid., 25 and 50.
[7] Ibid., 13.
[8] Ibid., 29.
[9] Ibid., 25 and 282.
[10] Ibid., 30–2.
[11] Ibid., 49 and 164.

embodiments of human possibility. As such, Niebuhr's inherent absolute is a normativity of the future, but predominately a future outside of history.

Anthropology: Niebuhr summarizes his biblical anthropology in three
points: the human person is created in the image of God, the human
person is a creature, and the human person is a sinner.[12] Creation in the
image of God accounts for the possibilities of freedom, self-transcen-
dence, and infinite potential. As sinners, however, human persons
usurp God and deny their creatureliness or they practice will-to-power,
i.e., pride, self-interest, and exploitation. Niebuhr's consciousness of
sin includes a deep suspicion of human rationality, for it, too, is fallen.

Since reason is constitutive of the "rules of justice," the fallen nature
of rationality results in structures of justice which are built on self-
interest, exploitation, and pride. This evaluation of social orders established on rational justice is heightened by the sharp distinction which
Niebuhr makes between individuals and groups. While it is difficult
for individuals to approximate the self-giving love of Jesus in their
relationships, "Groups have never been unselfish in the slightest degree."[13]

Who decides what justice is: Niebuhr suggests that structures and definitions of justice are established by depraved, self-interested, rational
men who are situated in positions of influence in specific cultures: "The
perspective of the strong dictates the conception of justice by which
the total community operates and necessitates social conflict through
the assertion of the rights of the weak before justice is corrected."[14]
Niebuhr counters this reality with the possibility that human persons
can transcend their own fallen reason to value the interests of another
as equal or more compelling than their own. Niebuhr defines such
imaginative justice as a justice which goes beyond equality to the needs
of others. In fact, disciples ought to influence the operating structures
and rules so as to restrain powers of domination. Thus Niebuhr holds
to the possibility of an ever more just social order, which approximates
community under conditions of sin.

Goal of justice: The goal of justice is a state of brotherhood in which
there is no conflict of interests.[15] Since both perfect justice and love are
impossible in this world, all justice here is relative, that is, the best
possible harmony within the conditions of sin, but not unconditionally
just. Calculations of competing interests, specifications of rights and

---

[12] Niebuhr outlines his anthropology in distinction to a Catholic and liberal Protestant approach. See ibid., 46–54.

[13] Ibid., 243.

[14] Ibid., 320.

[15] Ibid., 50.

duties, and the balancing of power provide guidelines for the best available approximation of community, given the conditions of sin. Since conflicts of interests are simply part and parcel of human personal and social living, justice seeks to restrain domination and to balance power in order to minimize such conflicts.

Mediating principles: Since justice in Niebuhr's understanding always stands under the judgment of love and the more perfect possibilities of human community, all the principles of justice are provisional and correctable.[16] Niebuhr's writings offer five principles of relative justice. First, "some balance of power is the basis of whatever justice is achieved in human relations. Where the disproportion of power is too great and where an equilibrium of social forces is lacking, no mere rational or moral demands can achieve justice."[17] Will to power threatens personal and social relationships. Hence justice must seek to restrain power and privilege, so that in each specific time and place, power is balanced in a social order.

Second, the struggle for social justice involves the use of coercion, political pressure, or police force.[18] In Niebuhr's understanding, this principle includes a duty to resist tyranny as well as an obligation to use power to establish order. Niebuhr admits that moral persuasion or self-giving love would be better, but believes that they are unable to be effective in a sin-ridden world. Still he urges the minimal amount of coercion necessary and a preference for mutual consent. However, since persons with privilege or advantage do not readily recognize claims which advance the interests of others, some kinds of coercive power (i.e., laws or taxation which equalize privilege) are typically required.

Equality is a third principle of justice. Equality is the best passageway between justice in this world and the ideal of Christian love, for it is both the pinnacle of justice and it "implicitly points toward love as the final norm of justice."[19] In Niebuhr's understanding, equality provides guidelines for both process (e.g., impartiality in determining need) and substantive concerns (e.g., equal civil rights).

The promotion of freedom is a fourth principle. Even though freedom is central to human persons, freedom must be regulated by justice, community, and equality. Without these, freedom will become license to exploit and dominate others.[20] Niebuhr finds this especially true in the economic and political spheres.

[16] Ibid., 17. By "provisional" Niebuhr does not necessarily mean arbitrary; rather provisional principles may in fact reflect what is genuinely human.

[17] Ibid., 207; cf. 35 and 52.

[18] Ibid., 34–5.

[19] Ibid., 14.

[20] Ibid., 95.

Niebuhr's final principle addresses the constitutional protection of human rights for all persons, especially those persons who are exploited and dominated.[21]

Attention to the structures of justice: Niebuhr's approach stresses structural dimensions of justice. Since history, power, and reason are corrupted by the will to power (sin), structures, laws, and institutions established on justice are necessary to restrain concentrations of power in a group as well as to protect society and its citizens from selfishness.[22] Neutrality in the face of structural dimensions of society only serves the advantage of the powerful. In contrast to liberal Protestantism's stress on individual character, Niebuhr holds that social systems and institutions are the true guarantees of justice in society. Still, structures remain temporary, partial, and correctable in light of the city of God, the ideal of love, and human possibility.

The relationship between specific just actions and justice: Niebuhr rejects the possibility of articulating "a universally valid concept of justice from any particular sociological locus of history."[23] Rather, just actions are historical manifestations of self-giving love, which transcends and judges any concrete historical enactment of justice. Specific just actions can never fully embody that perfect justice which is self-giving love, for an always more perfect historical approximation is possible. Niebuhr maintains that principles of justice transcend specific deeds of justice. Some principles may even become universal norms to the extent that they have their source in common human experience. Relative or this-worldly justice refers to those historical possibilities which are transcended by disinterested love.

Method: Niebuhr begins with a juxtaposition of the historical realities of social sin (self-interest, exploitation, and injustice) and love's more perfect possibility for community. Niebuhr probes this juxtaposition to suggest a balance of power and a way of compromise. Niebuhr relies on the Bible, the rational analysis of competing rights and interests, and the complexities of the specific situation for suggestions concerning the historical enactment of justice in this situation.[24] Niebuhr's method of justice-making then relies on a reasoning believer attentive

---

[21] Ibid., 34 and 196–9.

[22] Ibid., 12, 28, and 173.

[23] Ibid., 16. This is the basis of his major criticism of past attempts to set forth a so-called natural law, namely, that they incorporated the culturally conditioned into the universal.

[24] Ibid., 16-18. In his introduction, D. B. Robertson describes Niebuhr's method as including "the elaboration of ideal possibilities, the harsh and unlovely facts of the case and the search for any redeeming element in the situation." See ibid., 21.

to the Christian vocation to love, the concrete situation, the texts of the religious tradition, and human knowledge.

Self-critical mechanism: The historically constituted nature of justice standing under the judgment of the city of God or of love, which is future and outside of history, contributes to an inherently self-critical approach to justice in three ways. First, Niebuhr's approach to justice assumes that any historical enactment of justice could always be more just. Consequently there are no definitively just actions or structures. Second, this conception of justice harbors a built-in suspicion of justice as a manifestation of individual and collective self-interest. Third, Niebuhr specifically invites believers to be critical of their own claims for justice. However, he warns against outright dismissal of one's own claims. Rather, he invites believers to entertain the claims while resisting illegitimate self-interest.[25]

Niebuhr's description of justice as "approximation of brotherhood under conditions of sin" summarizes three central facets of justice as restraint of self-interest. First, justice must attend to the harsh realities of human inhumanity and sinfulness, for love apart from justice is not enough. Second, justice can only be approximated in this world, for true justice transcends this world. Third, human inhumanity and sinfulness require attention to the realities of conflicting interests, the inclusion of coercion as a strategy, and the dismissal of an ethic of love as naive. Niebuhr's awareness of individual and collective inhumanity, self-interest, or sinfulness situates any discussion of justice in a context of blunt and this-worldly realism.

JUSTICE AS FAIRNESS (JOHN RAWLS)

The publication of John Rawls' influential book A Theory of Justice *in 1971 must be seen in the context of revolutions against the establishment in 1968. The idealism of the time converged in agreement that everybody deserved a fair share of the goods and benefits of a society. Western European societies had a strong awareness of the need for structural change based on the fundamental equality of people which was readily accepted—at least ideally. The enthusiasm of the newfound freedom and opportunity also instilled optimism that these ideals could become a reality in a relatively short period of time. Barriers that for centuries had segregated people into different classes and social groups were torn down. Free and equal access to education was an essential part of the movement for equal opportunities. It was assumed that justice contained a*

---

[25] Ibid., 28.

claim to a certain state of affairs that was not yet a reality, but could become a reality through change.

According to Rawls, justice is the first, i.e., the most important, virtue of social institutions.[26] For him all justice is social justice. He holds, "the primary subject of justice is the basic structure of society";[27] that is, for Rawls justice is not a virtue of individuals, but of institutions. Rawls does, however, understand justice as a virtue and not as an obligation or a process. The "principles of social justice . . . provide a way of assigning rights and duties in basic institutions of society and they define the appropriate distribution of the benefits and burdens of social cooperation."[28] Justice thus provides "in the first place a standard whereby the distributive aspects of the basic structure of society are to be assessed."[29] Rawls completely focuses on distributive justice. He presumes that under concrete historical circumstances it is difficult, if not impossible, for people to choose just principles because they are influenced by the unequal conditions that have come about in historical situations. Therefore, just principles could only be chosen in an initial position in which no one would know in what kind of a historical position they might end up. Rawls thus describes the original agreement as "the principles that free and rational persons concerned to further their own interests would accept in an initial position of equality as defining the fundamental terms of their association."[30]

Rawls admits that his notion of rationality is based on economic theory. Consequently he assumes that rational is defined as "taking the most effective means to given ends."[31] In the area of justice, Rawls presumes that the given end is a furtherance of self-interest of free individuals. He is convinced that in the initial position free and rational people would understand that they can best further their own interests by giving everybody a fair share, by appropriately distributing rights and duties, benefits and burdens. While Rawls carefully disavows utilitarianism, his theory is certainly rationalist and individualist and maybe even pragmatist. For Rawls, justice is not essentially an ethical term, but rather describes organization and efficiency. The basic underlying presumption suggests the most efficient is most just and the most

---

[26] John Rawls, *A Theory of Justice* (Cambridge, Mass.: Harvard University Press, 1971) 3 and 6.

[27] Ibid., 7.

[28] Ibid., 4.

[29] Ibid., 9.

[30] Ibid., 11, cf. 19: the principles of justice are "those which rational persons concerned to advance their interests would consent to as equals when none are known to be advantaged or disadvantaged by social and natural contingencies."

[31] Ibid., 14.

just is most efficient, at least under the primordial conditions of the initial position.

Basis of the claim: The first basis of the claim to justice is the equality of all in the original position. Historically conditioned inequalities cannot be used to justify advantages of individuals and groups. According to Rawls, "each person possesses an inviolability founded on justice."[32] The second basis of the claim is the conviction that only just agreements are rational and thus effective means to further people's interest.

Inherent absolutes: Rawls' hypothetical original position assumes that inequalities of birth, historical circumstance, and natural endowment are undeserved. Furthermore, society's goal as a cooperative venture for mutual advantage can only be reached if everyone is treated fairly. Fairness is the most effective and thus the most rational means to reach the goal of society and to further self-interest.

Anthropology: Rawls' theory of justice is based on an understanding of the human person as autonomous and rational. For him, a free and rational individual is central. Society is the result of agreements between free individuals who are concerned to further their own interests. The source of injustice consists in the advantages which people gain due to natural and social chance.

Who decides what justice is: An agreement or social contract of free, rational people in the original position determines justice. Concretely, this amounts to a free and voluntary agreement of all autonomous and rational people even beyond the boundaries of the present generation. Rawls thinks that rational people who want to further their own interests would voluntarily agree to the two principles of justice that he offers.

Goal of justice: Since for Rawls society is a "cooperative venture for mutual advantage,"[33] he considers the goal of a just society to be the mutual advantage of everyone. To reach this goal, rights and duties in basic institutions of society need to be assigned fairly, the benefits and burdens of social cooperation would be appropriately distributed.[34] Fair and appropriate here mean equal or unequal if inequalities are "to the greatest benefit of the least advantaged."[35] The long-term effects of this so-called difference principle are a redressing of unequal situations.[36]

---

[32] Ibid., 3.

[33] Tom L. Beauchamp, "Distributive Justice and the Difference Principle," *John Rawls' Theory of Social Justice: An Introduction,* ed. Elizabeth H. Smith and H. Gene Blocker (Athens: Ohio University Press, 1980) 136.

[34] Rawls, *Theory of Justice,* 4.

[35] Ibid., 302.

[36] See Beauchamp, "Distributive Justice," 137: "The difference principle rests on the view that because inequalities of birth, historical circumstance and natural endowment are undeserved, society should reduce inequalities by selecting its

Mediating principles: Rawls' theory does not focus on the formulation of material principles or precepts, but rather on working out formal (structural) principles that govern the basic structure of society.

Attention to structures of justice: Since Rawls sees justice as a virtue of social institutions, his theory of justice focuses exclusively on the basic structure of society as a public system of rules governing the basic institutions.[37] Rawls worked out two formal principles of justice for institutions:

> [1] Each person is to have an equal right to the most extensive total system of equal basic liberties compatible with a similar system of liberty for all. [2] Social and economic inequalities are to be arranged so that they are both: a) to the greatest benefit of the least advantaged, consistent with the just savings principle and b) attached to offices and positions open to all under conditions of fair equality of opportunity.[38]

The relationship between specific just actions and justice: While Rawls concentrated on the political and economic sphere, he seems to assume that his theory of justice equally applies to all spheres of life. If the basic structures are not just, no other actions can be just either, no matter how just they might be in their own right.

Method: Rawls' theory of justice belongs to the social contract theories (cf. John Locke). But his beginning point is not the "state of nature." Rawls postulates a hypothetical original position and a veil of ignorance. In this original position no one is able to design principles to favor their own condition since no one knows in which position they will find themselves in life. Rawls assumes that the principles of justice on which the people in the original position would agree would replicate and preserve this original fair situation in this concrete world.

Self-critical mechanisms: Rawls is aware that structures do not remain just over time. Thus periodic regulation and correction of the basic structure of society by the principles of justice is essential. Rawls does not, however, seem to be aware of a need for self-criticism of his own philosophical thinking.

In this analysis we can hardly overlook that Rawls' ideas were developed in a period of enthusiastic new beginnings and unparalleled structural change in many societies. While Rawls undoubtedly remains caught in his overall liberal horizon peopled with self-interested, ra-

---

naturally disadvantaged members and redress their unequal situation." In Rawls' own words, "to redress the bias of contingencies in the direction of equality" (Rawls, *Theory of Justice*, 100).

[37] Rawls, *Theory of Justice*, 7, 55 and 84.

[38] Ibid., 302.

tional individuals, his optimistic idealism shaped a theory which sought to avoid many of the pitfalls in rationalism and individualism. Rawls' description of justice as fairness with special attention to the least advantaged challenges persons to put themselves in the shoes of another with the recognition that no one fully deserves their actual position in life.

JUSTICE AS FAIR PROCESS (ROBERT NOZICK)

Already in grade school children assume that if the rules and procedures are followed, then the outcome is just. This perception is connected to an environment which holds that following procedures is more important than the resulting distribution of income or opportunity. The process achieves justice and justice suffers when the procedures aren't followed.[39] *Procedural justice furthermore associates fairness of procedures with the opportunity to speak to an issue in public hearings, litigation, voting, or talk shows. Actual influence on the decision itself takes second place to voice. Because the procedures are deemed fair, the consequences of social allocation system are assumed to be just.*[40]

In his work *Anarchy, State and Utopia*,[41] Robert Nozick focuses on procedural requirements for fairness in exchange among individuals. Nozick seeks a justice which concerns itself with the underlying principles behind any given distribution of resources or "holdings." His book must be read first of all as a response to the work of John Rawls, published three years earlier. In addition, Nozick's treatment of justice occurs in the course of his argument for a minimalist state against those who hold that a more extensive state is necessary to redistribute resources among its citizens according to need, merit, usefulness, or equality. Hence, for Nozick, justice belongs to the sphere of individual exchanges including contracts. He admits that his entitlement conception of justice in holdings is only a part of a total theory of justice.

According to Nozick's theory, justice resides in the generating principles governing the distribution of resources, not with the final outcome. Nozick holds that any distribution can be just, as long as the procedures

[39] Bonnie Gershkon, "Justice Defined," *Loyola: The Magazine of Loyola University Chicago* (Spring 1998) 25.

[40] Tyler and McGraw, "Ideology and the Interpretation of Personal Experience," 115–28. See also Tom R. Tyler, "The Psychology of Leadership Evaluation," *Justice in Social Relations*, ed. Hans Werner Bierhoff and others (New York: Plenum Press, 1986) 310–1. Moreover, Ronald L. Cohen, "Procedural Justice and Participation," *Human Relations* 38:7 (1985) 643–63, describes the "fair process effect" with those who have participated in the legal decision-making process.

[41] Robert Nozick, *Anarchy, State and Utopia* (New York: Basic Books, 1974).

which actually or historically brought about that distribution were just. Justice depends on how the distribution came about, not what the distribution is. Nozick distinguishes this historical theory of justice from those substantive approaches to justice which concern themselves with a final outcome or end-state.

Basis of the claim: The basis of an individual's claim to justice is entitlement through acquisition, transfer, or rectification. Nozick emphasizes the freely chosen nature of this entitlement with his summary expression, "From each as they choose, to each as they are chosen."[42] In other words, justice is the product of free exchange among individuals entitled to make these exchanges. Self-interested and rational persons voluntarily come together as a protective agency to protect their individual claims, to adjudicate conflicting claims,[43] and to mutually agree upon procedures which assure entitlement for those in the group.[44] These mutually determined procedures provide principles of justice. They do not, however, address an ideal end-state which ought to exist.

Inherent absolutes: Nozick understands individual liberty and free choice as an absolute foundation of his understanding of justice. In fact, liberty has priority over equality,[45] which fact leads Nozick to place himself among libertarian thinkers. The central place accorded to individual liberty explains Nozick's justification of a minimal state. Nozick's minimal state only functions to protect against force, theft, fraud in transactions, and to enforce contracts.[46] A minimalist state cannot coerce citizens to aid other citizens (e.g., taxation) or prohibit activities for the citizens' own good (e.g., smoking). Since no central body exists with the authority to redistribute holdings, justice can only regulate procedures governing exchange contracts between free persons.[47]

The absolute nature of individual liberty is also connected to another foundation, namely, that past choices and actions can legitimately lead to differences in entitlement, i.e., things are not equal. Nozick's equation of justice with procedures rests on an absolute conviction that the world is just and persons get what they deserve, even when it is different from what other persons get. With this foundation, justice is served when the procedures are followed. Finally, Nozick holds that private property or holdings are an absolute.

---

[42] Ibid., 160.

[43] Ibid., 12–15.

[44] See Ronald L. Cohen, "Power and Justice in Intergroup Relations," *Justice in Social Relations,* ed. Hans Werner Bierhoff and others (New York: Plenum Press, 1986) 65–86, for a discussion of group boundaries and scope of justice concerns.

[45] Nozick, *Anarchy,* 167.

[46] Ibid., 149.

[47] Ibid.

Anthropology: In the anthropology which undergirds this approach to justice, individuals are autonomous, rational, self-interested agents with natural assets and natural rights. People are entitled to their natural assets (resources and abilities) and to whatever flows from these assets. Since holdings flow from natural assets, people are entitled to their holdings. Differences in natural assets or the holdings that flow from them may not be equal, but they are not unjust.[48] Natural assets and holdings provide power to influence and to initiate social exchange. Individual natural rights include liberty and choice, holdings or property, and the right not to be injured by others.[49] A minimalist state protects only these natural rights. With this anthropology, a central headquarters which distributes resources and holdings justly is a logical impossibility. Thus justice must focus on keeping social exchanges free from coercive interventions external to the exchange itself, including those of an expansionist state.

Who decides what justice is: The historical process of acquisition and transfer of holdings is a major determinant of justice. "Justice in holdings is historical; it depends upon what actually has happened."[50] In other words, the historical process determines justice.

Goal of justice: Since Nozick's understanding of justice focuses on holdings or property and their historical entitlement, he describes a wholly just world as one in which persons are entitled to the holdings which they have:

> 1. A person who acquires a holding in accordance with the principle of justice in acquisition is entitled to that holding. 2. A person who acquires a holding in accordance with the principle of justice in transfer, from someone else entitled to the holding, is entitled to the holding. 3. No one is entitled to a holding except by (repeated) applications of 1 and 2.[51]

When each person's holdings are just, then the distribution of the holdings is also just. Nozick's theory of just entitlements in holdings envisions the free exchange of mutually beneficial resources for long-term personal benefit and defense of self-interest.

Mediating principles: With these goals in mind, Nozick sets forth principles which generate a just world in which persons are entitled to the holdings which they have. First, persons must be able to acquire and transfer resources. Second, Nozick maintains a prohibition against harm, that is, one's situation ought not be harmed or made worse.[52]

[48] Ibid., 255.
[49] Ibid., ix.
[50] Ibid., 152.
[51] Ibid., 151.
[52] Ibid., 178.

This principle does not require that a situation improve, no matter how miserable the situation might be. Third, "past circumstances or actions of people can create differential entitlements or differential deserts to things."[53] These differential entitlements may not be equal, but they are not unjust.

Fourth, Nozick advances a principle of rectification of injustice in holdings if past injustices contributed to the current distribution of resources. Although this principle suggests more questions than ways out of the injustice, Nozick appeals to historical information about the past unjust situation and the subsequent course of events as a beginning.[54] Finally, Nozick does set forth a limited principle for qualified and impartial parties to adjudicate competing procedural claims.[55]

Attention to the structures of justice: Nozick's focus on procedural justice gives a certain emphasis to those structures which underlie resulting patterns of justice. However, Nozick's attention to historical entitlement to holdings and freedom of choice avoids other structural considerations. For example, Nozick never raises questions like the following: Is the structure of private property the only inherently just structure for holdings? Have the historical practices of domination and exploitation in market economies rendered free exchange impossible? Are there other dimensions of human life which do not fit exchange structures? How do race, gender, class, or religious institutions shape social exchange? These foundational questions of structure in the 1990s did not arise in Nozick's approach from two decades earlier, although it seems unlikely that these questions could find a place within Nozick's anthropology.

The relationship between specific just actions and justice: Nozick's reaction to Rawls' substantive notion of justice and his consequent insistence on procedural justice does not allow for a universal or transcendental reality which is justice. Rather, justice is just procedures. There is no substantive justice behind this specific instance; there is no concrete expression of a universal justice. Nozick's position is certainly univocal, that is, just process is just process and nothing else.

Method: Like Rawls, Nozick's theory of justice belongs to the social contract theories (cf. John Locke). Thus Nozick's beginning point is a state of nature described in Locke's words as "a state of perfect free-

---

[53] Ibid., 155.

[54] Ibid., 152.

[55] Ibid., 101–8. Within the context of Nozick's argument for a minimalist state, the procedures apart from redistribution of resources are the subject matter of the adjudication. In addition, protective agencies, not the state, adjudicate these procedures. See also Cohen, "Procedural Justice," 643, for a broader sphere of action for unbiased third parties and a broader understanding of procedures and their creation.

dom to order their actions and dispose of their possessions and persons as they see fit, within the bounds of the law of nature, without asking leave or dependency upon the will of any other man."[56] The propensity of human persons to invade other's rights results in conflict and the need to protect one's own rights or to defend self-interest. Persons freely come together in voluntary associations for the mutual enforcement of rights and protection of self-interest. The members agree to and abide by the procedures for fair process in defense and enforcement. These voluntary associations and their resulting procedures for fair process give rise to Nozick's understanding of justice as entitlement and its mediating principles.

Self-critical mechanism: In his preface, Nozick presents his work as a beginning effort marked by convictions and argumentation as well as doubts, conjectures, and side connections. He invites others to interact with him in this project. In this way Nozick marks out a place for self-criticism in dialogue with a community of scholars. In addition, the principle of rectification of injustice in holdings introduces a self-critical mechanism into his system. Nozick, however, shows no self-critical awareness with reference to the state of nature.

Nozick's theory presents an understanding of justice which resonates with Western individualistic cultures. Justice as entitlement provides a welcome emphasis on protection of individual rights and holdings and thus legitimates the status quo. Justice as adherence to the procedures apart from any outcome justifies the absence of public agreement on the content of justice, while explaining how pluralistic societies can hold together. Nozick's theory recalls that justice cannot begin with a clean slate, but must begin with the existing situation in its concrete historical evolution.

JUSTICE AS VIRTUE (ALASDAIR MACINTYRE)

Some people claim that they deserve their possessions by virtue of their hard work and that it would be an injustice to require them to share a part of their income with others through higher taxes. Others consider it an injustice that the poor are deprived of dignified living conditions since they do not deserve to be poor. They call for a just distribution of wealth through higher taxes. The problem is, however, that the rights, entitlements, or deserts that different people demand in the name of justice are irreconcilably opposed to each other. The question then arises how a decision can be taken between them. In this

---

[56] Nozick, *Anarchy,* 10 quotes from John Locke, *Two Treatises of Government,* ed. Peter Laslett (London: Cambridge University Press, 1967) section 4.

dissonant competition for attention and advantage, contemporary Western so-
cieties use and sometimes misuse the word "justice." This apparent agreement
ends with the word itself and the sheer unbridgeable difference of meaning
dooms its users to isolated planets. In societies reduced to sound bites, the
word "justice" has become a shorthand way of investing one's own claims
with an irresistible authority.

Alasdair MacIntyre starts from the presupposition that people in
contemporary Western societies are nothing more than heirs of frag-
mentary traditions and practices, because communal goals and shared
narratives no longer exist. People are rather confronted with rival
claims to justice which lead to irresolvable conflicts. MacIntyre mentions three examples: the just war discussion, the abortion issue, and
the debate about equal opportunity.[57] According to MacIntyre these discussions are irresolvable because their proponents claim that their argu-
ments are based on rational universal principles, independent of any
context. He takes up the task to demonstrate that these allegedly universal principles were originally part of a concrete social-historical context. Each concept of justice is part of an overall system of thought[58] on
which its validity depends. According to Norman O. Dahl, MacIntyre
argues "that there is no tradition-neutral conception of practical rationality that can be used to settle disputes about justice. Through an
examination of four philosophical traditions, he argues that the conception of justice of each is linked to its own theory of practical rationality."[59]

MacIntyre's work is a fundamental critique of libertarian philosophers such as John Rawls. He seeks: (1) to demonstrate the contextual
particularity of the principles which they claim as abstract and universal; (2) to replace their focus on abstract autonomous individuals by
concrete persons shaped in communities; and (3) to redirect their focus
from rules, the origin of which is lost, to the virtues and the *ethos* which
contextualize their meaning.

[57] Alasdair MacIntyre, *After Virtue: A Study in Moral Theology* (Notre Dame, Ind.:
University of Notre Dame Press, 1984) 6–7.

[58] This is the particular focus of Alasdair MacIntyre, *Whose Justice? Which Rationality?* (Notre Dame, Ind.: University of Notre Dame Press, 1988) 389: "The enquiry
into justice and practical rationality was from the outset informed by a conviction
that each particular conception of justice requires as its counterpart some particular
conception of practical rationality and vice versa. Not only has that conviction been
reinforced by the outcome of the enquiry so far, but it has become evident that conceptions of justice and of practical rationality generally and characteristically confront us as closely related aspects to some larger, more or less well-articulated,
overall view of human life and its place in nature."

[59] Norman O. Dahl, "Justice and Aristotelian Practical Reason," *Philosophy and
Phenomenological Research* 51 (1991) 153.

MacIntyre is a main proponent of communitarian virtue ethics. In his 1981 publication *After Virtue,* he ends with the awareness that we live in a fragmented world and all we can do is wait for a new St. Benedict to make a new synthesis. However, in his 1988 study *Whose Justice? Which Rationality?* he demonstrates a clear preference for a coherent ethical tradition, namely, Aristotelian-Thomistic philosophy. Some commentators see MacIntyre as a nostalgic classicist and a reactionary thinker who would like to move back behind the Enlightenment era.[60] Others maintain that he is more dangerous than that.[61] Still others highlight his significant contribution to twentieth-century thinking on justice.

Basis of the claim: MacIntyre severely criticizes Rawls and Nozick for seeing the basis of the claim to just treatment in "need" and "entitlement" respectively. He accuses them of having privatized and individualized the claim. MacIntyre, however, follows Aristotle in making desert or merit the basis of the claim to justice. While partially based on past actions and suffering, this view mainly concentrates on the future. Justice is thus determined on the basis of a person's merits[62] with regard to his or her contributions to the community's striving for the common good. The basis of the claim is thus contributive, merit-oriented, and communitarian. "While all must share in the good . . . it is clear that more is owed to . . . outstanding contributors. They merit more than the rest. This is Aristotle's principle of 'proportionate' equality."[63]

Inherent absolutes: One of MacIntyre's most basic *a priories* is the assumption that the community has precedence over the individual. His position is also teleological which means that a common project, i.e., the common good, is essential, even constitutive of communities. For MacIntyre the decline of teleological conceptions is the basis of the modern fragmentation which he deplores.

---

[60] This is the view defended by Jef Van Gerwen, *Denk-wijzen 6: Een inleiding in het denken van A. Schopenhauer, S. Kierkegaard, K. Marx en A. MacIntyre* (Leuven-Amersfoort: Acco, 1991) 120–1.

[61] See, for instance, Charles E. Larmore, "Review of *Whose Justice? Which Rationality?* by Alasdair MacIntyre," *Journal of Philosophy* 86 (1989) 442, who calls MacIntyre's critique of modern ethics in the name of earlier traditions "at all points unfair."

[62] Desert is embedded in a "human community in which the notion of desert in relation to contributions to the common tasks of that community in pursuing shared goods could provide the basis for judgments about virtue and injustice" (MacIntyre, *After Virtue,* 251).

[63] Charles Taylor, "Justice After Virtue," *After MacIntyre: Critical Perspectives on the Work of Alasdair MacIntyre,* ed. John Horton and Susan Mendus (Cambridge: Polity Press, 1994) 37.

MacIntyre shows how the growing sense among many different schools of modern philosophy that no "ought" can be derived from an "is" is not the slow dawning of a context-free logical truth, but rather the correlate of the decline or rejection of the conception central to much ancient philosophy that human life was defined by a telos.[64]

Another important *a priori* is the view that what is good precedes what is right. Something is right or just because it is good, not vice versa.

Anthropology: MacIntyre sees human persons primarily as social beings. Community precedes the individual who is formed by families and other groups with a shared vision of what is good. Thus morality is not seen from the perspective of rules, but of virtues. Virtues enable persons to understand the function and authority of rules.[65] In line with Aristotle virtues are those qualities the possession of which empowers persons to contribute to the common good. The lack of virtues frustrates movement toward that *telos*.[66]

Who decides what justice is: MacIntyre is strongly convinced that justice is always related to a particular type of community, be that the Greek *polis* for Aristotle or the *civitas Dei* for Augustine.[67] He is therefore opposed to abstract universal principles and abstract autonomous individuals characteristic of the libertarian approaches. Thus those who shape a community by their contributions as a result of their virtues indirectly share in determining the shape of justice. Nevertheless MacIntyre understands virtue as doing what the accepted order requires. Consequently the decision of what constitutes justice is received by the individual person as a result of a living tradition and not directly determined by individuals.

MacIntyre is fully aware that it is difficult, but not impossible, to decide rationally between rival claims of justice because each claim is formulated in its own conceptual terms. This does not lead necessarily to relativism and perspectivism. He is rather convinced that it is possible to make universal claims "from the standpoint of a tradition,"[68] after engaging in dialogue within and between traditions. His criterion is "successful tradition," i.e., "one that can solve all the problems raised

---

[64] Ibid., 16.

[65] See MacIntyre, *After Virtue,* 119.

[66] See ibid., 148. See also Dahl, "Justice and Aristotelian Practical Reason," 153, who describes another and more individual-centered dimension to virtue: "Aristotelian justice focuses on treating people as they deserve to be treated, desert being determined by the extent to which people achieve excellence across the range of activities, many of which are tied to social roles."

[67] MacIntyre, *Whose Justice? Which Rationality?* 389.

[68] Alasdair MacIntyre, "Précis of *Whose Justice? Which Rationality?*" *Philosophy and Phenomenological Research* 51 (1991) 152.

by its external and internal critics and explain the plausibility and mistakes of its rivals."[69]

Goal of justice: The goal of justice is the *telos* of human life which is so central to MacIntyre's approach and which is so fatefully absent in modern societies. In Aristotle's view, for the individual this goal is *eudaimonia*,[70] that is, happiness; for the community it is the common good. Of what does this common good consist? For Aristotle and the medievals, the common good was the good life which culminates in the contemplation of the divine.[71]

Mediating principles: MacIntyre's focus on practical rationality shows his conviction that moral life can only be learned in concrete practices. Thus moral practice is a coherent and complex form of socially learned, cooperative human activity which leads to the realization of the inherent goods. The virtues are the fruit of moral practice. A second mediating principle calls for a narrative tradition which gives meaning to these virtuous practices. A tradition has its origin in a constitutive narrative about the community or society which offers a goal and in which the members of the community can identify themselves. Traditions provide the context within which moral practices have their meaning. "A living tradition . . . is an historically extended, socially embodied argument and an argument precisely in part about the goods which constitute that tradition."[72]

Attention to the structures of justice: In MacIntyre's view, persons are rather shaped by families and institutions in general. Also, his concepts of virtue and desert evidence the structural orientation of his approach. Desert is seen as "the discharge of the duties of one's assigned place within the institutions of a determinately structured community."[73] Since MacIntyre always relates justice to a particular type of community, his undivided attention to the importance of structures is evident.

> So theories of justice and practical rationality confront us as aspects of traditions, allegiance to which requires the living out of some more or less systematically embodied form of human life, each with its own specific modes of social relationship, each with its own canons of

[69] Dahl, "Justice and Aristotelian Practical Reason," 157: "The truth about justice is what accords with a successful tradition." Dahl criticizes MacIntyre for not taking seriously enough "the possibility of more than one successful tradition."

[70] MacIntyre, *After Virtue,* 176.

[71] Ibid., 175.

[72] Ibid., 222.

[73] See MacIntyre, *Whose Justice? Which Rationality?* 162, where he speaks about the agreements of Gregory VII's concept of justice with that of Aristotle.

interpretation and explanation in respect of the behaviour of others, each with its own evaluative practices.[74]

Insofar as MacIntyre is Aristotelian he presumes that human life is structured through a hierarchy of goods.[75]

The relationship between specific just actions and justice: In his comments on MacIntyre, Charles Taylor speaks of the distinction between "absolute" justice and "local" justice. Absolute justice is the answer to the question: "What is the distribution corresponding to the demands of the (highest) transcendent good?" Local justice deals with the issue: "What is the balance of indebtedness in our particular community?"[76] Taylor concludes: "Real life participants are raising questions of local justice or of local and absolute justice together; academics speak only of absolute justice."[77] MacIntyre, however, prefers just actions to an abstract concept of justice.

Method: MacIntyre's method includes attention to the following components: communal narrative, concrete sociohistorical context, communal worldview, "the concrete," the contribution of individuals to the common good, and the common good *(telos)*. The pursuit of the *telos* happens within the context of a communal narrative.[78]

Self-critical mechanism: Self-critical mechanisms have a central place in MacIntyre's approach insofar as he is convinced that each conception of justice is linked to its own conception of practical rationality and to a specific community. This cautions against absolutizing any one position. On the other hand, MacIntyre is not in favor of relativism. He is convinced that universal claims can be made from the standpoint of particular traditions. The criterion he suggests is the success of a tradition. This is, however, a dangerous concept since he does not take seriously enough the possibility of more than one successful tradition. Moreover, when MacIntyre talks about the common good and a shared *telos*, what kind of communities (city? country? continent?) are his reference point and, hence, how universal is his concept of universality?

MacIntyre stresses a historically embedded and socially located understanding of justice. This understanding is inextricably bound up with a shared narrative of a people. Human persons are social by nature and by membership in a community with a formative narrative. Perhaps a most significant contribution is MacIntyre's insistence that justice is a virtue practiced by human persons in pursuit of the common good.

---

[74] Ibid., 391.
[75] See Dahl, "Justice and Aristotelian Practical Reason," 155.
[76] Taylor, "Justice After Virtue," 40.
[77] Ibid., 41.
[78] MacIntyre, *After Virtue*, 225.

JUSTICE AS SOCIALLY CONSTRUCTED
(MICHAEL WALZER)

Newspaper articles and coffee break conversations also reveal a certain tolerance of multiple understandings of justice co-existing together. What is just for me isn't necessarily just for you. What is just practice in the business world is often not just practice in one's family. What is just in the United States is not just in Iran. There is no one concept of justice nor one set of principles to direct justice action. This may not be good or the way it ought to be, but that's the way it is. It might be easier if we could all agree on what justice is or what the standards for justice are. Sometimes it seems like a talk show approach where each person's experience is given equal weight because it is their experience. Consequently individual persons or nations take justice into their own hands. Most times not even the United Nations can agree about the justice of trade sanctions or war crimes. We just don't agree about what justice is and it is unlikely that we ever will. We are just too different.

Michael Walzer's 1983 book *Spheres of Justice: A Defense of Pluralism and Equality*[79] emerged from a course which he taught at Harvard University with Robert Nozick. Like Nozick, Walzer's concern is the distribution of social goods or distributive justice. Walzer would also agree that there is no single center for distribution. Nor is there a universal medium of exchange or set of criteria for allocating resources. Unlike Nozick, however, Walzer's concept of distributive justice rests on the radical particularity of human communities which construct shared understandings of justice. Justice is the shared social meaning of particular men and women in particular communities.[80] Before joining those critics of Walzer who maintain that such an approach is devoid of the kind of transcendental dimensions necessary to avoid cultural relativism, we will look more thoroughly at his understandings of justice.

Basis of the claim: For Walzer any claim to just distribution of social goods rests on the existence of human communities which are capable of structuring the distribution of social goods and on membership in some human community. In Walzer's own words, "The primary good we distribute to one another is membership in some human community. What we do with regard to membership structures all our other distributive choices."[81] This foundational nature of membership and of

---

[79] Michael Walzer, *Spheres of Justice: A Defense of Pluralism and Equality* (New York: Basic Books, 1983).

[80] Ibid., 313. See also Glen Stassen, "Michael Walzer's Situated Justice," *Journal of Religious Ethics* 22 (Fall 1994) 375–6; and Tyler T. Roberts, "Michael Walzer and the Critical Connections," *Journal of Religious Ethics* 22 (Fall 1994) 334 and 338.

[81] Walzer, *Spheres of Justice*, 31.

human communities requires that any adequate theory of justice accounts for and regulates both boundaries for determining membership and some provision of inclusiveness. Only in this way can communal life be viable and can persons share in other social goods.

Inherent absolutes: Walzer builds his theory of distributive justice on three self-evident absolutes: pluralism, equality, and social construction of shared meanings. By pluralism Walzer means that "there is no single set of primary or basic goods conceivable across all moral and material worlds."[82] Rather, goods are endowed with social meanings determined by particular and historical human communities, that is, communities share understandings which they have socially constructed over time and place. Distinct socially constructed meanings signal separate and equal spheres. A sphere is not a separate sociopolitical community. Rather, it is a distributive justice arena in which different social goods with different social meanings are portioned out for different reasons according to different procedures. In addition to membership, Walzer identifies ten such distinct and equal spheres: (1) security and welfare, (2) money and commodities, (3) office, (4) hard work, (5) free time, (6) education, (7) kinship and love, (8) divine grace (9) recognition, and (10) political power. Pluralism, equality, and socially constructed shared meanings form the foundation for mediating principles which will be examined shortly.

Anthropology: Walzer speaks of persons-in-the-social-world, that is, human persons are constituted by one another or by membership in a community. Persons-in-the-social-world are capable of acting on their own behalf, of constructing social meaning, and of structuring decisions with regard to the distribution of social goods. Recognition of such agency in one's self requires a corresponding recognition of agency in others. Mutual respect extends to participation and contributions in meaning-making, decisions, and actions. As persons-in-the-social-world, concrete identity is shaped by the shared meanings and history developed through membership in a specific community. Persons-in-the-social-world differ with regard to social goods.

Who decides what justice is: The people who constituted the particular community determine the shared understandings of justice. These shared understandings are forged from the general will, the actual historical knowledge of a specific people. Participation shapes the shared meanings and the common life as questions of identity and difference are argued and adjudicated. Consequently the shared meaning of justice may differ from sphere to sphere, although some social meanings may coalesce across times and arenas.

[82] Ibid., 8.

Goal of justice: According to Walzer, if justice would be realized, this world would become communities of character, that is, "historically stable, ongoing associations of men and women with some special commitment to one another and some special sense of their common life."[83] The task of the communities of character entails faithfulness to the shared meanings which they have determined. Communities of character are threatened when one social good becomes a means of domination, that is, when the possession of that good gives access to other social goods in other spheres. For example, money ought not to influence the distribution of political power, kinship, or divine grace. Therefore faithfulness to shared meanings in any one sphere entails the distributions of social goods in such a way that no one social good can serve as a means of domination in other spheres. Walzer is convinced that this vision of a just and egalitarian society is within our reach and already hidden in our concepts. The goal of communities of character, however, can only be reached with membership participation both in the creation of communal shared meanings and in safeguarding the boundaries of particular social goods.

Mediating principles: Walzer's mediating principles of distributive justice emerge from his three absolutes, his anthropology, and his goal.

First, each sphere has its own principles and shared meanings, that is, the substance of distributive justice is constructed in its own sphere. Consequently it can be critiqued by internal principles, but not by other external substantive meanings of justice. The self-determination of persons-in-the-social-world requires mutual respect and recognition of distinct meanings or relative autonomy of the distinct spheres.

Second, the distribution of social goods in one sphere cannot determine the distribution in other spheres. This principle of complex equality holds that no social good (for example, political power) should be distributed to men and women who produce another social good (for example, money) merely because they possess money and without regard to the socially constructed meaning of political power.

Third, according to the principle of difference, different social goods are distributed to different groups for different reasons and in accordance with different criteria. Walzer does note that free exchange, desert, and need are open-ended criteria for distribution which work in some spheres, but none of the three would be effective in all spheres.

Fourth, a community alone decides admission and exclusion. However, since persons have rights and claims only by virtue of membership in community, self-determination with regard to membership is not absolute. Rather, the external principle of mutual aid also governs

---

[83] Ibid., 62.

decisions of membership inclusion. Mutual aid requires positive assistance when it is urgently needed by the inquirer and when the risks and costs are relatively low for the provider.

Attention to the structures of justice: Walzer's awareness of the structured nature of justice is linked to his concept of justice as historically and socially constructed, and to his awareness of the domination of one social good into other spheres. His mediating principles articulate qualities for the structuring of just distribution rather than the criteria, procedures, and actions for that distribution.

The relationship between specific just actions and justice: Walzer states that he attempts to give an account of the parts of distributive justice, namely, social goods and the spheres of distribution. Walzer understands his work as imminent and phenomenological, that is, it is appropriate for the people whose common life it reflects.[84] From this perspective, Walzer seems interested in just actions and structures and not justice at all.

Walzer also holds that social goods carry shared social meanings. A way of doing philosophy includes living in a concrete sociopolitical community and interpreting "to one's fellow citizens the world of meanings which we share."[85] These shared meanings are not universal ideals, but rather the actual and historical knowledge of the people. Thus, for Walzer the task of interpretation focuses attention on the concrete and particular actions along with the conviction that the concrete bears meaning. Thus, just actions bear justice much like Catholic sacramental symbols of water and oil bear God's life-giving presence when they are used in constitutive communicative action. In this way justice is more than the structures of possibility for concrete distribution.

Method: According to Walzer the experience of subordination occasions the desire for a better equality or the experience of injustice urges the search for justice. Glen Stassen characterizes Walzer's method as dialogical, interpretative, and intuitive-reflective.[86] The dialogue takes place between the historically experienced understandings of communities and the philosopher's efforts at highlighting inherent moral meaning. The dialogue takes place between the practice in specific social contexts and explanations for the core values or principles which hold the practice together. This method is interpretative in its efforts to articulate the meanings present in concrete practices of sociopolitical communities. Walzer speaks of correcting "groping intuitions" through reference to models constructed on "more certain intuitions." This

---

[84] Ibid., 26.
[85] Ibid., xiv.
[86] Stassen, "Michael Walzer's Situated Justice," 378–9.

approach is reflective because it assumes the validity of social practices to bear meaning and then seeks to bring the meanings to light. In addition, rhetorical dimensions surface in Walzer's method. First, he argues against the domination of money into other spheres. Second, his goal is a coherent, credible, convincing explanation for separate spheres of distributive justice as a means of reducing domination.

Self-critical mechanism: The dialogical and the rhetorical dimensions of his method provide mechanisms for self-criticism. Both dimensions rely on the historical community in which he and the readers of his works are located. Initial interpretations are returned to readers for further dialogue or affirmation. Only plausible convincing interpretations resonate with these audiences.

Walzer's approach to distributive justice highlights the foundational nature of membership in human communities which construct shared understandings of justice based on their particular, historical knowledge and concrete actions. Walzer resists the equation that historical construction signals relativism because the concrete bears meaning which transcends the particular. Like legal justice, Walzer stresses the participatory and structural dimensions of justice. Like justice as obligation, Walzer emphasizes the relational foundations of justice. Furthermore, Walzer recognizes that justice is both socially constructed by communities and radically concrete.

JUSTICE AS LIBERATION
(FEMINIST AND LIBERATIONIST AUTHORS)

The 20 percent poorest inhabitants of the earth own 1.4 percent of its wealth, a drop from 2.3 percent in the past thirty years. The 20 percent richest inhabitants have enjoyed an increase from 70 percent to 85 percent of the earth's wealth. Three hundred fifty-eight billionaires of the world own more than the annual total income of the countries in which 65 percent of the world's population live. The richest are rapidly becoming richer and the poorest are rapidly becoming poorer. This process is a reality despite the enormous efforts of governments, non-governmental organizations, churches, and individuals. The fact that the efforts to help improve the situation in poor countries seem to be in vain discourages many people of good will in affluent Western countries and leads them in turn to blame corruption and mismanagement, ethnic instability, and the arms race in the poor countries themselves. There is a very real danger of an upsurge of classism among people who have taken up the cause of the poorest of the poor. The only escape from this danger might be to take seriously the reality of poverty.

Latin American liberation theologians and feminist-liberationist theologians make surprisingly little use of justice terminology or of explicit justice theories. This may not blind us to the fact that justice is at the heart of their concerns. But they raise their justice concerns in different terminology. For them, "justice" functions as a liberal or libertarian concept; hence it is an integral part of those structures responsible for the oppression of women and whole continents. Those who have defined what justice is in the past centuries have been representatives of a male-dominated, (neo)colonialist liberal structure which has restricted its justice concerns to the interests of the dominant group. So conceived and practiced, justice belongs to and works for the people in the center in ways which subjugate and marginate persons at the periphery of that center. When feminist-liberationist theologians use justice terminology and content, they rely on the biblical tradition of justice. The focus of the following analysis will be their presentation and integration of biblical justice.

Basis of the claim: According to Gustavo Gutiérrez, "the reciprocal relationship between God and the poor person is the very heart of biblical faith," and, "our relationship with God is expressed in our relationship with the poor."[87] Consequently the only way of being in loving relationship with God is being in just relationships with our neighbors.[88] This reciprocity characteristic of the biblical perspective maintains that humans are created in the image and likeness of God. As creation-centered and as God-centered, the feminist-liberationist basis of the claim for justice is the most universal and non-restrictive basis possible. Like the God of the Bible, liberation justice takes a preferential option for those who usually are denied the recognition of their creation in the image of God, namely, the poor, oppressed, and disadvantaged. Even if they are advocates for these groups, authentically liberationist thinkers remain alert to the ever emerging situations of oppression. Feminist-liberationist theologians are not pessimists, because they are convinced that the "history from which biblical faith springs is an open-ended history, a history open to the future. . . . Hope is an essential element of a faith in accord with the Bible."[89]

Inherent absolutes: Feminist-liberationist theologians do not hide their faith stance. Thus, faith in a God who has created men and women in

---

[87] Gustavo Gutiérrez, *The Power of the Poor in History: Selected Writings* (London: SCM, 1983) 8. In support of this he points to Prov 17:5: "To mock the poor is to insult his creator."

[88] Gustavo Gutiérrez, *A Theology of Liberation: History, Politics and Salvation* (London: SCM, 1977) 194–203.

[89] Gutiérrez, *The Power of the Poor in History*, 6–7.

God's own image and likeness and who wants them to have lives in keeping with that dignity is the foundational absolute for their approach. The reciprocity between our relationship with God and with the poor becomes a consequent absolute.

Anthropology: Because human persons are created in the image and likeness of God, feminist-liberationist anthropology seeks an integrated, holistic view of the human person. Both the dignity of the human person and the interdependence of human persons are central. Enrique Dussel has explicated the incarnated aspect of this anthropology with the English expression "sensibility," or human fleshiness.

> Many heretics . . . forgot the dignity of the "flesh"—as has a whole modern capitalist culture, beginning with Descartes. Sensibility, as pain or pleasure, the "skin" as the locus of cold or torture, remind us that injustice, sin, the oppression of the poor, crucify those poor in their sensibility. The morality of dominators denies the value of the body precisely in order that it may continue to dominate it and exploit it without a feeling of guilt.[90]

Feminist theologians are in full agreement with this stress on the dignity of the flesh.

Who decides what justice is: By their recourse to the biblical notion of justice, feminist-liberationist theologians reject the limited access to the process of defining justice, which is typical in Western libertarian concepts of justice. They point out that existing injustice effectively excludes the poor and oppressed from the efforts of defining justice.[91] One can only truly speak of justice if those at the periphery have the opportunity to participate actively in the process of defining what justice is.

Goal of justice: Within such a biblical perspective, justice requires the kind of activity that characterizes God's behavior toward the poor and oppressed. The goal is the creation of a new person in a new society.

Mediating principles: Preferential option for the poor seems to be the major mediating principle. This implies that for feminist-liberationist theologians mediating principles are not mere theories, but they require praxis and concrete involvement.

---

[90] Enrique Dussel, *Ethics and Community* (Maryknoll, N.Y.: Orbis Books, 1988) 61–2 and 66–7.

[91] Dussel is emphasizing this in discussion with representatives of discursive ethics like Karl-Otto Apel. See especially Horst Sing, "Eröffnet der Dialog zwischen Karl-Otto Apel und Enrique Dussel einen plausiblen Zugang zur Überwindung absoluter Armut in der Dritten Welt?" *Diskurs und Leidenschaft: Festschrift Karl-Otto Apel zum 75. Geburtstag,* Concordia. Reihe Monographien 20, ed. Raúl Fornet-Betancourt (Aachen: Verlag der Augustinus Buchhandlung Aachen, 1996) 295.

Attention to structures of justice: For feminist-liberationist thinkers, justice is a thoroughly structural reality. Enrique Dussel pointedly states, "Latin American theology . . . considers the structure in which the sin of the world conditions our own personal sin."[92] According to Gustavo Gutiérrez, "The poor are a by-product of the system in which we live."[93]

The relationship between specific just actions and justice: The expression "doing justice" already refers to concrete actions which bring about a more just society. These actions build up a just community in the future and express relationship with God. For feminist-liberationist thinkers, human dignity and relationship with God (rather than justice) are concretized in specific just actions.

Method: The starting point of feminist-liberationist approaches is praxis, involvement in the struggle for liberation. Thus justice theory is a secondary reflection on an existing praxis. This sequence gives emphasis to the perspective of the oppressed who are engaged in the struggle.

Self-critical mechanisms: Feminist-liberationist thinkers are constantly subjecting their theories to the critique of the praxis. In this way they try to avoid a theoretical superstructure that has lost touch with reality. In constant dialogue with the poor, the theories are subjected to the tribunal of their practicability and helpfulness in what they are intended to achieve.

Feminist-liberationist theologians are not surprised that the efforts of the past thirty years to root out poverty have not borne fruit. All the good will in the world will not be able to bring about a just social order as long as structures like capitalism ensure that the rich become richer. Moreover, the present situation, which does not allow people of the periphery to have influence in how justice is defined, presents a further stumbling block. These convictions point to a requirement that justice attend to the most disadvantaged (cf. Rawls) as well as to social structures and to participation (cf. Walzer and Justice as Law). Similar to Catholic Social Teachings, justice as liberation points to God's creation and covenant relationships with persons which ground an understanding of the human person, especially the marginated, as persons of dignity and relationality. Justice as liberation, however, offers additional characteristics of justice, including attention to bodiliness and hope. In addition, feminist-liberationist ideology criticism highlights that any specific understanding of justice can be used to legitimate those in positions of power. Thus the very process of defining justice includes the danger of including some persons and excluding others.

---

[92] Dussel, *Ethics and Community*, 2.
[93] Gutiérrez, *The Power of the Poor in History*, 44.

CONCLUSION

This survey of key contemporary approaches to justice surfaced a number of characteristics which an adequate understanding of justice must include. A faith-based understanding of justice relies on a relational God and an anthropology that stresses the constitutive dignity and relationality of the human-person-in-community. Within this anthropological and theological framework, justice needs to include attention to structures that facilitate or impede just action. Members of the human community must participate in the construction of the meaning of justice and in the creation of processes to ensure just action. The human community must find ways to include and attend to the needs of the least advantaged. An adequate approach to justice must recognize concrete and bodily dimensions of justice. Furthermore, justice does not begin as a transcendent ideal, but as a historically evolving practice in a context of individual and collective inhumanity and hope.

6

The Context for Justice as Participation

An ethic of justice as participation in the human community relies on a certain coherence between theology, anthropology, ethics, and public policy. Questions concerning the God of justice are connected to other questions concerning the constitution of the human community, how people ought to live together, and which policies promote a just and inclusive community. Beliefs about God are integrally related to the character, values, behaviors of the human community and those social structures which make it easier or harder to act justly. For example, a community believes that God intervenes on behalf of those unjustly treated and that God has invited believers to take up this mission in the world. These beliefs are linked to values and behaviors such as advocacy, resistance to injustice, and defense of human rights. This constellation of values, behaviors, and beliefs urges the establishment of policies which make unjust treatment difficult and just action desirable.

In this chapter we set forth our understanding of a coherent context for an ethic of justice as participation. We describe this context for justice with attention to five dimensions: (1) authentic human living, (2) the God of justice, (3) the sacramentality of existence, (4) a vision of the endtimes city of God, and (5) normativity of the future. In this endeavor, we are not content with merely repeating the traditions of Catholic Social Teachings, the Scriptures, the experience of practitioners, or the systematic writings of contemporary experts in justice as they have been passed on to us. Rather, we approach these traditions with particular attention to those dimensions which contribute to a liberating and inclusive ethic of justice. The presence of multiple metaphors for

God in the traditions as well as long-standing practices of interpretation in both Catholic Social Teachings and the Gospel of John open the door to this strategy.

An Anthropological Context for an Ethic of Justice as Participation

In this section we set forth an anthropological context coherent with an ethic of justice as participation which will be presented in the next chapter. Babies are born into a concrete, particular human community already structured by language, patterns of economic systems, political convictions, and social customs. Infants are immersed into a network of relationships, pre-determined assessments of differences, and a defined configuration of ideas, values, and behaviors. This world constitutes personal identity and provides the contours for authentic human living.[1] Relationships with parents, family, neighbors, peers, and colleagues constitute personal identity and determine authentic human living. Bodily health and integrity, sex, and race constitute personal identity and provide the contours for authentic human living. Social location in an ethnic group, a neighborhood, a religious tradition, a language group, a historical era, and a nationality constitute personal identity and provide the contours for authentic human living. This constellation of diversities constitutes each and every person as original, unique, and valuable in their particularity; in fact, persons are not fundamentally equal in spite of differences, but these very differences are at the heart of their equality. Opportunities for intellectual, aesthetic, and freely chosen activities with consequent self-reflection, accountability, and responsibility constitute personal identity and provide the contours for authentic human living.

In short, the constitutive dimensions of authentic human living are embodiment, relationality, accountable agency, difference, and social location.[2] Although we have addressed the definitive character of these

---

[1] We use the term "authentic human living" to refer to an adequate anthropology. The expression highlights the dynamic, concrete, relational, and self-reflective character of an adequate anthropology. The dynamic character includes awareness of human flourishing or thriving. Furthermore, the dynamism of human living embraces both present survival and promise of a future. The concrete character includes attention to embodiment, social location, and actual sustainability. The relational character shifts the focus of anthropology from individuals to human community. The self-reflective character entails an awareness of dignity and accountability for actions in keeping with that dignity.

[2] Our position is heavily indebted to Louis Janssens, "Artificial Insemination: Ethical Considerations," *Louvain Studies* 8 (Spring 1980) 3–29. Our approach differs

dimensions of human living, a word about each of the dimensions may be clarifying at this point. We will address the five dimensions, one after the other, while insisting that the order is not an order of priority or of importance, for all five dimensions are essential to personal identity and constitutive of authentic human living.

First, relationality debunks the myth that relationships are essentially voluntary choices,[3] while recognizing that some specific relationships may be chosen voluntarily. Already in conception we were created through a relationship we did not choose, yet which determined some physical, relational, historical, self-reflective identity, and unique dimensions of our identity and living. Our pre- and postnatal environment has been a network of relationships, healthy and diseased, graced and sinful, nurturing and stifling. Relationality also means that the very structure of our humanness requires that others respond to us and we respond to others.[4] The structure of relationality is the basis of faith, of religious experience, and of the invitation to relationship with God. This inherent relationality lurks behind the awareness that human living and cosmic thriving are integrally connected. The constitutive nature of relationships surfaces as well in the human longings for community, just relationships, and solidarity among peoples. Although living as a local or universal human community may be a struggle, it is a requirement of authentic human living. Since relationality is definitive for all persons, equality, mutuality, interdependence, and reciprocity ought to characterize relationships. Similarly, collaboration, participation in decision-making, and inclusion as members of the human community flow from relationality as a constitutive dimension of authentic human community.

The second constitutive dimension stresses that persons do not *have* bodies but *are* embodied.[5] Gender, race, and ethnicity are bodily realities which circumscribe personal identity. Embodiment shapes personal

---

from the anthropology of Catholic Social Teachings on two points. First, we insist that all five dimensions are constitutive of authentic human living, whereas Catholic Social Teachings hold that bodiliness, relationality, and social location are necessary for "full human development" of subjectivity which preexists and which is served by the others. Second, our focus is on the concrete human person and authentic human living, whereas Catholic Social Teachings tend to discuss abstract human nature or generic humanness.

[3] See the discussion of Nozick and Rawls in Chapter 5.

[4] See Martha Heineman Pieper, *Intrapsychic Humanism: An Introduction to a Comprehensive Psychology and Philosophy of Mind* (Chicago: Falcon II Press, 1990).

[5] In feminist anthropology "our bodies/ourselves" or "body-self" has been used to express this constitutive awareness. See Susan A. Ross, "Extravagant Affections," *In the Embrace of God: Feminist Approaches to Theological Anthropology,* ed. Ann O'Hara Graff (Maryknoll, N.Y.: Orbis Books, 1998) 108–21, esp. 110.

sense of worth, value, and identity. Furthermore, the societies in which persons exist assign meaning and value to sexual, racial, and ethnic embodiment, that is, gender, race, and ethnicity are social constructs[6] into which persons are born and from which embodied identity emerges. At times the assigned social meaning becomes the basis for unjust discriminatory practices. Gender, race, and ethnicity may be the most significant contributors to bodily identities, but size, weight, "attractiveness" with their socially constructed meanings mediate value, worth, and dignity. Identities are forged by resisting or by complying with prescribed embodied identities. Embodiment also refers to the concreteness and particularity of human persons and communities. Embodied activity both creates and expresses personal identity and authentic human living. The constitutive nature of embodiment requires that the fulfillment of basic human needs cannot be left to happenstance. Rather, food, clothing, shelter, water, and health are necessary for authentic human living.

The third constitutive dimension of human persons is social location, that is, the historical and cultural situations within which persons and communities live. World War II and the disestablishmentarianism of the late sixties profoundly changed the world and separated persons who were born before from persons who were born after these events. Northern Europeans and tropical Central Americans are shaped by their geographic and ethnic locations. Survival itself requires that rural Americans and inner city urban dwellers approach daily living differently. The sights and sounds of a sacramental religious tradition shape different persons than a religious tradition of words and concepts. Available vocabulary and sentence structures configure our ability to make sense of the world. Social location, along with embodiment, highlights the particularity of human persons and communities. Persons do not exist in general, but as embodied and socially located, that is, as concrete, particular persons and communities.

The fourth dimension, difference, underscores the particularity of each and every person. Difference emerges from the concrete, specific constellation of relationships, bodily characteristics, social location, and personal appropriation for each and every person. In fact, the worth, dignity, and equality of human persons rests in difference. As a result, difference cannot be used as the basis of discriminatory practices. Difference is thus not an incidental flavor or external dress to humanness which can be overlooked or penetrated to get to essential

---

[6] The social construction of gender, race, and ethnicity becomes problematic not because meaning is assigned, but in cases when the assigned meaning restricts participation in the human community.

and abstract "humanity"; rather, difference is constitutive of the human person and authentic human living. When we understand difference as constitutive of human persons and communities, then equality and respect must characterize the interactions between persons and communities.

The fifth dimension, accountable agency, highlights the integration and appropriation of relationality, embodiment, social location, and difference into reasonable, meaningful, espoused identity and agency. For both individuals and communities, this movement to wholeness entails self-reflection and accountability to commitments and decisions. However, self-reflective identity and accountable agency can only emerge from an actual network of embodied relationships in a specific cultural and historical location. Agency and identity emerge from interaction and differentiation; thus persons and communities become aware of an originality forged in relationality, embodiment, and social location. In this context sin can be described as the denial or violation of any of these dimensions in a person or community; for example, the imposition of a specific culture on other communities. Sin can also entail the refusal to embrace and integrate dimensions into agency and identity; for example, disregard of bodily limits. Accountable agency highlights accountability, responsibility, and commitment of specific persons or groups with regard to justice and injustice.

Embodied, socially located agents in relationship, fundamentally equal in their originality, are images of the Divine Persons; that is, human persons are the sacraments of God and symbols of God's presence. This sacramentality of authentic human living underscores the dignity of human persons. The rituals and actions of daily living extend the continuing creating, liberating, and transforming activities of God into specific times and places. Unsurprisingly, then, authentic human living is replete with creativity, healing, resiliency, and transforming agency. Social location is transformed into a concrete arena for God's intervening action. Embodiment and materiality are transformed into particular disclosures of God's ongoing activity. Relationships are transformed into mediations of divine love and justice. Differences are transformed into revelations of Trinitarian life.

A THEOLOGICAL CONTEXT FOR AN ETHIC OF JUSTICE AS PARTICIPATION

In this section we set forth a theological context coherent with the above anthropology as well as the ethic of justice as participation presented in the next chapter. The living, dying, and raising of Jesus of Nazareth embodied the creating, liberating, and transforming activity of God in this world. The ethnic and religious Jewishness of Jesus was a paramount instance of the concrete particularity of God's liberating and transforming activity. In Jesus, God revealed Godself in the concrete particularity of first-century Jewish and Greco-Roman history.[7] Since God's revelation in Jesus is preeminent, then we can expect that concrete, particular, historical presence and action continue to make present the Divine Persons. To the extent that God's revelation in the particularity of Jesus is paramount, the value and worth of all that is created, bodily, historical, and particular, is affirmed.

The relationship between Jesus the Christ and God, albeit qualitatively distinct, reveals both the relationship with God in Jesus to which human persons are invited and the normative characteristics of relationships within the human community. Some characteristics include mutual indwelling, accountability, inclusion, participation, and public witness. Since Jesus the Christ, like the God of the Hebrew people, intervened and took the side of those marginalized by the religious and political structures of that time, the People of God are expected to continue the pattern of concrete intervention on behalf of those sidelined by social structures. Since Jesus also identified with those marginalized by religious and political structures of first-century Israel, the body of Christ today is expected to continue the activity and presence of the God of Jesus among those persons marginalized by economic and religious structures in this historical era.

Through the Spirit, God has revealed Godself as never fully exhausted or constrained by any concrete, particular embodiment or sacrament. The Spirit then is God resisting absolute identification with one historical particularity.[8] That is, while Divine Activity requires embodied specificity, Divine Activity can never be reduced to one single activity, just as interpersonal love can never be reduced to one specific action. In this way the Spirit is a universal Spirit who blows where it will and whose comings and goings are beyond human control.

The Spirit is a name for God as Longing or Desire for what could be or for a better world. The Spirit is God who stretches our comfortable boundaries and narrow worldviews to encompass an in-breaking future city of justice and peace. The Spirit is God who calls the human community into an alternative future and uncharted territories. The

---

[7] Gavin D'Costa, "Christ, the Trinity and Religious Plurality," *Christian Uniqueness Reconsidered: The Myth of Pluralistic Theology of Religions* (Maryknoll, N.Y.: Orbis Books, 1990) 16–29, esp. 17–18.

[8] See ibid., 17–19.

Spirit is God who leads and guides believers into the future of what Jesus did in the past. The Spirit is God who arouses and activates the People of God into ever-new embodiments of divine living which can never be fully embodied. The Spirit is God who renews or re-creates institutions, structures, and patterns into the inclusive and universal city of God. The Spirit is the divine activity seeking embodiment and particularity, while remaining more and beyond any specific activity. The Spirit is the universal God seeking and transforming concrete historicity.

The universal God of all is also ongoing Creative Activity and Personal Creator. Although it is possible to imagine a static Creator of all things in the beginning, for us Creator is a name for God as ongoing, creating activity at work wherever life is emerging and nurtured. The emergence of all life through relationships reveals a Creator God who generates life-giving relationships. Names like Parent, Father, or Mother depict this creating and life-giving God. The Creator is God who initiates covenant relationships and bonds of personal intimacy and whom we name Lover, Friend, or Beloved. God's abundance in creating the world and gratuity in offering a covenant provides the context for our approach to justice as participation. Justice becomes a gracious offer of inclusion and participation in response to God's abundance.

The Creator is God who invites but never coerces, who engages but never discards. Thus relationships in the inclusive and participatory community are personal, free, and mutual. The Creator is divine creative activity seeking embodiment and particularity; that is, the Creator relies on concrete, historical participation in ongoing creating activities, in life-giving relationships, and in the building of community. Ongoing creative activity thus embodies or mediates the Creator. Thus interdependence and participation characterize the relationships between the Creator and those created in God's image. Interdependence, inclusion, and participation then ought to characterize relationships in the inclusive and participatory community.

The universal God of all is also ongoing Liberating Activity which reached a high point in Jesus of Nazareth. But because the universal God cannot be confined to any particular instance, God as Liberating Activity is Gracious Intervention on behalf of those oppressed by the unjust social systems throughout the Hebrew Scriptures and continuing until today. God as Liberating Activity is known in resistance to oppression and injustice by those who are oppressed and by those who identify with them.

God who is Liberating Activity calls to conversion and judges those who oppress persons in the name of economic, religious, or political gain. God who is Liberating Activity calls to conversion and judges all those structures, institutions, and patterns which cut off or deny an existence or a future to (parts of) the human community. God who is Liberating Activity seeks the conversion and transformation of the sinner and the sinful structures, not condemnation. The call to conversion may emerge in a clash between socialization and religious traditions. For example, belief in one creator of all may clash with socially prescribed value based on gender or income. The call to conversion may come from the concrete insight that embodiment challenges complicity in unjust structures. For example, persons who are working and are still poor challenge the widespread demand for inexpensive products which is typically met through low wages. The conversion process may be initiated through opposing practices presented by Christian traditions and the culture. For example, "the equality of all" conflicts with the practice of "disposable persons."

God who is Liberating Activity offers hope and the inauguration of a new creation in the face of religious, political, economic, and social injustices. The relational nature of this universal God who is Liberating Activity seeks embodiment and particularity of the people of every age. Thus persons and communities of all ages and nations are invited to become the sacraments of the concrete activity of the universal God who is Liberating Activity.

Although we have looked at dimensions of the universal God's relationships with the human community, the transforming, creating, and liberating activities of God are personal. God is Transforming Spirit, Creator, and Liberator. When the Trinity is understood as a tri-personal God whose difference actually constitutes personal distinction and whose difference cannot be collapsed into oneness without destroying the image of God as Trinity, then difference becomes integral to personal identity and the foundation of participation in community. Since human persons are created in the image of God, difference is integral to authentic human living and requires equitable treatment. Furthermore, personal identity requires community of difference. Participation in the human community is a requirement of justice.

Similarly, the image of God as Trinity attempts to articulate the completion, the fullness, or the universality of God. In this view, for both the Trinitarian God and authentic human living, fulfillment or completeness rests in diversity, not in oneness. This in turn provides a theological foundation for the fullness of God's redemptive action not only in Jesus Christ, but also in the diverse body of Christ throughout ages and cultures. On a related but practical level, completeness in diversity discourages both conformity to sameness and reliance on universal principles for application to differing situations. Rather, a central question becomes: How ought different persons to live together well without destroying personal identity forged in difference?[9]

The trinity of distinct persons seeks concrete embodiment in every age and community so that revelation can be continued. This revelation occurs wherever differences and particularity come together in relationships with a future for the human community. This revelation occurs whenever difference and particularity join in common action toward the city of God. This revelation occurs whenever concrete and particular claims invite encounter and respect. Symbolic action celebrates difference, confirms the tension between diversity and oneness in order to create an openness for the renewing Spirit of God. Perhaps more importantly, symbolic action transforms space, time, and relationships in the enactment of an alternative world, that is, the city of God. In such enactment of the endtimes in-breaking of the city of God, symbolic action legitimates alternative voices, plans, and perspectives.

A Sacramental Context for an Ethic of Justice as Participation

A sacramental worldview is built on the conviction that the concrete materiality of the cosmos, authentic human living, historical unfolding, and social location are sacramental.[10] Materiality bears Divinity and makes encounter with God possible.[11] Human persons cannot encounter

[9] The demands of justice which arise from social location and difference indicate that action on behalf of justice in this framework requires the development of skills in resistance, conflict mediation, and trust in struggle. It is at this point as well that a reading of the Gospel of John as the product of struggle may also provide some indication of how the Johannine community lived together well in difference.

[10] We recognize along with Roberto S. Goizueta, "A Ressourcement from the Margins: U.S. Latino Popular Catholicism as Lived Religion," *Theology and Lived Christianity*, The Annual Publication of the College Theology Society 45, ed. David Hammond (Mystic, Conn.: Twenty-Third Publications, 2000) 3–37, esp. 5–10, that modernity has separated the sign from the symbolized. In turn, this has led to a devaluing of materiality, an overemphasis on the rational, and the construction of meaning apart from the concrete. Against this tendency Goizueta argues that materiality is intrinsically connected to the symbolized.

[11] See David Hollenbach, "A Prophetic Church and the Catholic Sacramental Imagination," *Justice, Peace and Human Rights: American Catholic Social Ethics in a Pluralistic Context* (New York: Crossroad, 1988) 181–202, esp. 194–5. Imagination is the source, which is derived from experience and root metaphors. "Thus the Roman Catholic sacramental principle suggests that the normative structure of Christian experience and Christian imagination is concretely expressed in symbolic actions of the church's sacramental life. . . . The sacramental principle is an important counterweight to the excessively futurist and critical approach of a purely eschatological theology."

God or embody God's ongoing creation, redemption, or indwelling presence apart from materiality. Doctrines of creation, incarnation, and indwelling intrinsically connect materiality to divinity. Gathering community, sharing bread and wine, anointing with oil, extending forgiveness, making promises, and pouring water are symbolic actions in and through which Divine Activity is embodied and concretized in this time and place.[12] This approach to sacramentality is a logical implication of the incarnation and recognizes that materiality has the capacity to bear the divine.[13]

Our approach to justice is situated in this sacramental worldview. Consequently, justice is realized in and through just actions and structures. As sacraments effect what they symbolize, just actions effect the city of God and embody the justice of God. Because just action is equivocal, symbolic action, the city of God is realized. Just action is a visible eschatological symbol of the future city of God. At the same time this sacramental dimension grounds justice in the here and now in contrast to conceptions of justice as a God-given endtimes reality, which therefore is unachievable through human effort in this world. Just actions, then, are the embodiment of intimate, mutual relationships with God and with all persons; they are the concretization of divine presence, covenant, and mission.

VISION AS A CONTEXT FOR AN ETHIC OF JUSTICE AS PARTICIPATION

Attention to vision provides another dimension of the context for this approach to justice, linked to the sacramental approach. Christian traditions are replete with metaphors of vision. The city of God, the reign of God, a new heavens and a new earth (new creation), the messianic banquet and risen life (resurrection of the body) occur frequently in the Scriptures. In addition, the Gospel of John introduces the reader to a just and inclusive community.[14] Contemporary theologians and practitioners of justice have articulated their vision in terms of a better world, a re-creation of a world in which there are no ex-

---

[12] For the difference between equivocal, symbolic language in contrast to univocal, materialistic language, see Sandra Schneiders, *The Revelatory Text: Interpreting the New Testament as Sacred Scripture* (San Francisco: Harper, 1991) 33–7.

[13] Langdon Gilkey, *Catholicism Confronts Modernity: A Protestant View* (New York: Seabury Press, 1975) 196–7, describes the link of sacraments to justice: "the divinely granted capacity to allow finite and relative instruments to be media of the divine and to endow all of secular and ordinary life with the possibility of divine creativity."

[14] See above, 76–78.

cluded ones, a future for humanity, and God's vision for the redemption of creation.[15]

The notion of vision which provides the context for an understanding of justice has the following characteristics: (1) it is already present in human longings, desires, and hopes; (2) it carries the seeds of transformation; and (3) it provides some content.

Vision is already present in human longings, desires, and hopes. As we saw in the analysis of the justice survey (see Chapter 2), longings and desires for a more just and inclusive community moved the respondents to action on behalf of justice. Attention to longings recognizes the insights of affective, intuitive awarenesses, not only rational analysis and principles. Visions sometimes surface in loss, absence,[16] or a negative contrast between what is happening and Christian traditions.[17] The absence of what ought to be can lead to a vague but real insight about what ought to be. Such insights need a language or images which religious traditions can provide. Attention to desires affirms that the same Spirit who dwells in unfolding history and social situations[18] also dwells in the creating waters and the liberating activities of God.

A vision carries the seeds of transformation in one of two ways, both of which are integrally connected to present concrete living. Sometimes vision emerges from reading the signs of the times in a way that sees in the present those glimpses and seeds which will transform contemporary situations into a future for humanity or the city of God.[19] Personal

---

[15] Miroslav Volf, "Eschaton, Creation and Social Ethics," *Calvin Theological Journal* 30 (1995) 130–43.

[16] See Tina Pippin, *Death and Desire: The Rhetoric of Gender in the Apocalypse of John* (Louisville: Westminster/John Knox, 1992) 89: "[Apocalyptic literature] is a literature of desire, which seeks that which is experienced as absence or loss," quoting Rosemary Jackson, *Fantasy: The Literature of Subversion* (New York: Methuen, 1981) 106.

[17] See Edward Schillebeeckx, *God Among Us: The Gospel Proclaimed* (New York: Crossroad, 1983) 185, who points out that such awareness comes in concrete transformative action on behalf of justice, not simply in theories or principles.

[18] Hollenbach, "A Prophetic Church," 191, recognizes the presence of the Spirit in creative and charismatic imagination which emerge from outrage at existing social situations in light of the call coming from the Christian faith.

[19] Gustavo Gutiérrez, *A Theology of Liberation: History, Politics and Salvation* (London: SCM, 1977) 14–15: "Moltmann wrote that theological concepts do not 'limp after' reality. . . . They illuminate reality by displaying its future. In our approach, to reflect critically on the praxis of liberation is not to 'limp after' reality. The present in the praxis of liberation, in its deepest dimension, is pregnant with the future; hope must be an inherent part of our present commitment in history. Theology does not imitate this future which exists in the present. It does not create the vital attitude of hope out of nothing. Its role is more modest. It interprets and explains these as

and institutional vision statements typically suggest a path into the future based on a reading of the seeds and signs of the times. Other times a vision is a given into which we enter, much like the gratuitousness of relationship extended to us. Here the vision is not an extension of present possibilities into the future, but rather the future reaching out to meet the present as an annunciation of something more or as a disjuncture from what is.[20] Visions of this type tend to be collective and formative of a movement, such as the vision of racial or gender equality. Such inspired movements have a life of their own which invites participation in its ongoing creation and transformation.

The Christian religious traditions provide a sketch of the content for vision[21] as well as link the vision to creation and the endtimes. In the beginning and at the end basic human needs are satisfied. Peace marks relationships between nations, persons, and the cosmos. Justice flourishes in the economic, political, legal, and social realms. Human persons participate in the very life of God. The widow, the orphan, the

---

the true underpinnings of history. To reflect on a forward-directed action is not to concentrate on the past. It does not mean being in the caboose of the present. Rather it is to penetrate the present reality, the movement of history, that which is driving history toward the future. To reflect on the basis of the historical praxis of liberation is to reflect in the light of the future which is believed in and hoped for. It is to reflect with a view to action which transforms the present. But it does not mean doing this from an armchair; rather it means sinking roots where the pulse of history is beating at this moment and illuminating history with the Word of the Lord of history, who irreversibly committed himself to the present moment of mankind [sic] to carry it to its fulfillment. . . . It [liberation theology] is a theology which is open—in the protest against trampled human dignity, in the struggle against the plunder of the vast majority of people, in liberating love and in the building of a new, just and fraternal society—to the gift of the Kingdom of God." See also Reimund Bieringer, "The Normativity of the Future: The Authority of the Bible for Theology," *Bulletin European Theology: Zeitschrift für Theologie in Europa* 8:1 (1997) 52–67.

[20] In an oft quoted text, Archbishop Oscar Romero emphasizes participation in a vision not of one's own creation as well as the largesse of the vision: "It helps, now and then, to step back and take the long view. The Kingdom is not only beyond our efforts, it is even beyond our vision. We accomplish in our lifetime only a tiny fraction of the magnificent enterprise that is [God's] work. Nothing we do is complete, which is another way of saying that the Kingdom always lies beyond us. No statement says all that should be said. No prayer fully expresses our faith. No confession brings perfection, no pastoral visit brings wholeness. No program accomplishes the church's mission. No set of goals and objectives includes everything. . . . We are prophets of a future that is not our own."

[21] Laurent A. Parks Daloz and others, *Commonfire: Leading Lives of Commitment in a Complex World* (Boston: Beacon Press, 1996) 140–5, discuss religion and family as sources of imagination, especially when religious understandings and practices could be interpreted as accounting for inclusion, diversity, and participation. Cf. Hollenbach, "A Prophetic Church," 193, who notes that the moral imagination of Christians is shaped by fundamental symbols and doctrines of Christian faith.

poor, and the stranger are included in the common life. Persons are recognized as the image of the Creator, with consequent dignity and rights. This dimension of vision intersects with the sacramental dimension described above. The Christian religious traditions provide a sketch of God's vision for the world, and human persons are invited to embody and participate here and now. Hence the vision is not static, but one which invites participation in continuing creation, liberation, healing, and transformation.[22]

Visions serve several functions.[23] First, vision engages the imagination and the affective dimensions of the human community. Since rational approaches to justice typical of the modern age have not brought about just communities, the inclusion of the imagination and the affections in an approach to justice seems warranted. Second, vision urges transformation and challenges the status quo. Even the most mundane vision in a corporate world suggests something other than what is. A vision of equality for women challenges all social systems established on hierarchy or patriarchy. Visions by their very nature present an alternative to the existing realities.

Third, because vision arises out of experience and practice, all persons have access to vision. A vision does not require a specific kind of education, race, gender, or class. In fact, persons who live at the margins of dominating systems are often more ready to recognize a vision, an alternative pattern, because they are not locked into the status quo. Their position at the margins actually enables them to see things differently. Fourth, vision integrates diverse components into a whole. A vision holds together doing and dreaming, correcting injustice and facilitating justice, illuminating present realities and articulating future goals, accomplishing tasks and making meaning. The vision of a world in which all persons have access to the fulfillment of their basic human

[22] Volf, "Eschaton, Creation and Social Ethics," 133–8, holds that the eschatological vision is God's vision for the redemption of creation; hence the vision is a goal of human ethical behavior. Thus it is not a return to the Garden of Eden, but human participation in ongoing creation.

[23] Beverly Wildung Harrison, "The Dream of a Common Language: Towards a Normative Theory of Justice in Christian Ethics," *The Annual of the Society of Christian Ethics* 29 (1983) 1–25, delineates four functions of the vision of justice as "rightly ordered community": (1) The vision shapes the goal of Christian community as a collective direction (intellect). (2) It animates the passion (emotions). (3) It provides a sense of purpose, vocation, or lifestyle (self-evident direction). (4) Through the practice of justice, it provides hints of what justice is (action). Pippin, *Death and Desire*, 92–100, has identified these functions of vision: (1) to destabilize the rational world by allowing silent voices to speak and unconscious desires to be enacted, (2) to confront the known world with an alternative real world which dissolves the boundary lines between the imaginary and the symbolic, and (3) to awaken desire.

needs suggests actions which can be done, injustices which can be corrected, structures which facilitate just distribution, criteria which evaluate the present situation, a goal to accomplish, and meaning for action on behalf of justice.

Vision is a component of the context of justice, but the creation and evolution of just community requires more than vision. Persons and communities also need disciplined staying power to maintain the struggle toward an embodiment of the vision.[24] Disciplined staying power relies on five things: (1) experiences which suggest and encourage alternative worldviews;[25] (2) shared convictions that the current situation is not as it ought to be and that persons are capable of bringing about change;[26] (3) thoughtful reflection which gives rise to theoretical articulations; (4) institutionalized support in the form of shared values, patterns, social roles, and structures;[27] and (5) skill development for effective action. Furthermore, a vision requires insights from social and behavioral sciences with regard to approaches and techniques which are actually able to translate a vision into a concrete structure or behavior. Thus vision remains one important component of the context of justice, albeit one that has been overlooked in recent centuries.

NORMATIVITY OF THE FUTURE

Eschatological inclusion of women and of persons who are blind, deaf, or poor requires reversal of social destinies now. Liberation the-

---

[24] Walter Brueggemann, "The Call to Resistance," *The Other Side* 26 (November/December 1990) 44–6, esp. 46.

[25] Joanne Martin, "When Expectations and Justice Do Not Coincide: Blue Collar Visions of a Just World," *Justice in Social Relations,* ed. Hans Werner Bierhoff and others (New York: Plenum Press, 1986) 317–35, esp. 330–3, proposes two explanations of why visions of just worlds tend to be variations of the familiar: (1) prospect theory holds that our cognitive limits mean we cannot imagine what is too far removed from current realties; (2) availability theory holds that, if a thread is not available cognitively, then it is hard to imagine, since imagination retrieves from memory what has been experienced and expected to recur. Martin holds that prior participation in central aspects of visions is necessary for the sense of a vision.

[26] Patricia O'Neill, "Cognition and Citizen Participation in Social Action," *Journal of Applied Social Psychology* 18 (1988) 1067–83, holds that action for change requires belief that the world is not just and that we have the power to change it.

[27] David Hollenbach, "Justice as Participation: Public Moral Discourse and the U.S. Economy," *Justice, Peace and Human Rights: American Catholic Social Ethics in a Pluralistic Context* (New York: Crossroad, 1988) 71–83, esp. 73: "As a result of the culturally fragmenting effects of modern individualism, we have lost a coherent moral vision as well as the kind of coherent institutions of communal life needed to sustain such a vision."

ologies hope that God will remain faithful to the promise of justice and love and thus keep history open to the fulfillment of the promises. The very struggle for justice is an expression of the eschatological hope. Justice is a dimension of the city of God which calls the People of God to embody the endtimes reality in each new era.[28] Justice continues God's action in the world and in Jesus and fulfills the eschatological reign already begun in Jesus.

Normativity of the future is not a rejection of normativity of the past or present.[29] For example, the age old tradition of God as creator of all suggests norms which recognize life as a promise stretching into the future as well as norms which promote solidarity among peoples and nations. Similarly, the God who initiates covenants suggests norms of participation. Immediate experiences and feelings of outrage at injustice suggest norms urging action and transformation of existing injustices.

In the midst of the historically situated statements of justice directed primarily to the economic order, there are flashes of insight which provide an existence and a future for the human community (access of all to basic human resources). Even in the rhetorical laments against socialist unions and state controlled production, there are glimmers of the future city of God where justice, peace, and love provide the guiding principles (creation of opportunities, education, and skills so persons can contribute to the human community). Even in ideologies of hierarchy, patriarchy, and Eurocentrism there are moments when the dream of a just and inclusive community is recalled (participation, social anthropology). It is these insights, glimmers, and moments that hold the in-breaking of the future providing norms for just living today.

---

[28] Hollenbach, "A Prophetic Church," 192, provides five conclusions for the movement from vision to ethical behavior: (1) Concrete proposals for social policy cannot be deduced from Christian general ethical principles. (2) Negative criticism is also not sufficient for communal engagement of Church and society. (3) Positive proposals for action must be linked to identity. (4) Shared identity and shared action are linked in a synthesis that occurs within the living Christian experience. (5) Ecclesial sacramental imagination provides access to symbols and myths which can promote shared identity and shared actions.

[29] Although Hollenbach, "A Prophetic Church," 192, essentially critiques ethical systems built on a normativity of the present and calls for a link with the past, some of his comments about the function of the future (teleology and eschatology) may prove valuable. "An ethic that starts and ends with the boundaries of the present conflict-ridden situation cannot fail to lead to insoluble puzzles. Ethics is meant to transform the human condition from what it is to what it could be, not simply to help us better understand the conflicting values of our world."

CONCLUSION

Chapter 6 has described a coherent theological and anthropological context for an understanding of justice as participation. In addition, we have set forth three further dimensions of our approach. This approach to justice as participation is played out in a world which bears traces of the divine presence and effects the endtimes vision of the city of God characterized by justice and inclusion. We embrace this vision dimension, for we are convinced that a vision engages the emotions, challenges the status quo, is accessible to all, and offers an integrated glimpse of a complex whole. Furthermore, we believe that the eschatological vision which breaks into the present world in "longings and glimmers of what could be" provides norms from this future to guide practices of justice today.

Justice as participation is coherent with those understandings of God which highlight God's universal invitation to enter into relationship with Godself and to continue the works of God, namely, creation, liberation (intervention), and resistance (judgment) to injustice. The image of God as a trinity of persons constituted in their difference provides additional theological underpinnings for justice as participation. Finally, our description for justice as participation is connected to an anthropology which recognizes the following constitutive characteristics: embodiment, social location, relationality, fundamental equality in originality, and accountable agency. These characteristics shape the description and give contours to the requirements of justice as participation.

7

Justice as Participation in the Human Community

Lakewood is a diverse neighborhood of sixty thousand within a larger urban setting. Twenty-two buildings and store fronts are the home for seventeen different religious traditions. As a port of entry neighborhood, forty-five different ethnic groups bring nearly forty native languages to its stores and classrooms. Half-a-million-dollar homes are situated next to thirty six-unit modest apartment buildings. Such ethnic, religious, and economic diversity is celebrated as the identity/character of Lakewood. More residents rent homes than own them. Excellent public transportation, proximity to a lakefront, and a fine university make this area a prime site for upscale development.

Over time a variety of community groups (developers, religious congregations, home owners, tenants, grass roots organizers, city government, ethnic alliances) have developed skills and resources to influence and shape public policy with regard to neighborhood vision, priorities, and strategies to reach the vision. A five-year neighborhood plan articulates the vision of an ethnically, economically, religiously, and culturally diverse neighborhood. Religious groups search out ways to link inclusion and justice to the central mysteries of their traditions as well as to explore the ethical implications of these beliefs as communities of faith in this specific neighborhood. Some issues such as child care, drug and gang prevention are universally embraced, although specific strategies for addressing the issues diverge. Other issues, such as gentrification, dislocation of low income families, living wage jobs, affordable housing, and ecologically sensitive development are hotly debated in the public forum against the backdrop of the articulated vision. Alongside these long-term issues, the citizens seek creative and immediate responses to persons who are homeless, hungry, and without access to health care.

As long as all the community groups are strong in skills, resources, and networks of relationships, decisions and strategies emerge from public discourse. Conflict and attentiveness remain central to the embodiment of a just and inclusive community. Sometimes a group will try to negotiate a decision behind closed doors. Other times connections to larger systems and decision-making bodies frustrate or complicate local activities. At times, attitudes and values emerge in ongoing struggles which the agreed-upon vision challenges. Still, structures, processes, and people actively exist to hold up the vision, to embrace diversity, to maximize participation, and to effect the required changes. The wide variety of interest groups, the collaboration of Church and civic arenas to facilitate a public space for discussion and conflict, as well as engaged citizens committed both to the vision and to the transformation of injustice into justice provide necessary resources. Lakewood is not yet fully the city of God, but the vision is taking hold in the formation of structures, procedures, and endeavors as well as in the hearts and actions of the people.

Against the backdrop of this local vision for a just and inclusive community, this chapter seeks to describe justice within the contexts of the previous chapter, namely, a relational God engaged in this world, authentic human living, a sacramental worldview, attention to the end-times city of God, and the inclusion of norms derived from that vision. In other words, this approach to justice takes place within the contours of a shared Christian identity and a living Christian experience.

We will first articulate an understanding of justice in descriptive narrative. Then we will address the same ten questions to "justice as participation" which were posed to the twentieth-century understandings of justice in Chapter 5. In the final analysis this approach to justice seeks the transformation of human communities into the city of God. Hence we are interested in moving from an adequate narrative to just actions and public policies. To that end, this chapter sets forth values coherent with this approach to justice, before formulating mediating principles which can be used to evaluate whether personal activities and public policies are just. Mediating principles or middle axioms are concrete, sensate stages on the way toward a just and inclusive community. As such, they are visible and tangible sites between a vision like the city of God embodied in a local just community and those detailed action plans or strategies outlining how the group will attain a just and inclusive community. An example of a mediating principle would be when persons who are homeless influence public policy on affordable housing, then a local community knows they are on the way toward a just and inclusive community. In the final chapter, we will see if these values and mediating principles can point a direction in the dilemmas posed in the first chapter.

JUSTICE AS PARTICIPATION IN THE HUMAN COMMUNITY

Justice concerns itself with life in common: What constitutes a just community? How ought different people to live together justly? How ought communities to be organized so that it is easier for people and groups to do just action?[1] This approach to justice considers the justice of personal actions and decisions according to their contribution to or hindrance of a just and inclusive community. The practice of justice is a condition of possibility for life in common.

With regard to the question "What constitutes a just community?" the previous chapters point to a just and inclusive community, a community in which all persons count, contribute, and participate in building the city of God. The Scriptures highlight the intimate relationships between God and the human community in their descriptions of the city of God, the messianic banquet, and the Indwelling Spirit. The normativity of a just and inclusive community flows from a God of abundance who gratuitously invites, initiates, and welcomes human communities into relationships of mutuality, reciprocity, and participation which stretch into the future by means of promise. Within these interactive covenant relationships, the Scriptures remind their readers that God's transformative action intervened on behalf of justice, called to conversion from injustice, and re-created one more time the promise of a just and inclusive community stretching into the future. The practitioners surveyed encountered this process in their hopes or longings for a better world.

With regard to the question "How ought different people to live together justly?" the previous chapters highlight an anthropology which describes human persons as inherently relational, as constituted in difference, as embodied and located in specific times and concrete places,

---

[1] This approach is based on the conviction that an adequate description of justice requires a coherence between theology (How is God just?), anthropology (What ought the just community to look like?) ethics, (How ought people to live together well?), and public policy (How do you structure a just community?). For example, in Catholic Social Teachings the theological framework accentuates God as a creator of all persons in God's own image and as the establisher of a covenant people. In Catholic Social Teachings the requirements of justice emerge from the resultant dignity and relationality of the human-person-in-community. Since God is Creator God, these requirements in justice are God-given demands.

and as interdependent agents and as images of God invited to take up God's transformative action on behalf of justice. The Gospel of John presents an image of an inclusive community characterized by a variety of leadership roles, including representative figures from various ethnic groups, economic statuses, social locations, and genders. The prophets describe a people whose relationship with God requires provision for basic human needs, social and economic justice at the city gate, and attention to widows, orphans, strangers, and the poor on the margins of Hebrew social life. Other passages include justice as a fundamental dimension of the vision of the city of God and a hallmark of those believers who are wise. The practitioners of justice linked their dreams for a better world to participation, inclusion, and equitable treatment for all members of the human community. Similarly, the United States Bishops concluded that the inherent relationality of authentic human community makes certain demands of justice:

> Basic justice demands the establishment of minimum levels of participation in the life of the human community for all persons. The ultimate injustice is for a person or group to be treated actively or abandoned passively as if they were nonmembers of the human race. To treat people this way is effectively to say they simply do not count as human beings. This can take many forms, all of which can be described as varieties of marginalization or exclusion from social life.[2]

With regard to the question "How ought communities to be organized so that it is easier for people and groups to act justly?" the previous chapters have drawn on the insights of the human and organizational sciences as well as the Scriptures and magisterial teachings. The Torah, laws, and social roles such as priest, prophet, and king belong to the organizational structures of the Israelite people. The Christian Scriptures stress adherence to the teachings and commandments of Jesus and Spirit-based charisms, although a variety of offices is mentioned in one or another of the texts. Catholic Social Teachings highlight values and general principles that contribute to economic, political, and social living in common. Typically, Catholic Social Teachings do not suggest strategies which will flow from these general principles and values, in part because of the concrete and particular character of local political, social, and economic situations. Our study of contemporary theories of justice (see Chapter 5) offered some theoretical models for a more just organization of communities. The practitioners and ministers of justice

---

[2] National Conference of Catholic Bishops, *Economic Justice for All: A Pastoral Letter on Catholic Social Teaching and the Economy* (Washington, D.C.: National Conference of Catholic Bishops, 1986) section 77.

described their concrete effort to change social structures and to treat all persons justly.

In light of these questions and the work of the previous chapters, we conclude that a community is just when:

- diverse persons and groups are engaged in equitable, mutual, and participatory relationships which build up networked communities and effectively find ways to include persons who have been marginated;

- diverse persons and groups have access to the resources necessary for humane and authentic human living;

- the way society or the specific human community is organized (social structures, patterns of behavior, attitudes, institutions, and social roles) facilitates inclusive and participatory membership for all persons, particularly those at an experiential distance (the ones we do not know);

- processes of developing structures, decision making, influence peddling, and conflict resolution are equitably and consistently engaged in and practiced;

- concrete, particular actions realize justice;

- unjust structures, relationships, resource availability, practices, and processes are transformed into a future for humanity;

- human persons and communities are accountable for and responsible agents of a just and inclusive community.

The following description will develop each of these seven aspects of justice. The aspects are so integrally connected that the seven-fold separation merely distinguishes and clarifies, rather than divides into kinds or progressive levels of justice. The aspects are explicitly described within the context of theology, anthropology, vision, sacramental worldview, and normativity of the future.

First, diverse persons and groups are engaged in equitable, mutual, and participatory relationships which build up networked communities and effectively find ways to include persons who have been marginated. This aspect of justice is rooted in the long Jewish and Christian traditions of an abundantly relational God who includes human persons in the divine life and participates in human living in ways that are revealed as God's justice. God is a trinity of diverse persons constituted by mutual, equal, and reciprocal relationships. Creation in the image of God, covenant relationships, baptism into the body of Christ, and the call into an intimate relationship with God that has a future are all faith statements confirming an awareness that human persons are included in divine living. God's identification with humanity including the incarnation of Jesus, God's intervention on behalf of persons who are oppressed including judgment and the redemption in Jesus, God's indwelling Spirit and grace, as well as the images of Word, Wisdom, and Life are likewise faith statements of God's participation in human living. Human longing for participation and inclusion may well be the indwelling presence of the city of God.

As the Gospel of John highlights and a sacramental worldview confirms, what is said of God's relationship with Jesus can also be expected of relationships within the human community. As a result, authentic human communities strive to embody the mutual, equal, and reciprocal relationships which constitute a community of diverse human persons. Authentic human communities incarnate the creation of all in the image and likeness of God in efforts to build a human community in which all are welcome, in which the abilities and gifts of all are embraced, and in which all participate. The just and inclusive community includes attention to the least advantaged[3] in order to level the historically constructed playing field of human community.

The essentially social dimension of authentic human living confirms this vision and sacramental worldview. Because human persons are essentially social, inclusion in the human community and participation are necessary for authentic human living.[4] In other words, engaged membership[5] and active participation[6] are basic requirements of justice.

---

[3] We would describe the "least advantaged" as persons whose race, gender, class, ethnicity, sexual orientation, or religious faith are used to marginate or exclude. We would also link this attention to the stories in the Christian traditions which show a God who intervenes on behalf of the oppressed, a Jesus who identified with the marginated as well as the Christian mission which continues the creating, redeeming, and intervening activities of God in the body of Christ.

[4] In Neh 5:1ff. the poor protested that they were not getting their due. The fact that they were members of the People of God, rather than poverty itself, provided the basis for their complaint against exclusion.

[5] According to Alasdair MacIntyre, *After Virtue: A Study in Moral Theology* (Notre Dame, Ind.: University of Notre Dame Press, 1984) 205: "individuals are never able to seek for the good or to exercise virtue only *qua* individual, for the story of a life is always embedded in the story of those communities from which that life derives an identity." See also David Hollenbach, "Justice as Participation: Public Moral Discourse and the U.S. Economy," *Justice, Peace and Human Rights: American Catholic Social Ethics in a Pluralistic Context* (New York: Crossroad, 1988) 71–83, esp. 82: "To be a person is to be a member of society, active within it in many ways through diverse sets of relationships. . . . The meaning of justice rises from this link between personhood and social participation." Michael Walzer, *Spheres of Justice: A Defense of Pluralism and Equality* (New York: Basic Books, 1983) 80, emphasizes the relational foundations of justice: "The primary good we distribute to one another is member-

Since human relationality comprises both the involuntary and voluntary relationships, specific practices of inclusion and participation are responsive to varied and concrete circumstances of voluntary friendship as well as involuntary citizenship in the human community. Justice is then a requirement of both interpersonal face-to-face and distant relationships.

This vision of justice as engaged membership and active participation in the human community provides a basis for ethical norms.[7] Inclusion in the human community entails recognition of the diversity of persons and groups as constitutive of the human community, and intentional incorporation of persons who have been disadvantaged by prior or existing patterns of social organization. For example, a Chicago neighborhood project coming from the World Parliament of Religions attempts to mobilize local churches around issues of hunger by inviting the various religious traditions to ponder and share the meaning of food in their own tradition. From the sharing, the religious communities begin to clarify their own traditions, appreciate the diversity, and act together to end hunger, but in congruence with each tradition's religious meaning of food.

Participation in social relationships minimally entails voice in self-definition, involvement in the articulation of meaning and purpose, collaboration in building up networks of groups, and cooperation in decision-making concerning whose voice counts in decisions about who gets what, who gives what, and on the basis of which criteria. As a requirement of justice, participation further indicates practices of

---

ship in some human community. And what we do with regard to membership structures all our other distributive choices: it determines with whom we make choices and from whom we require obedience and collect taxes, to whom we allocate goods and services." Also cf. John Rawls, *A Theory of Justice* (Cambridge, Mass.: Harvard University Press, 1971) 230: "We say that a person is someone who can be a citizen, that is a fully cooperating member of society over a complete life. . . . A society is not an association for more limited purposes; citizens do not join a society voluntarily but are born into it, where, for our aims here, we assume they are to lead their lives."

[6] Hollenbach, "Justice as Participation," 83, points out that discomfort in the face of marginalization may in fact be the beginning of consensus around participation. In her comments on social analysis, Beverly Wildung Harrison, "The Dream of a Common Language: Towards a Normative Theory of Justice in Christian Ethics," *The Annual of the Society of Christian Ethics* 29 (1983) 1–25, esp. 15, raises the question whether the state of life into which we are born is just. Structures and institutionalized patterns of power privilege some, so that other groups must live without appropriate self-direction and without participation in the human community.

[7] Survey respondents confirmed a link between membership in the human community and justice. See above, 35.

equality,[8] mutuality, and reciprocity.[9] The way in which two persons play double solitaire actually could be a learning tool for participative action. When Mary and Pat play, they play for themselves and try to disadvantage each other by their choices of moves. When Kylene and Martha play double solitaire, they consult and collaborate with each other so as to facilitate the other person's game. Mary and Pat rarely win the game, while Martha and Kylene win most of their games.

Second, diverse persons and groups have access to the resources necessary for humane and authentic human living. Access to resources focuses on needs of human persons in community, with concrete attention to embodiment. As such this aspect of justice takes up the traditional concerns of distributive justice. God created embodied human persons in God's own image and likeness. In Jesus of Nazareth, God became human flesh and blood (incarnation) with the promise that bodies would be raised up at the end of time. Resurrection of the body at the end of time stands, then, as a dimension of the vision which calls for just living here and now.

Jewish and Christian traditions have long linked justice and embodiment. The prophets of the Hebrew Scriptures insisted that faith in God showed itself in the doing of justice to the widow, the orphan, and the poor. God's justification of humanity was embodied in Jesus, who liberated persons embodied in illness, blindness, deafness, and other kinds of disablement. This same Jesus fed the hungry and in John identified himself as Bread of Life and Life-giving Water. The mission of the Church as body of Christ is the continuation of the justifying and liberating activities of God's action in Jesus.

Taken together these Christian traditions proclaim that bodies matter,[10] for embodiment is the place of encounter with the divine. This

---

[8] Simone Weil, *Waiting for God,* trans. Emma Craufurd, intro. Leslie A. Fiedler (New York: Harper/Row, 1973) 139–45, when discussing love of neighbor, describes justice as "behaving as though there were equality, when one is the stronger in an unequal relationship."

[9] Reciprocity describes practices in which persons and groups *contribute* work, talents, and resources as well as *receive* work, talents, and resources, so that the community flourishes. Reciprocity opposes exploitation.

[10] Roberto S. Goizueta, "A Ressourcement from the Margins: U.S. Latino Popular Catholicism as Lived Religion," *Theology and Lived Christianity,* The Annual Publication of the College Theology Society 45, ed. David Hammond (Mystic, Conn.: Twenty-Third Publications, 2000) 3–37, esp. 23–4, points out that a failure to see the bodiliness of another tends to reduce persons to abstract essences. In this light, one cannot over-emphasize the link between embodiment and justice. Perhaps a contemporary identification of justice with the legal system or even economic systems comes from a retreat into abstraction which allows the relegation of issues such as food, water, shelter, clothing, health to individual choice.

foundational expression of a sacramental worldview is confirmed by the anthropological recognition that embodiment is a constitutive dimension of the human person, along with relationality, accountable agency, difference, and social location in time and place. The present and future thriving of human and cosmic embodiment surfaces requirements of justice. The demands of justice include access to what is necessary to meet basic human needs such as food, clothing, shelter, education, health care, and safety.[11]

Religious freedom, meaning and purpose, forgiveness, work, belonging to a community, love, social capital, and self-esteem are additional resources connected with other constitutive dimensions of the human person; access to these resources is required in justice.[12] As a requirement of justice, cosmic-embodied thriving also necessitates stewardship of the earth's resources for present and future generations. Justice entails an environment in which each and all have access to those resources needed for the unfolding of their person, vocation, social roles, and contributions to community life. As a requirement of justice, access to resources necessary for humane and authentic living further indicates practices which foster dignity, worth, and healing. Jan, in his position as pastor, finds himself asked for money for basic human needs. Rather than giving money or food, Jan finds a way to employ the person so that he is able to earn money. The present and future thriving of human and cosmic embodiment provides the foundations for eliminating torture, genocide, forms of sexual exploitation, and discrimination based on racial or gendered embodiments.

Access to resources necessary for humane and authentic human living includes attention to equity and justice. For instance, when children play and eat together, issues tend to be resolved by absolute equality in the piece of candy or in the time allotted to a favorite toy. Equality in access to resources, however, does not typically end up in justice. Not sameness, but fairness or equity often provides a more fitting standard of justice.[13] Equitable treatment demands personal action which does

---

[11] Cf. the "I am" sayings from the Gospel of John, wherein Jesus identifies himself as Bread of Life (food), the Gate (shelter, safety), Light (education), and Life (health care).

[12] It is noteworthy that the survey respondents (see above, 37) gave "access to power" only limited affirmation as a description of justice.

[13] Robert Folger, "Rethinking Equity Theory: A Referent Cognitions Model," *Justice in Social Relations,* ed. Hans Werner Bierhoff and others (New York: Plenum Press, 1986) 145–60, describes equity as follows: across persons there should be a comparable rate of compensation for contributions to an exchange, i.e., an equivalent outcome/input ratio. Folger holds that equity primarily deals with distributions of resources. It would seem, however, that it could also deal with conditions of

not discriminate on the basis of relationships (e.g., life status, association), embodiment (e.g., gender, race, ethnicity), social location (e.g.,
class, language, national origin), or accountable agency (e.g., religion).
Justice as equitable treatment recognizes that difference requires fair
treatment, which is not always the same treatment. In addition, difference
is not an ethical tool for evaluations of better and worse or superior and
inferior. Equitable treatment also requires ending that which disadvantages someone on the basis of difference or which treats persons un-
fairly by treating persons in the same manner.[14] For example, equal
reduction of property taxes or income taxes advantages only those who
have property or income. Furthermore, decreasing tax funds for public
works and services disadvantages citizens who must rely on public
services such as police protection and education because they do not
have the resources to hire private security forces or attend private
schools.

*Third, the way society or the specific human community is organized (social
structures, patterns of behavior, attitudes, policies, institutions, and social
roles) facilitates inclusive and participatory membership for all persons, particularly those at an experiential distance (the ones we don't know).* Justice is
more than access to those resources required for authentic human
living and relationships characterized by mutuality, participation, and
inclusion. Justice is more than personal or group effort. Justice also concerns itself with patterned behavior, attitudes, policies, institutions,
social roles, and systems which promote or hinder inclusive, participatory communities,[15] that is, structural justice. Something of this awareness is behind the comment of Dom Helder Camera: "When I give
people bread, they call me a saint; when I ask why they are hungry,
they call me a communist." Camera's comment implies that feeding
people does not address the social attitudes, economic policies, and

---

access to resources which shape the input to outcomes ration. See *Oxford Unabridged
Dictionary*, "equity": "The original notion was that of 'in equity' being understood
to be one given in accordance with natural justice, in a case for which the law did
not provide adequate remedy or in which its operation would have been unfair."

[14] Justice as equitable treatment has an affinity to the Thomistic understanding
that justice concerns itself with that which "is due in relationships of equity."

[15] Social structures are independently operative patterns of relationships between
foundational components of a social system. These behaviors, attitudes, values,
roles, institutions, and norms are interconnected, have a life of their own, and will
continue to function whether individuals are aware of them or not. As such, social
structures are resistant to change and are the locus of social problems. When social
structures change, they tend to change together. See Bronislaw Malinowski, *The
Ethnography of Malinowski: The Trobriand Islanders* (London and Boston: Routledge
and Kegan, 1979) 79.

political institutions which make it impossible for persons to provide food for themselves.

This structural justice, on one level, is an extension of access to resources because it seeks an organization of the common life which regularizes access to resources. Structural justice recognizes that personal and communal just actions become easier when patterned behavior, attitudes, policies, institutions, social roles, and systems encourage and support just practices. For instance, a sociologist once commented that the inclusion of women ministers in diocesan pastoral meetings has structurally altered the role and influence of women in the Church to such an extent that the prohibition against women's ordination will eventually disappear.

The development and implementation of such structures relies on the human sciences and public discourse in order to determine which institutions and policies actually promote just action. Patterned behavior and social roles are embodiments of justice; socially promoted attitudes and social systems are enactments of justice. Similar to bread and wine which realize and express the body of Christ, structures and institutions both realize and express justice. Structural justice concerns itself with social organizations to facilitate the in-breaking of a just and inclusive community characterized by access to resources as well as mutual, participatory, and inclusive relationships.

Such attention to a socially constructed organization of life in common underscores social location as constitutive for the human community. The human community is always located in a specific time and place, in concrete language patterns, as well as in its patterns of economic, political, social, and religious life. The patterns and institutions which organize life in common are constructed by specific communities over time and are constantly undergoing revision. Organized common life is never a clean slate, but rather has contours which make it easier or harder to act justly or to facilitate inclusion and participation of all in the human community. The current situation of Catholic hospitals in the United States illustrates the limitations stemming from social location. The vision of Catholic hospitals as continuing the healing ministry of Jesus is situated in a context where increasing numbers of persons who are poor need medical attention, while the costs of medical treatment rise and the need for federal grants increases. Within these confines, hospitals are challenged to pay employees just wages and to provide competent and competitive medical care. Since all life in common is organized in some way, a central issue for hospitals and other institutions becomes what kind of structures best promote and encourage just and inclusive community.

Our Christian traditions show us a God who revealed Godself in structures. God made a covenant which formed the Israelites into a people with a law and a land. God promised to be present in the institutions of kingship, priesthood, and prophecy. The Israelites experienced God in patterns of war making, in attitudes of elitism, in the policies surrounding clean and unclean, as well as in the social roles of widow, orphan, and stranger. God's presence in these structures of life in common comforted and challenged the Israelites. God intervened to end slavery in Egypt. God called the Israelites to conversion in the practices of war making and economic exploitation. God established a new people after the Flood, after the Exodus, after the Exile, and after the destruction of the Temple.

These new creations set forth a vision of the city of God—a city structured as a just and inclusive community:

> No more shall the sound of weeping be heard in it,
>   or the cry of distress.
> No more shall there be in it
>   an infant that lives but a few days,
>   or an old person who does not live out a lifetime;
> for one who dies at a hundred years will be considered a youth,
>   and one who falls short of a hundred will be considered accursed.
> They shall build houses and inhabit them;
>   they shall plant vineyards and eat their fruit.
> They shall not build and another inhabit;
>   they shall not plant and another eat;
> for like the days of a tree shall the days of my people be,
>   and my chosen shall long enjoy the work of their hands.
> They shall not labor in vain,
>   or bear children for calamity;
> for they shall be offspring blessed by the LORD—
>   and their descendants as well.
> Before they call I will answer,
>   while they are yet speaking I will hear (Isa 65:19b-24).

This vision of the city of God as an organization of life in common only hints at the patterned behavior, attitudes, policies, institutions, social roles, and systems which need to be in place for this vision to become concrete. Similarly, today's human communities can draw some norms from the vision of the city of God for the patterned behavior, attitudes, policies, institutions, social roles, and systems which ought to realize the vision of the just and inclusive community. For example, today's just and inclusive community ought to include policies that facilitate home ownership, systems of health care for the vulnerable children and aging, economic institutions that link work with self-sufficiency for the meeting of basic human needs, and networks of relationships that support persons in distress and delight.

Thus structural justice requires that human communities develop and implement policies which provide reasonably thorough access to resources necessary for authentic human living. Human communities are challenged to find ways to reward behavior that embodies justice and discourages behavior that realizes injustice.

This aspect of justice compels human communities to evaluate and re-structure existing political, economic, and religious institutions so that they actually promote just action and restrain exclusive, elitist activities. Human communities need to examine social roles and re-shape them in light of the vision of participatory membership for all. As a requirement of justice, the common life must be organized to encourage practices which embody inclusion, equity, mutuality, and reciprocity. Consequently, hierarchical patterns in social roles need to be distrusted when difference provides the criteria for subordination or superiority.

Fourth, processes of developing structures, decision-making, influence-peddling, and conflict resolution are equitably and consistently engaged in and practiced. This aspect of justice, that is, procedural justice,[16] turns its attention to processes and procedures, particularly their formation and practice. Whereas structural justice focuses on the existing institutions and patterned behavior, procedural justice entails three foci: first, the processes through which the structures came into existence; second, the access of persons to the processes; and third, the consistent, equitable practice of the processes. For example, with regard to laws, procedural justice is concerned with processes through which laws, precedents, and policies are established. The variety of legislative, executive, interpretative, and judicial processes offers the possibility of a broad range of citizen participation. Procedural justice includes a concern about access to the process of law-making. Who gets invited to participate in the processes of law-making? Whose voice is spoken or heard? What are the criteria for access to these processes? Procedural justice also attends to those legal processes which provide consistent, equitable administration of the laws.

---

[16] For our evaluation of Robert Nozick, *Anarchy, State and Utopia* (New York: Basic Books, 1974), see above, 125–9. We noted that an exclusive consideration of process and procedures without content can actually serve to legitimate the status quo and justify the absence of public agreement on the content of justice, while explaining how pluralistic societies hold together.

As with structural justice, procedural justice does not begin with a clean slate, but must begin with the existing situation in its concrete historical evolution. Therefore, the work of procedural justice involves adjusting what is already in place, maximizing the hidden potential for justice in current practices, and replacing what is unable to provide justice in process, access, and practice with inclusive and participatory processes. These realities are consistent with the understanding of authentic human community as embodied, socially located, and fundamentally relational.

The vision behind procedural justice could be described as a banquet, the messianic banquet at the end of time. Banquets are successful and enjoyable when the plans and furnishings have been settled, when the guests have access to good food, wine, and conversation, and when predetermined arrangements run smoothly. Behind the glow of success, however, linger other procedural questions like: Who received an invitation? What were the criteria for inclusion? Who decided where each person would sit?[17] The messianic banquet in the Scriptures further suggests that banquet tables are places of encounter with Divinity where there is room enough for all. The God whom we encounter at the messianic banquet is a God of Abundance who provides a feast of rich food and well-aged wines (Isa 25:6), who serves the best wine last (John 2:10), and who provides so much bread that twelve baskets are filled with leftovers (John 6:13).

Since vision has ethical implications, procedural justice is accountable to the human community characterized by access to required resources and mutual, participatory, and inclusive relationships, that is, the messianic banquet at the end of time. Some of these ethical mandates for procedural justice include the establishment of processes for decision-making, policy formation, and legislation which maximize broad-based inclusion and varying kinds of participation. In addition, processes need to intentionally seek out the insights and contributions of those affected by the corresponding decisions, policies, or laws. In order to ensure equitable access to the formation and practices of processes, laws, and decisions, the least advantaged in the social organization need to be intentionally included and recognized. Furthermore, attention to the voice of the least advantaged requires processes to restrain the collusion of influence peddling between the economic, political, religious, and social systems. For example, urban development has a past record of establishing a coalition of business leaders, developers, lending institutions, and politicians. This coalition has

---

[17] In this regard the parable of the guests at the wedding feast in Luke 14 is instructive.

chosen and approved sites and plans without publicizing information or seeking input from citizens and small business in the area so as to avoid grass roots influence in the process itself.

Procedural justice urges the enactment of approaches to resolve conflict in both the formation and practice of processes. This understanding of procedural justice further indicates practices which promote equity, participation, collaboration, and attention to the least advantaged. The consistent and equitable practice of processes in all social organizations is necessary for procedural justice. For example, differences between students in classroom settings necessitate that evaluation practices and learning procedures be adjusted so that the differently advantaged are able to participate in an equitable fashion.

Equitable treatment also calls for legislative and institutional protection of difference and prohibition of discrimination, because equal access legislation can favor those in positions of influence and can further marginate other persons whose influence is disadvantaged. Procedural justice concerns itself with questions about how resources are distributed and how the equitable contribution of persons to life in common can be fostered. For example, how do procedures foster the equitable availability of education? How can the election process ensure equitable representation from the races, classes, and genders which comprise the nation and state?

Fifth, concrete, particular actions realize justice. This aspect of justice highlights just activities as concrete instances which both cause justice to break into the world and express justice. Justice as effective action,[18] then, stresses action in the context of a sacramental worldview. As has been noted previously, this sacramental worldview is an extension of the incarnation of God in Jesus of Nazareth as well as an embodiment of the image and likeness of God in human persons. The body of Christ animated by the Indwelling Spirit for mission provides a vision behind justice as effective action. This body of Christ continues and in the Spirit accomplishes the creating, saving, and transforming action of God in the world.

Justice as effective action concentrates on the concrete, specific practices of everyday living. The actual embodiment of justice in action takes on an importance beyond mere good intentions, for the practices must actually bring about justice. For example, the story is told about some farmers from the United States who toured agricultural regions

---

[18] This approach to justice has its roots in Thomas Aquinas' definition of justice, namely the "what's right." Recall that for Thomas, the intention to do justice did not make something justice, but the actual "what's right" in the relationship of equity. Liberation theology's understandings of justice also emphasize concrete just action.

of Mexico. The malnourishment of rural children inspired the farmers to donate some cattle to the farmers in the region, so that their children would have an additional source of protein. Five years later, the children were more malnourished than before because the cattle were being fed with the corn which the families previously used for corn tortillas. While the farmers had good intentions, their action did not effect the just access to nourishing food which they intended.

Justice as a universal becomes accessible in particular activities. Concrete just activities transmit meaning which transcends the particular activity.[19] This kind of sacramental unity between symbol and symbolized is countercultural in its celebration of the unity of materiality and non-materiality. The ordinary and daily activities on behalf of justice become a privileged place of encounter with God who acts justly as well as the continuing incarnation of the God who intervened on behalf of the marginated, called the oppressor to conversion, and gave a new Spirit to dry bones. These same ordinary and daily activities on behalf of justice also effect or actually bring justice into existence in specific social locations. Justice as action then responds to historical situations and communities in order to effect or embody justice for this time and place. For instance, while writing this book the authors kept a daily log of just and unjust experiences which they encountered in the ordinary unfolding of living. This focused attention caused them to practice justice more regularly and to develop the necessary skills to be effective.

Within the context of a sacramental worldview, the vision of the body of Christ animated by the Indwelling Spirit for mission provides some ethical implications of justice as action. Justice as action requires the doing of justice.[20] Consequently, the purpose for study groups, university courses, Catholic Social Teachings, discussions, plans, and programs is the practice of justice. Similarly, while practices of justice occasion concepts and theories about justice, priority is given to effective just action. The practices of justice can involve resistance to injustice or building justice. Effective action requires the development of skills, competencies, and proficiencies. For example, citizens who wish to influence neighborhood development plans need skills in social analysis, competencies in organizing community hearings, and proficiencies in articulating common concerns and alternatives. Only then will their efforts become effective action on behalf of justice.

---

[19] Walzer, *Spheres of Justice*, xiv.

[20] Cf. Mic 6:8, "What does the LORD require of you / but to do justice, and to love kindness, / and to walk humbly with your God?"

Sixth, unjust structures, relationships, resource availability, practices, and processes are transformed into a future for humanity, into a new creation. Transformative justice stresses two points. First, existing injustice, whether in structures, relationships, practices, processes, or in access to resources, must be transformed into justice. Second, the transformation process does not merely repeat or remake the past embodiments, which may well have been just at some point or place. Transformative justice is linked to the just practices of God, namely, intervention on behalf of those who are marginated, a call to conversion directed to the oppressor, and a new beginning, that is, a new heaven and a new earth. As persons who digested and spoke the word of God, the prophets carried on God's transforming action on behalf of justice. Furthermore, they embodied a self-understanding as agents accountable to the word of God and the new creation in their own historical situation, shaped by political, economic, and religious systems.

The awareness of injustice is certainly a beginning point of action on behalf of justice.[21] The practitioners of justice who were surveyed frequently referred to the experience of "something being wrong with the picture" as a source of their motivation to work for justice. Young adult and adult immersion experiences typically build in exposure to persons whose lives are riddled with injustice. Unjust economic structures were the occasion for the majority of the documents known as Catholic Social Teachings. Rawls approached his theory of justice from the vantage point of veiled ignorance with regard to one's social advantage in an effort to minimize the injustice he saw in the existing social order.

Transformative justice expects that the process of moving from injustice in structures, relationships, resource availability, procedures, and practices entails the creation of something new. This something new results from a complex interaction between the Creating Spirit, specific injustices in their historical and social locations, and the competencies or resistances of persons in their communities.[22] Consequently, this new creation cannot be a repeat of the past. For example, when Lori moved to Florida, she took up the ministry of building community among persons who were not included among the socially advantaged. This ministry of building community underwent transformations over time based on current needs, available resources, and personal gifts. First, a monthly talent show filled the storefront. Then, a folk dance group, followed by a swing dance group brought people together. Then a

---

[21] Karen Lebacqz, *Justice in an Unjust World* (Minneapolis: Augsburg Publishing House, 1987) 112, appears to hold that injustice is the beginning point for justice.

[22] The social location of just and inclusive communities cannot be identified with Walzer's separate spheres of justice (see above, 135–9).

speakers' bureau of persons with AIDS provided information and inspiration to community and school groups. Then she worked with foster parents to design their own support group and in-service for certification. Another new creation is probably lurking in the wings. The shift in the Christian scriptural traditions from the first creation in a garden to the final re-creation of the city of God at the end of time illustrates the impossibility of merely repeating past just arrangements in the future.

Justice as transformation into the city of God entails some ethical implications. Because the awareness of injustice is a beginning point for transformative justice, sustained contact with persons who have been unjustly treated provides a necessary motivation and a foundation for efforts to plant a new creation. Awareness of injustice can also fuel the desire to resist injustice. Transformative justice also requires the development of creative competencies and intuitive directions. Practitioners of transformative justice also need to develop an openness to surprise and difference. Too often the base tendency is to associate with those persons and read those articles which confirm already held positions. In addition, justice as transformation requires the development of skills in social analysis, of capacities for complex thinking and abilities to collaborate with diverse interest groups. For example, a project called "Common Ground" brought together persons who differed on the issue of abortion. Together they learned to clear away misunderstanding so that they could legitimately and honestly disagree.

Seventh, human persons are accountable for and responsible agents of a just and inclusive community. In our approach to justice as participation in the human community, justice as accountable agency stresses personal contribution to and responsibility for the just and inclusive community. As such, it takes up the concerns traditionally embraced by contributive justice. As agents, human persons have potential for self-consciousness and self-reflection. Yet, and probably more significant, the essential relationality of human persons interweaves personal responsibility with the formation of a just and inclusive human community.[23] Thus, human persons are accountable for nurturing the vision and substance of justice as well as those structures and processes which foster the possibility of a just and inclusive community.

Finally, one cannot speak of justice as accountable agency without addressing sin in the context of just practices. God's covenant relationship with Israel required both divine and human accountability to justice. God's intervention on behalf of the oppressed and judgment of the oppressor were expressions of accountability to the covenant. Similarly

[23] Cf. Ivan Boszormenyi-Nagy, *Invisible Loyalties: Reciprocity in Intergenerational Family Therapy* (New York: Brunner/Mazel, 1984).

the prophets called the kings and the people of Israel to do justice in accountability to the covenant. The image of final judgment in the Christian traditions points to an ultimate accountability, which Matthew 25 presents as the collective provision for basic human needs.

Because relationality is constitutive of authentic human living, justice as accountable agency cannot be separated from the establishment of a just and inclusive community. Justice thus demands a deliberate engagement in those decisions which structure institutions, policies, and systems for participation, inclusion, equitable treatment, and human thriving. It includes the personal accountability for the creation of an environment in which domination, violence, discrimination, and irresponsibility are unimaginable. For example, persons and communities must take up the struggle both to pass legislation that prohibits violence and to resist social expectations that promote violence as a response to conflict, hostility, or anger.

Another dimension of such engagement includes the assessment of that which currently hinders the establishment of a just and inclusive community. Such an assessment can uncover personal complicity in the marginalization or oppression of other persons. In some instances Christians and the institutional Church benefit from structures of racism, classism, and sexism or are socialized into accepting what is as what must be. For example, churches and Christians regularly employ women, persons who are poor, and ethnic or racial minorities for entry level positions with minimal or no benefits. The institution benefits from social structures, attitudes, and policies which link certain races, classes, and genders with certain types of work. This benefit and socialization blinds Christians to their complicity in supporting these unjust structures. Sometimes these employment decisions are understood as charitable help.

Accountable agency entails the embrace of calls to conversion. Conversion is mediated by negative contrast experiences or by participation in efforts to transform unjust exploitation into just practices. For example, an experience of gender discrimination can lead to a life committed to ending all discrimination. The call to conversion is also mediated by a longing for justice or by texts of the Scriptures and Catholic Social Teachings. In the scriptural presentation of justice, God's judgment called the oppressor to conversion. When the oppressor failed to respond with conversion, judgment became condemnation.

Thus, justice as accountable agency must include attention to sin, both as the practice of injustice and the embrace of powerlessness in the face of injustice. The concept of sin includes an awareness that accountable agents choose to practice exploitation, to deny humanness to some persons, to hoard resources, to structure the social playing field in their favor, to exclude different voices from influence, to embrace justice in the abstract, or to refuse involvement in the transformation of injustice. Some justice practitioners mismanage food pantries to their own advantage. Some ministers of justice ignore the voices of persons whose style and strategy differ from their own. Some Christians hate persons of other religious traditions or races. Some Christians deny the dignity and equality of the aged and children and sinners. Some Christians refuse to use their gifts and time to develop just employment opportunities.

Ten Comparative Points

By way of summary, the development of this approach to justice as participation is analyzed according to the ten comparative points introduced in Chapter 5.

Basis of the claim: The basis of the claim of justice as participation rests in the conviction that by virtue of their creation, all are members of the human community. Because the Christian faith tradition confirms that all persons are created by God and that all are invited and welcomed into intimate and reciprocal relationships with the Divine Persons, participation in the human community is a justifiable claim on social organizations and personal practices.

Inherent absolutes: The above claim to justice as participation in the human community assumes the following: First, God is an engaged and relational God, who graciously invites communities to participate in God's own life and mission of justice (intervention, judgment/call to conversion, and new creation). Second, human community expresses the constitutive relationality which characterizes human persons. Third, this approach to justice assumes a sacramental worldview. Fourth, a just and inclusive community is a community in which all persons count, contribute, and participate in building a future for humanity. Fifth, numerous visions in the Scriptures and in human longing for a just world articulate these general contours and their implications for just practices in this time and place.

Anthropology: Justice as participation understands that human persons are created in the image and likeness of God and constituted in relationality. They are embodied, socially located, and accountable agents who are fundamentally equal in their originality.

Who decides what justice is? Since justice as participation is theologically rooted in God's gift of covenant and participation in God's own life, the determination and discernment of just practices is dialogical.

In community and in the Spirit, the members of the human community decide which practices embody the just and inclusive community of God. Furthermore, the above aspects of justice recognize the complex interaction necessary for authentic public participation in the political, religious, economic, and social spheres. This approach to justice requires attention to structures and procedures so that the inclusion and participation of all persons is facilitated. Given the historical and social location of human communities, consistent and deliberate regard to the least advantaged is highlighted.

Goal of justice: The goal of justice as participation is the building of a just and inclusive community which embodies the endtimes vision of the city of God in specific times and places.

Mediating principles: The mediating principles which provide concrete steps on the way to the embodiment of justice as participation in the human community are spelled out in a subsequent section of this chapter. They emerge from the seven aspects of justice as described in the section above.

Attention to structures of justice: Structural and procedural justice are two of the seven aspects of justice. This central role that structures have for justice emerges from an awareness of the historically and socially constructed nature of a just and inclusive human community.

The relationship between specific actions and justice: Concrete just action effects the justice which it signifies. Thus the relationship between specific actions and justice is a sacramental relationship. Justice is only known and embodied in particular and concrete just practices.

Method: This approach to justice as participation begins in the experience of the concrete struggle to do justice as Chapters 1 and 2 illustrated. The wisdom gleaned from those engaged in this struggle enters into dialogue with the wisdom of the human faith communities over time expressed in the Scriptures, Catholic Social Teachings, and other classic contemporary articulations of justice. The dialogue is transformed into just practice and not merely new insights or feelings. This approach to justice recognizes and celebrates the context of its endeavor. That is, the communities engaged in this method are particular communities with specific understandings of God, human persons, and sacramentality, with their vision of a better world and its ethical requirements of justice. An image of this method resembles a feedback loop in interaction with its social location: the circular progression of experience, the human and Christian traditions, for action influencing and influenced by specific human communities.

Self-critical mechanisms: This approach has a number of built-in mechanisms for self-criticism. The key place given to incarnation and sacramentality as well as the inclusion of a normativity of the future point to an awareness of future and divine in-breaking which challenge and change understandings of justice as participation. Similarly the place given to continuous conversion, dialogue, and concrete injustices requires self-critical mechanisms.

VALUES AND JUSTICE AS PARTICIPATION

The understanding of justice as participation in the human community emphasizes some values which are specifically connected to the seven aspects clarified earlier in this chapter. A value is an intangible good that has worth in and of itself and which can only be encountered in concrete, embodied instances. General ethical norms protect and encourage values. For example, the value of human life is protected by a general norm such as "respect life." Or the value of solidarity is encouraged by a general norm such as "build community." The following paragraphs offer an initial and partial listing of some values that are linked to each of the aspects of justice as participation in the human community.

Relational justice accentuates the values of inclusion, mutuality, reciprocity, solidarity, equality, friendship, and preferential option for the poor. Justice as access to resources includes the values of stewardship, embodied life, present human thriving, future human flourishing, and fairness in distribution of resources. Both structural justice and procedural justice underscore the values of equity in processes as well as in institutions, policies, or actions. Structural justice also points to organization, regularity, and coordination as values, while procedural justice indicates collaboration and cooperation as values.

Justice as effective action accents concrete embodiment, sacramentality, difference, development, wisdom, and acquisition of competencies for effective action as values. Transformative justice suggests values such as openness to change, hope, healing, liberation, struggle, resistance, and resiliency. Justice as accountable agency highlights the values of self-reflection, knowledge, freedom, meaning, dignity, respect, initiative, conversion, and integrity. At times, these values will conflict with one another in efforts to determine a specific just practice appropriate to the situation. Still, attention to values can provide a way to move the description of justice as participation into concrete practices of justice.

MEDIATING PRINCIPLES AND JUSTICE AS PARTICIPATION

Mediating principles or middle axioms provide another way of moving the description of justice as participation to those concrete practices which build up a just and inclusive community. As described earlier in this chapter, mediating principles are visible and tangible sites between the vision of the city of God and action plans detailing how a group will embody the just and inclusive community. As with values, this section will suggest several mediating principles for each of the aspects of justice as participation.

A just and inclusive community is on the way toward embodying relational justice characteristic of the city of God when:

- middle-class persons include persons of other races, classes, religious traditions, and nations among their friends;

- personal, work, neighborhood, and church relationships are characterized by mutuality, reciprocity, and equality;

- intentional communities who share resources and living arrangements in common thrive within the larger community;

- the least advantaged in a community contribute their time and talent as well as participate in decision-making;

- persons embrace interdependence and solidarity as preferable to independence and self-reliance.

A just and inclusive community is on the way toward embodying justice as access to resources characteristic of the city of God when:

- all persons have equitable access to basic levels of education, health care, food, clothing, and shelter;

- wages and salaries provide equitable access to the fulfillment of basic human needs;

- stewardship of resources is practiced in simple living, food cooperatives, clothing exchanges, and investments;

- persons network their social resources to multiply influence and power;

- attention is given to the development of gifts, talents, and resources so that persons can participate in and contribute to building up a just, inclusive community.

A just and inclusive community is on the way toward embodying structural justice characteristic of the city of God when:

- social structures actually promote and support a just and inclusive common life;

- laws and social attitudes do not tolerate the exploitation of persons from any race, class, gender, ethnic origin, or religious tradition;

- the boards of religious, social, and economic entities are mandated to reflect the diversity of the communities in which they are situated;

- collaborative and participative social arrangements replace hierarchical social arrangements;

- the social organization protects the advocacy for and voice of the least advantaged.

A just and inclusive community is on the way toward embodying procedural justice characteristic of the city of God when:

- all participate in the formation of social policies and institutions;

- all have consistent and equitable access to influence, information, and protection under the law;

- public discourse fosters dialogue and discourages polarization between positions;

- all have access to the development of skills in conflict resolution, negotiation, literacy, anti-racism training, and collaboration;

- processes for negotiating competing claims are practiced.

A just and inclusive community is on the way toward embodying justice as effective action characteristic of the city of God when:

- citizens have access to the development of skills in social analysis, community organizing, legislative lobbying, mediation, building community, and resistance;

- discussions and good intentions give way to practices and actions which embody justice;

- practitioners of justice can articulate the vision and draw on the arts to inform and inspire persons to just practices;

- attention is focused on righting the immediate injustice and changing the structures which allow the injustice to persist;

- practitioners of justice network with regional, national, and international groups.

A just and inclusive community is on the way toward embodying transformative justice characteristic of the city of God when:

- laws and institutions are viewed as social constructions which can and must be changed through legislation, non-compliance, and non-reception;

- hope and abundance shape idealism, intensity, and commitment to transformative action;

- social and ecclesial communities practice resistance to unjust practices and structures;

- middle-class Christians embrace the power linked to their location at the intersection or margins of Church and society (the challenge of privilege is to use it to bring about change);

- conversion is welcomed as a tool for transformation of unjust practices (personally and structurally);

- ending unjust practices is linked with structural change.

A just and inclusive community is on the way toward embodying justice as accountable agency characteristic of the city of God when:

- middle-class Christians believe that they are able to be agents of just practices and they initiate such practices;

- Christians take it upon themselves to learn the skills necessary for effective and transformative action on behalf of justice;

- personal agency includes accountability for the creation of conditions of possibility for a just and inclusive community;

- the accountable agent finds ways to respect and empower the agency of others;

- the agent of just practices collaborates with others and the Spirit of transformation, rather than acting alone.

CONCLUSION

This chapter has set forth our understanding of justice as participation both as a local vision and as a description developed in seven dimensions. An adequate understanding of justice as participation recognizes an inherently relational dimension. Structural and procedural dimensions are essential. Furthermore, justice as participation is concerned with access to resources. For justice as participation to become a concrete reality, effective action and action which transforms unjust deeds and structures into just behavior and patterns are necessary.

Finally, justice as participation requires agents who are accountable and responsible to the human community. We also saw that justice as participation could be linked to specific values and spelled out in mediating principles. We will now test whether this understanding of justice can provide a viable response to the dilemmas with which we began this study.

8

The Practices of Justice

The case studies presented in Chapter 1 surfaced some dilemmas which white, middle-class Christians encounter when they try to practice justice in their lives. We return to these cases from the perspective of the approach to justice set forth in the Chapters 6 and 7. The understanding of justice as participation in the human community in its sevenfold aspects, consequent values, and mediating principles suggest contours for just practices in the specific situations. In other words, the situations provide some limited test cases for the implementation of this approach to justice. Two caveats are in order. First, the small number of situations which are treated in this chapter invites other practitioners of justice to explore the implementation of this approach to justice in other situations. Second, the social location of the authors as well as those with whom and among whom we write challenges practitioners and theoreticians of justice in other social locations to nuance and expand this understanding and implementation of justice.

CASE STUDY: A CHANCE ENCOUNTER

As they came out of a board meeting for a neighborhood food pantry, Mary and Julie met a couple walking in the cold March night. The couple knew Julie from the food pantry and asked if they could stay overnight in the pantry because they had been locked out of their apartment until they paid the rent and it was too cold to sleep outside. Insurance regulations prohibited overnight guests in the pantry, so Mary and Julie tried to find a place in an area shelter. There weren't any beds left in one. Another didn't take people after nine P.M. The couple had been in a third when they were locked out the last time and couldn't return for two months. Another shelter only took women and children. Both Mary and Julie considered inviting them home with them, but neither had talked to the people they lived with about such a possibility and didn't feel they could make such a decision individually. By this time the couple decided to ride the subway all night to stay warm, leaving Mary and Julie engulfed in ambiguity, guilt, and self-blame for their individual failures in responding to the gospel call of justice.

Such ambiguity, guilt, and self-blame reflects a kind of religious socialization largely coherent with the context set forth in Chapter 6. Familiarity with an engaged and relational God provides a worldview within which Mary and Julie are invited or even expected to intervene on behalf of persons unjustly disadvantaged. An understanding of persons as social and embodied provides a context within which Mary and Julie evaluated absence of shelter on a cold March night as wrong. The sense of the ways things ought to be (vision) finds something wrong with the picture of a couple locked out of their apartment because they didn't pay the rent. A sacramental worldview is reflected in the identification of these neighbors with God. On some level, then, Mary and Julie are immersed in a context which supports an approach to justice as participation in the human community. The disjuncture between this context and the inability to implement specific practices of justice responsive to the couple's homelessness led to feelings of guilt, ambiguity, and self-blame. Several aspects of justice as participation in the human community, however, suggest a path out of the dilemma.

A network of relationships beyond shared human community brought Mary, Julie, and the couple together. Julie had a working relationship with them from the food pantry. When this concrete relationship is added to her position as a social service provider and to their positions on the food pantry board, Mary and Julie become part of the network of relationships to which the couple legitimately turn in a situation of having been left out in the cold. Relational justice, however, does not consider face to face relationships as the sole provider of just practices. Even though Mary and Julie are primary links in this network of relationships, they do not bear sole responsibility for sheltering the couple.

This encounter raises two foundational questions of justice: What does a just and inclusive community look like with regard to shelter? How does a just and inclusive community organize itself so that either temporary homelessness does not happen or it can be resolved effectively if it does happen? With regard to the first question, a just and inclusive community does not necessarily entail the abandonment of the social structures of owning and renting. Rather, a just and inclusive community envisions viable access to shelter through a variety of structures, such as renting, owning, or cooperatives as a dimension of difference in authentic human community. The just and inclusive community, however, implements ways to restrain abuse and exploitation by renters and owners alike. Consequently it would support policies around affordability, property damage, and protection for life and livelihood.

The organization of a just and inclusive community with regard to issues of homelessness entails effective structures and procedures. Effective policies and procedures to end temporary homelessness include programs to develop skills in property stewardship, renters' associations, mediation processes, and legislation. As an extension of food pantry services, structural justice challenges Mary and Julie to create a mentoring process to develop skills in stewardship of property or job related skills. Justice as effective action urges Mary and Julie to collaborate with a local renters' association to leverage for just practices with regard to excessive rent, substandard housing, and temporary eviction. Procedural justice invites Mary and Julie to develop a structure for the mediation of longer-term solutions in housing conflicts, which would bring together a renter, an owner, and a social services provider with a mediator. In an effort to prevent similar situations from occurring, structural justice nudges Mary and Julie to learn about existing legislation which protects owners or renters and then join with others to influence new legislation which prohibits temporary eviction without mediation.

As Mary and Julie engage these issues, procedural justice requires the active involvement of persons who have experienced or resorted to temporary eviction. These policies and procedures aimed at transforming unjust practices into a more just and inclusive community require the participation of other groups, such as the food pantry board, neighborhood organizations, and the parish community.

Even if all of the above policies and procedures were implemented, temporary homelessness could still occur. Consequently Mary and Julie need to explore emergency backup shelters for situations to which existing shelters cannot respond. Possible emergency shelter options include a kind of sanctuary for homeless neighbors located or constructed on parish property, or the establishment of a network of homes in the neighborhood, including Mary and Julie's homes, to provide emergency shelter in their own homes under agreed upon circumstances (cf. shelter networks for survivors of domestic violence).

The resolution of temporary eviction requires access to resources which protect human bodies from the cold, which provide connection to other persons, and which promote a sense of home in the face of homelessness. Mary and Julie had information concerning various area shelters, which addressed the need of bodily protection. Their efforts to help the couple who had been evicted did provide some kind of human face to walk with them a while. However, a backup shelter in the local parish or neighborhood could afford access to a broader network of relationships for the couple as well as Mary and Julie. Within this local network the possibility of a sense of belonging in the face of eviction could more likely be realized.

Justice as accountable agency does challenge Julie, Mary, and the couple to assess and focus on their contribution to building the city of God. In the short-term, the couple contributed their own resourcefulness to find shelter on public transportation. In the short-term, Mary and Julie's efforts were thwarted by the interface of this immediate situation with larger social structures, namely, insurance regulations, food pantry inspection policies, and the Church as an institution. In this specific situation, Mary and Julie were more willing to open their homes to the homeless couple than to risk violating the laws and regulations of the larger social structures. This approach gives social structures and systems exorbitant power. Justice as accountable agency challenges persons to deliberately weigh basic needs of real persons against systemic requirements.

Accountable agency also involves assessment and implementation of personal contributions to long-term resolution of justice dilemmas. The couple who was homeless could maximize their contribution to a just and inclusive community by involvement in grass roots groups working for tenants' rights or by availing themselves of assistance in living and job skills development. Mary and Julie could maximize their contribution by developing skills required for effective action on behalf of justice and by involvement in structural change, including those described in the preceding paragraphs.

Although the focus of this situation is emergency shelter resulting from temporary eviction, the approach to justice employed in this book provides some contours for responding to related issues of homelessness. This case study highlights the following values as integral to the practice of justice in issues of homelessness and housing: participation, home and shelter, nonviolent conflict resolution, personal and institutional accountability, stewardship, solidarity, preferential option for the least advantaged, and human dignity.

The following mediating principles present markers which indicate progress toward a just and inclusive community. A community is becoming a just and inclusive community with regard to homelessness when:

- homelessness occurs infrequently and existing structures actually resolve the situation;

- mediation processes are the normative approach to housing conflicts;

- immediate housing needs of persons are weighed against institutional regulations and structural mandates;

- local churches provide sanctuary for the homeless traveler and neighbor;

- the voiceless persons who have been homeless and owners of rental property share voice and influence for proposed legislation;

- owners and renters alike resist exploitation of persons and embrace stewardship of property.

CASE STUDY: ENCOUNTERING POWERLESSNESS

Holy Family is a suburban parish comprised primarily of blue-collar and professional families with a parish staff of six ministers providing a wide range of social, educational, and religious opportunities. A group of interested parish volunteers makes up the social justice committee. The members stay involved as long as they want. Leadership roles are determined by consensus and time availability. The committee chair is not part of the finance committee or of any decision-making body of the parish. In the past year the committee has organized and sponsored some highly successful projects including a Christmas giving tree for an inner city sister parish, a Thanksgiving dinner for the needy and lonely in the neighborhood, holiday food baskets, and a children's winter coat drive. However, a lenten speaker series on "Justice in the Scriptures and Catholic Social Teachings" averaged eight persons an evening, most of whom were committee members. Publicity about a "Justice in the Marketplace" ministry formation program brought one inquiry. A subsequent social justice committee meeting surfaced frustrations and concerns about the viability of the committee, its mission, and its place in Holy Family Parish.

Since the Spirit makes herself known in the longings and hopes of believers, the frustrations and concerns voiced in the committee meeting most likely point to a communal vision of a better world or the city of God. In their current context the social justice committee has the time and leisure to move behind their frustrations and longings to articulate their vision of the just and inclusive community at Holy Family Parish. An articulation of this vision provides the committee with directions in determining future activities, a standard against which to evaluate these efforts, and a framework within which to examine their identity and role in Holy Family Parish. In other words, how ought a social justice committee to understand itself and function in a just and inclusive community?

The articulated vision of the social justice committee may well assume a theology and an anthropology which departs from the theology and anthropology of at least some members of the larger parish. For example, committee leadership in the areas of meeting basic human needs as well as of promoting education and formation for just practices requires a social anthropology. A holiday donation mentality more typically emerges from an individualistic anthropology which stresses voluntary choice and control in determining resource distribution (who gives what, who gets what, and according to which criteria). The interest and leadership taken by the committee, as well as their current frustration, imply beliefs about a God who is identified with the neighbor, who somehow keeps alive in their hearts the dream of a better world, and who invites their participation in continuing creation, liberation, and transformation. In contrast, a holiday donation mentality might imply an understanding of God as a benevolent superior who extends compassion to poor and inferior wretches through holiday generosity.

The social justice committee's place in this context of contrasting theologies and anthropologies must be linked to its self-understanding. Within a Christian sacramental worldview, the social justice committee is sacramental, that is, the committee expresses and effects the eschatological city of God. Through the social justice committee, Holy Family Parish expresses and becomes more of what it is already: a just and inclusive community embodying the city of God in this particular time and place. Such a self-understanding contradicts two prevalent views, namely, the role of justice practitioners as optional and as private. In contrast, a sacramental self-understanding locates just practices at the heart of the Church's mission. In addition, as an agent entrusted by the parish, the function of the social justice committee becomes the expression and actualization of the justice mission of the whole parish. In other words, this committee becomes leaven of transformation. As one concrete expression of this accountable agency, the committee fashions ways to include or stress images of an engaged, relational God and a social anthropology in public parish life. This can facilitate the experience of justice as integral in parish life and mission.

The description of justice in Chapter 7 recommends other functions for the social justice committee in Holy Family Parish. Since the parish has already incorporated some efforts to provide for basic human needs, the aspect of justice as access to resources could be expanded to include other resources. For example, the social justice committee may well devise programs for mothers mentoring mothers, or for making parish facilities or personnel (e.g., a parish nurse) available, or for developing job skills (e.g., computer classes), or for providing education (e.g., scholarships and tutoring), or for financing start-up businesses (e.g., church-sponsored entrepreneurial efforts). This expanded role links personal and social resources with people who have limited access to them. At times the social justice committee can be a resource for persons and groups in the parish who seek to shift their understanding of justice from an exercise in voluntary sharing to the creation of structures of self-sufficiency.

Because inclusion in the human community is the most important resource, justice as relationality challenges the committee to find ways for the Holy Family parishioners to enter into friendships with persons who are poor or oppressed. Mentoring, big sister or foster grandparent programs, cultural heritage programs, potlucks, and shared festivals could provide opportunities for friendship to unfold. Both justice as relationality and as access to resources urge the social justice committee to include persons who are least advantaged as consultants, organizational developers, and evaluators.

Furthermore, given its self-understanding, the social justice committee must address its marginal position within the parish structures. In order to express and effect the just and inclusive community, the social justice committee—as an agent of just practices accountable to Holy Family Parish—must have a voice and influence in parish decisions and practices. Voice and influence cannot be equated with the only voice or influence; however, influence with regard to financial choices, voice in liturgical rituals, and a place in the accountability structures integrate justice into the lifeblood of the parish. Such integration runs the risk of either domesticating the voice of justice or actually transforming the parish into a just and inclusive community.

Voice, influence, and a place in the structures assume the ability to act effectively, that is, justice as effective action requires the development of skills. Skills in social analysis, in listening to the least advantaged, and in identifying key players move speech into a credible voice. Skills in organizing communities as well as knowing and articulating the Christian traditions turn insight into influence. Skills in resisting both the depreciation of perspective and the co-option of an alternative view into a mainstream position preserve the possibility of conversion.

The development of such skills transforms a certain well-meaning naiveté into justice as effective action.

Both the structural inclusion and development of skills rely on an embrace of the marginality which currently characterizes the social justice committee at Holy Family Parish. The embrace of marginality enables the social justice committee to maintain a critical distance which keeps alive justice as transformation. What does embracing marginality mean? To embrace marginality means an acceptance and a home in two worlds. The bilingual practitioner of justice can speak the language of persons who are working poor and of parishioners who are wealthy power brokers. They walk easily on the sidewalks of the institutional parish and in the alleys of those ignored by all institutions.

To embrace marginality, the social justice committee must let go of any plans to move into a dominant position in parish structures. That is, the embrace of marginality requires conversion, a shift in direction from setting one's sights on the power at the center to embracing a different power at the edges. The embrace of marginality resists co-option in favor of the power of creative tension which comes from living in two worlds. If the social justice committee would lose contact with the least advantaged, any credibility as their advocate would be lost. The tasks which flow from an embrace of marginality involve unleashing the powers discovered at the margins. From their place at the margins, the social justice committee offers a different perspective. They speak a word which will rouse the imagination. They advocate for those persons whose voice is absent. They hold up the vision of the city of God persistently and consistently. They dare to ask the irreverent question, how things could be done differently.

Although this scenario describes how one specific social justice committee understands itself and its role in a suburban parish, some values and mediating principles emerge which could be beneficial in related situations. The values of inclusion, participation, friendship, preferential option for the least advantaged, sharing resources, power, influence, and resistance are highlighted. The following mediating principles present guidelines for effective parish-based social justice committees. A local church is becoming a just and inclusive community when:

- the social justice committee has voice and influence in the financial and decision-making bodies of the parish;

- the parish staff includes a salaried person whose job expertise and passion include social justice ministry;

- parishioners have friends among a diversity of social classes, races, and ethnicities;

- the parish and parishioners share material, social, personal, and institutional resources with persons and parishes who are among the least advantaged;

- the social justice committee understands itself as a sacrament of God's justice and the voice of the least advantaged.

CASE STUDY: HABITS OF THE HEARTH

After some ten years of friendship and professional colleagueship, Sarah and Adam committed themselves to each other in a mutual and egalitarian marriage. Sarah and Adam had become friends while working on their doctorates in English and after finishing found good positions in neighboring universities. Because their research interests overlapped, sometimes they collaborated on research and writing projects. They quickly learned that their personal commitments to a just love in their marital relationship was not enough. Even though Sarah and Adam decided to keep their birth names, marriage congratulation cards and mail came addressed to Mr. and Mrs. Adam Smith. Even Sarah's medical records ended up filed under Adam's name. Whether through socialization, practice, or personality, Sarah was an excellent cook and had an artistic sense for beauty in the home. Whether through socialization, practice, or personality, Adam's energies focused on his work. Consequently, Sarah found herself volunteering to cook when it was Adam's turn because he had a pressing deadline at work; Adam found this a precious expression of Sarah's love, to which he responded with gifts and gratitude. Casual conversation with colleagues reflected similar patterns in those relationships. Sarah's colleagues took it for granted that she would go home early to take care of household affairs. Adam's colleagues expected that his wife would be the affirming presence as he worked through the emotions of professional politics and workload. Work and social contacts assumed that Adam's activities would take precedence in conflicts of date and time. Sarah was surprised when professional colleagues construed their professional collaboration as her secretarial and research assistance for Adam's ideas. Adam and Sarah's commitments to just marital love required constant vigilance and careful listening to one another's experiences in their relationship. Without these efforts, justice risked subversion by their own socialization and habits, as well as by socially expected patterns of domination, gender role expectations, and institutional structures.

Many justice theoreticians would not include one-to-one relationships in the realm of justice, but would situate them in the realm of love. The above shows that love is not enough in one-to-one relationships, since the social dimension of the human person implies that we as individuals and in our one-to-one relationships participate in and therefore are influenced by the structures and patterns of the social realm. We are convinced that withdrawal from the world into a private safe haven will not open the door to justice, but rather whole-hearted involvement in and transformation of the "hostile world."

In our story, Sarah and Adam have a clear vision and a strong determination to make their marriage relationship just in the sense of mutual and egalitarian. But they are continuously faced with the fact that the world around them opposes or at least subtly erodes their desired way of living. In the following discussion we therefore want to look for ways that could help Sarah and Adam resist and counteract the influences from unjust structures that undermine their commitment. We are thus dealing with how justice can be lived in face-to-face relationships within a social environment which does not support justice.

The commitment to a just marriage relationship is based on an egalitarian anthropology. The bottom line of their vision is the conviction that God created woman and man with equal dignity. They know and accept that as man and woman they are different, but they resist construing these differences into a hierarchy. Rather, they have committed themselves to deal with their differences in egalitarian ways. From the perspective of social and egalitarian anthropology, Sarah and Adam allow their differences to become constitutive for their unity as a couple instead of abusing difference to reinforce individual independence and superiority.

To their great surprise, Adam and Sarah's own spontaneous reactions are shaped by structures and patterns of a hierarchical and individualist anthropology. Consequently the practice of their own vision necessitates conscious resistance against influences from the world around and in them. This realization fosters an awareness that marriage and friendship relationships are lived in a social context and are influenced by patterns and structures of the society we live in. Both the persons entering into a relationship and the relationship as such participate in social life which cannot be reduced to a private relationship. Married couples and committed friends need support from communities if they are to sustain a countercultural vision in the midst of indifference, ignorance, and opposition. Ideally they could find such support in a Christian community where preaching centers on God as Trinity. The proclamation of God as a threefold unity of persons who are constituted by difference and related to each other in egalitarian communion can provide a firm basis for all those who struggle to maintain their vision against demotivating and paralyzing forces.

The experience of Christian community will also help couples realize that a prevailing nuclear family model sets them up as a couple against the rest of the world. It predisposes their minds to look for solutions to their problems in their own one-to-one relationship and so deprives them of the support they need. In situations like that of Sarah and Adam, the relational dimension of justice is at stake. This dimension invites couples to move beyond the "we against the world" divide. They must realize that living out their vision of a mutual, reciprocal, and egalitarian community cannot be sustained solely by their own good intentions and their individual decision. Community support might be sought in a marriage support group at a local parish. Couples like Adam and Sarah may benefit from involvement in activities that help realize their vision and make it possible for others from the larger community to participate in their vision. For instance, they could take responsibility for remote marriage preparation for teenagers and for mentoring engaged couples in their immediate preparation for their wedding. They could get involved in lobbying for just legislation surrounding marriage, for instance, concerning insurance and tax regulations.

Their social anthropology reminds them that domestic life impacts social and public life. Their egalitarian anthropology provides a foundation for intolerance of all abuse and violence. Volunteering time at shelters, offering a temporary home to an abused child, and urging legislation which does not tolerate any kind of sexual violence in the community provide expressions of these anthropologies. In these activities couples can break the deadlock of their own apparent powerlessness and isolation. Thus they build up the kind of social environment which supports them in their vision.

Besides these activities to change the structures of their environment, couples also need to attend to the patterns and processes in their own one-to-one relationship. We shall concentrate on three areas in particular: communication, sexuality, and prayer. In order to increase justice in their verbal, non-verbal, and sexual communication, couples practice skills for egalitarian, mutual, and reciprocal communication. They learn to understand their feelings, thoughts, and judgments in the context of their own bodily, psychological, and spiritual needs. They learn to confront each other in loving and non-hurtful ways. Prayer together continuously challenges them to embrace the mystery of life and love as well as to accept their own limitations in living and loving.

In the story, Sarah and Adam seem open to the mysterious dimension of life. In their respect for each other's dignity and in their sensitivity for what hurts the other, they demonstrate a keen awareness that earthly, material realities are privileged places of encounter with the unfathomable mystery that we are to one another and that God is to us. Intimacy with God in prayer and liturgy prepares couples for intimacy with each other and with other individuals and communities. Their times of play and relaxation, their meals, and their sexual sharing with each other also become sacramental experiences. In all of this, couples realize that they are not only accountable to each other, but that they also have a responsibility to create an environment that supports mutual, reciprocal, and egalitarian relationships.

As we have seen, the most fundamental values which are at stake when couples or committed friends practice justice in their relationships are egalitarian status, mutuality, and reciprocity. These are based on respect for human dignity. When these values are threatened by unjust practices and structures, resistance becomes an important value.

Sarah and Adam have a clear vision of a just and inclusive marriage relationship. But in their daily lives they realize that, as individuals and as members of a world marred by injustice, the road to justice is long and covered with obstacles. Therefore mediating principles or intermediary markers along the way tell them whether they are traveling in the right direction. Couples have contributed to the creation of a context in which a mutual and egalitarian relationship can thrive when:

- each person and couple in the community is able to develop their gifts and talents;

- marriage is not exalted to a point of discriminating against other choices in life;

- the structures which advantage men over women are not tolerated any longer;

- men as the ones advantaged by society in marriage and friendship relationships embody mutuality and equality in relationships;

- those who violate human dignity through violence or sexual assault are denied access to those they could harm;

- survivors of violence and sexual assault are provided with the support needed to liberate themselves from their unjust situations.

CASE STUDY: HOSPITALITY IN DIVERSITY

Bethany is a Catholic faith community in a major university. A local parish's decision to exclude lay involvement and leadership within their community birthed this group. In response to this exclusion, the group sought to become a community resisting exclusionary structures and embodying inclu-

sion of diverse peoples.[1] *The initial leadership team provided for collaborative ministries and leadership opportunities for members through a structure of volunteerism. The team itself included a diversity of persons, some of whom may well have been excluded from membership in other Catholic communities. Although the official language of the community was English with a variety of accents, efforts were made to include music and readings in the native languages of the members. In keeping with the hospitality for which the scriptural Bethany is remembered, each liturgical event was followed by a simple reception for informal community building. This initial phase of becoming a community of resistance centered on the development of structures which would facilitate inclusion and diversity. Some signs of the success of this phase were seen in the following: (1) the leadership team was comprised of ten persons from six nations and was responsible for organization, decisions, and events; (2) community membership grew in numbers and in cultural, ethnic diversity; and (3) the per capita contributions of the community exceeded that of any other faith community in the university. But the story does not end here because an origin as a community of resistance differs from continuation as a community of resistance. The struggles to resist unjust, exclusionary practices have begun to change form. In spite of its diversity, the leadership team primarily consists of white Western persons. As a team they are committed to an inclusive, just community, but their perspective remains Western. For example, in the Western approach a structure of volunteerism affords opportunities for collaboration, inclusion, and participation. This policy, however, clashes with cultures where appointment empowers persons for service. Again in the Western perspective, potluck meals signify a coming together of equals; such an approach, however, excludes those who fear that their non-Western food is inferior and non-acceptable. These new struggles offer new opportunities to resist these more subtle exclusionary practices.*

Bethany Catholic Community was founded in response to an experience of injustice. As a result, much of its foundational myth centered on avoiding similar injustice and creating the conditions of possibility for a just community. Soon, however, the community needed to face the danger of assimilation into existing structures. In addition, the community needed to avoid perpetrating injustice in its own midst. The focus of the following discussion is therefore the formulation of a myth of

[1] The printed materials from this community state: "The goal of our community is to welcome people from various parts of the world who are bound together by English as a common language. We want to foster an atmosphere where people from different backgrounds and countries, people of different ages and walks of life, people affiliated with the university and people who have other affiliations can meet and experience Christian community together."

resistance which enables communities to become or to remain just and inclusive.

The theology on which Bethany Catholic Community is founded is strongly Trinitarian. This unity of three diverse but equal persons nourished the conviction that communities do not need uniformity in order to function well as communities. The Trinitarian theology was rather the source of the conviction that different people can live together well in respecting and celebrating diversity. Like the Trinity, Christian communities are places where persons are respected as fundamentally equal in their originality. Difference is thus not something to tolerate, to get used to, or even to get over, but a constitutive dimension of life in community. Bethany Catholic Community embraced an anthropology that respects and celebrates difference as life-giving and uplifting (cf. its intercultural selections of music). Its ideal model is not the organ where one single person plays all the different instruments, but rather the orchestra where many people are actively involved and where the difference adds to the beauty.

Bethany successfully resisted the danger of making its foundational response against injustice its myth. The experience of injustice rather became the occasion and the challenge to develop a myth that would enable its members to undo injustice and to do justice. This way it became possible not to interpret the original conflict in light of a dualistic scheme of good and evil, friend and foe. As a consequence, despite having been a victim of injustice, the community remained aware that it could become a perpetrator of injustice. From this flowed a need for ongoing self-criticism and transformation as a response to ever so subtle forms of injustice that are creeping up in its midst.

The foundation of this community included among its basic values active participation, multiculturalism, shared non-clerical leadership, voluntary unpaid involvement, and open access to decision-making. But will this be enough to resist becoming like a normal parish and tolerating unjust practices? Bethany Catholic Community and all communities with similar aspirations need a myth of resistance. Such a myth is found in the Gospel of John, a Gospel which some interpreters have characterized as resistance against processes of institutionalization which were in full force at the end of the first and the beginning of the second centuries. The Gospel presents the relationships between God and Jesus as well as between Jesus and the disciples as relationships of reciprocal love and friendship. John thus rejects the models of hierarchy and superiority. Within the community the Gospel awards every believer the equal status of disciple by avoiding the exclusive and hierarchical dimensions of apostleship. John also gives prominent roles to women. Those who approach Jesus are presented as including Jews,

Samaritans, and Greeks, people of high and low standing, those healed of paralysis, blindness, and even death, as well as those who love, deny, or betray Jesus. The Fourth Gospel also resists the ritualization of prayer and liturgy by focusing on relationships and service, for instance, foot-washing.

How can this Johannine myth of resistance help Bethany Catholic Community become a just and inclusive community? The Johannine vision highlights the centrality of relationships. Bethany can remain a just community if the quality of the relationships of its members continues to be the center of its life. The simple reception after each liturgy is a constitutive part of the life of the community which is holy and life-giving like the liturgical celebration. The centrality of relationality is expressed in a communicative arrangement of the seats in its chapel, in the openings that are made for active participation of all members, as well as in the acceptance extended to infants, children, and their needs. This focus on relationality culminates in welcoming new members with open arms and in giving them a voice in the shaping of the community. For Bethany, God is encountered in relationality.

Participation and inclusiveness are threatened in this community by a reluctance to offer time, talent, and friendship for the sake of the community. A tendency toward minimalism retains a certain force, from the early days of the community when survival dictated minimal activities. At this stage a reliance on the same people for certain services, a diminished effort to invite new people to participate in the planning, in the ministries, and in a preference for few activities, services, or requirements still reflect this early tendency. The Johannine story of the multiplication of the loaves is a challenge to Bethany's founders to let go of the myth of scarcity and to embrace the abundance, that is, God's gift when all are welcome to contribute. In this way the community can overcome the split into providers and consumers and can become a community where everyone contributes according to their own gifts and talents.

The structural shift from an exclusively volunteer model to a model of elected and officially commissioned representation on the parish team and in vital community ministries is necessary, because a volunteer model discourages participation from non-Western people. Other structural shifts include a policy that the same person does not exercise the same liturgical ministry in successive weeks. Such a policy could be a welcome remedy for the over-involvement of some members and provide the necessary room for others to develop their own agency by contributing their resources.

The leadership team of Bethany Catholic Community also needs to discern the charisms in the community and to direct its members to the ministries that correspond to their charisms. In addition, training and education need to be provided for the exercise of the respective ministries.

Participation in international networks of ecclesial and civil life, like Bread for the World, Amnesty International, and Doctors without Borders, will allow Bethany to keep its vision alive. Bethany could invite a pastor from another part of the world to be its pastor-in-residence for the duration of a semester or an academic year. At the same time it could establish contacts with a sister parish in one of the home countries of its present members for an exchange of friendship and vision.

The high turnover of Bethany's membership as a student community as well as the natural forgetfulness of people necessitates a retelling of its vision and values at regular intervals (e.g., at the beginning of a semester). Bethany can only be a just and inclusive community if its members are committed to ongoing conversion. This can provide a self-correcting mechanism that attends to the evolving issues of justice in the community and that counters the tendency toward assimilation into a regular parish, which new arrivals might expect to find there.

The values of Bethany Catholic Community are participation, inclusiveness, and respect for difference. Its life is based on relationality and it cherishes the value of friendship. Flexibility, openness to the future, and ongoing conversion are the transformation-oriented values of this community.

Since Bethany started out as a response to injustice, its original vision had a strong justice orientation. But soon the community had to realize that justice is a very complex reality and one that can never be achieved once and for all. Therefore, the following mediating principles provide measuring posts for the community to see whether it is on the road toward a just and inclusive community. A Christian community is resisting the dangers of being co-opted into normalcy when:

- it provides structures that increase levels of participation by its members;

- those who emerge from its day-to-day life as leaders commit themselves to enabling others to take their places;

- the values of a myth of resistance (e.g., participation and respect for difference) are the grounds of effective action;

- faith education and human development are made available to all;

- the members of the community recognize that injustices creep into their life as a community and they accept help to overcome injustice;

- the community resists the undermining of participation and inclusiveness by hierarchical or moralizing mechanisms of exclusion.

Bethany Catholic Community as we presented it here is an effort to embody the Trinity. In the early years of its existence it was possible to observe its development from a tenuous weekly ad hoc gathering to a real and stable community. Its sacramental celebrations clearly effected what they symbolized: Christian community. This is obvious from the broad range of friendships that have grown in the environment and from the ways in which community members collaborate, help, and enrich each other from their own rich resources. This wealth of goodness at the same time binds its members to resist the demise of friendship and to engage the challenges of the future.

CASE STUDY: PASSIONATE COMMUNITY

A group of young single and young married persons in their twenties meets biweekly for a meal, prayer, theological reflection, and sharing of concerns. The majority of the group spent at least a year after their undergraduate education as part of various Christian young adult volunteer programs. There they lived in community and volunteered in economically disadvantaged settings. Their volunteer experiences nurtured a longing for a just and inclusive community. Today the group struggles together about how to live simple lives. They purchase only what they need so as to provide jobs and income for the persons who are poor. They invest so that their savings can benefit persons and companies practicing justice. They support affordable housing, fair lending practices, and sustainable communities of diversity. Together they are organizing a local cooperative which buys durable chemical-free food in bulk from the producer at fair prices. In their biweekly meeting times they are consciously trying to connect their lives and just actions with the Scriptures and Catholic Social Teachings. They are trying to articulate foundations and surface inspirations for how they live. They struggle to create images and uncover principles which give language to the vision drawing them to its concretization. The group has found that coming together has fueled the desire for a just and inclusive community and developed real, concrete ways to live that vision already now.

Intentional communities such as these are typically steeped in a context which promotes justice as participation in the human community. Their history of activities on behalf of justice expresses and nurtures a relational, engaged understanding of God and a social anthropology. Their vision of a better world is reflected in their life in common, in a shared mission of service, and in efforts to create more just ways of living. The identification of God with neighbor grounds their struggle to connect their just practices with the Christian traditions. In addition to an engaged theology, a social anthropology, a vision, and a mission, the sustainability and viability of intentional just and inclusive communities require attention to two foci: first, an embrace of desire and longing for the presence of the Indwelling Spirit; second, the deliberate derivation of norms for just practices from a vision of the eschatological city of God.

A theology which recognizes the Spirit provides the opportunity to experience God's intimate presence, to celebrate transformation, and to legitimate the in-breaking of surprising longings or challenges. Such an embrace of the Spirit requires an openness to a relationship with the Spirit which a life of communal activism may not naturally uphold. Just and inclusive communities need literally to create room and space for the Spirit to move where it will. The designation of a quiet place offers room for an experience of divine indwelling intimacy. Challenges to slow down a frantic pace invite space for transformation. Receptive ears for intuitive insights, tears, or heartaches provide a crack through which the in-breaking Spirit can enter.

Communities can also turn to the arts as participants or as viewers and listeners. Music, theater, art, dance all afford highly effective ways to inspire, transform, or break through the hearts of persons engaged. Just and inclusive communities may experience the Spirit in hymn-sings or in theatre productions like *Les Misérables*. Or just and inclusive communities can engage art, song, or drama to allow a space for the Spirit to deepen their own understanding of their mission or to inspire others through their presentations.

Sometimes the Spirit benefits from a structure. For example, just and inclusive communities may offer room to the Spirit through a recurring question in their common prayer or household meetings. Possible questions might include: Where is the Spirit calling or challenging you? For what are you longing? How can we organize this activity to leave room for the Spirit to transform it? How did the Spirit surprise you this week?

The embrace of Spirit theology must resist two structures which have marginated the Spirit in the last two decades. As the commentary in Chapter 1 pointed out, the truths emerging in longings and desires have been minimized through rationalization and spiritualization. Consequently, an embrace of longings as the presence of the Spirit resists socialization into the preeminence of reason and a distrust of materiality. The Spirit has been further marginated within many churches through a neglect which deprives believers of concepts and vocabulary to describe or recognize experiences of the Spirit moving in their lives. A public worship and theology in churches which links the Spirit with transformation, indwelling presence, and surprise challenges believers to put their longings for a better world into action on behalf of justice. The neglect of the Spirit in local churches challenges intentional groups to invite their churches to encourage the seeds of a Spirit theology to grow. Lack of structural support privatizes the Spirit and impoverishes the Church.

A second challenge was posed for just and inclusive communities: the deliberate derivation of norms for just practices from a vision of the city of God. As has been noted, abundance characterized the eschatological images: more bread than could be eaten, vintage wine, length of years, resurrected life, and intimate, immediate relationships with God. Such abundance reflects a God who is always more than is expected and a Spirit who cannot be restrained by human plans or institutional patterns. This Spirit-linked abundance suggests some norms from the endtimes city of God for these just and inclusive communities.

Transformative justice invites these intentional communities to be transformed by the Spirit. This indwelling Spirit calls for a conversion in understanding of the task of justice, namely, a shift from justice as an obligation of discipleship to the very embodiment of the Spirit of Jesus. The Spirit of eschatological abundance seeks to transform taut intensity into playful graciousness. Justice as accountable agency reminds the communities that, with the Spirit, they are co-responsible to recognize the in-breaking of the city of God, to prepare its way, and to nurture its presence in this time and place. Justice as access to resources affirms that common life, simple living, and cooperatives may well be a way to express and to bring about the abundance of resources described in the eschatological visions of the city of God.

Since the focus of this situation is the sustainability and vitality of just and inclusive communities, the approach to justice employed in this book has surfaced some values and mediating principles for these contemporary embodiments of the city of God. This case study highlights values of beauty and aesthetic expression, divine-human mutuality, openness to the new and unexpected, embodiment and materiality, graciousness, community, human wholeness, and a humane pace of living.

A just and inclusive community is on its way toward an embodiment of the city of God when:

- the transforming Spirit provides contours for understanding communal experiences and is included in prayer, public meetings, and worship along with the engaged Creator and the liberating Savior;

- Christians brought together by a desire for community living and a longing for a just world are welcomed as key members of local communities;

- beauty, song, longings, and desires, alongside reason and knowledge, practices and rituals, prayer and silence, are all expected moments of encounter with divinity;

- the human embrace of abundance and indwelling intimacy actually can lighten and grace the burden of transforming injustice into justice;

- practitioners of justice can play, delight in beauty, and trust their intuition.

CASE STUDY: INVITING THE WORLD HOME

Angela and Peter live with their three children in a modest home which they own in a neighborhood of white-, pink-, and blue-collar families. After a lenten homily urging church members to participate in Operation Ricebowl, they start watching where the food they eat is produced and where the clothing they wear is made. Their amazement at inviting the world to the family table turns to dismay as they learn about the poverty in these same countries. Their coffee comes from Kenya, a country with an annual per capita gross domestic product of $1,200. Their bananas come from Honduras and Nicaragua, countries with annual per capita gross domestic products of $700 and $410 respectively. Their sugar comes from Haiti, a country with an annual per capita gross domestic product of $1,000. Angela's silk blouses come from China, a country with an annual per capita gross domestic product of $494. The children's turtlenecks come from El Salvador, a country with an annual per capita gross domestic product of $1,000, and where 2 percent of the population controls 90 percent of the country's wealth. Peter's flannel shirt comes from Guatemala, a country with an annual per capita gross domestic product of $980. In her closet Angela finds a dress from Sri Lanka, where the annual per capita gross domestic product is a mere $500, and skirts from Pakistan and India, countries with annual per capita gross domestic products of only $434 and $350 respectively. Even though the family does not consider themselves well off by U.S. standards, they know that it is financially difficult to raise their family on their annual income in a country where the per capita gross domestic product is $14,420. But how can they improve these economic realities for people half a world away whom they do not know? How can they engage the struggle to end global economic injustice?

Through a process of conscientization, the family in our story realized that their purchase of food and clothing was an unwitting participation in structures that caused exploitation and oppression. Angela,

Peter, and their children are good people who would be unable to inflict direct suffering on anybody. Becoming aware of the indirect effects of their actions was disturbing to them. Like many good people, however, the complexity of the economic system and their apparent powerlessness ran the risk of paralyzing them. Such a situation is laced with the danger of escapism rather than engaging the overwhelming complexity of global economics.

In the following discussion we will focus on two questions: How can middle-class Christians disengage themselves from complicity in global economic injustice? How can they engage effectively the struggle to end global economic injustice? Our goal is to point out concrete and manageable strategies that assist people to get actively involved in this endeavor.

The fact that Angela and Peter could be affected by the issue of a just distribution of the world's resources presupposes a basic goodness on their part. This goodness could be informed by faith in a God who created all persons equal, who stays involved in the world's affairs, and who has a special love for the poor. Furthermore, their goodness might be based on a deep conviction of dignity which implies that no one deserves to suffer and which compels people to end suffering wherever they can. Peter and Angela are convinced that the fundamental relationality of all persons calls for solidarity. But their frustration and the absence of advice when confronted with the implications of their consumer habits show that basic goodness and good intentions are not enough when confronted with injustice.

Angela, Peter, and similar middle-class Christians would benefit from confirmation that involvement in the struggle for justice is not optional, but rather a constitutive part of Christian faith in God. God is actively involved in the world through the prophets of old, through Jesus Christ, and through people today. God does not side with the rich and powerful, but with the poor. God does not condone exploitation and oppression, but seeks ways to liberate.

Middle-class Christians learn that human beings are created as social persons with a dignity that requires their basic needs to be fulfilled. Consequently, humanity is a community of destiny where no one can be truly happy at the expense of another, where the good fortune of one can be for the good of all.

This leads to the realization that often we are doing more than meets the eye. In the story, Angela realized that in the simple daily dinner of their family they were bringing the world to their table. How could they share resources with these global guests? How could they be in solidarity with those who were exploited for their benefit? How can their concern be made fruitful for poor people?

The understanding of justice as participation invites us first to look at relationality. In order to engage the struggle against injustice, Angela and Peter look for ways to shift their contacts with people of the Two-Thirds World from an anonymous consumer relationship to face to face friendship relationships. They could begin by collecting pictures and texts on the countries from which their food and clothing originate and post them on a family bulletin board. As a further step they could participate in immersion trips sponsored by their local parish to a sister parish in another part of the world. They could establish a pen pal relationship with someone from a country in the Two-Thirds World. They could offer a home away from home for Two-Thirds World students at a nearby college or university. They could seek personal contact with recent immigrants or asylum seekers. They could encourage their children to expand their circle of friends to include persons of other cultures. They could offer their children opportunities to learn the skills it takes to nurture cross-cultural relationships. This focus on friendship relationships would give them the opportunity to learn more about the cultures and the people who are providing such a vital part of their daily living. Instead of demonizing or idealizing these friends, they are challenged to develop an attitude of loving realism which accepts their strengths and weaknesses.

Middle-class Christians cannot take up the struggle for justice alone. They can tap into the social network that their church provides or tap into organizations which share similar concerns and values. In the course of their involvement they may well begin to question why the organization is more involved in feeding the hungry than in practices that address the unjust structures that cause hunger. They will question why their local parish is only involved in specific collections for the relief of natural disasters, but devotes no percentage of its annual budget to transform structures of oppression and exploitation. Such attempts at conscientization might encounter the tendency to revere those who are involved in direct relief as saints and to stigmatize those working for structural change as "Marxists."

In view of a response to exploitative practices in food production and making of clothing, middle-class Christians might request information from their churches. Such information could include the circumstances and human rights violations under which various producers have their goods produced in countries of the Two-Thirds World. Such information should be available to the public in all church buildings and via church-related newspapers and publications. The general availability of information about oppressive practices in the economic sphere will support churchgoers in their faith-inspired responsibility of boycotting the oppressing companies and businesses.

Boycotts have contributed to the end of unjust practices and to corporate economic reform. Gradually individuals and families, parishes and church groups will recognize that companies and businesses only have the power which consumers confer on them.

As a result, when buying a dress or a suit, middle-class Christians will ask the sales agent questions not only about the size, the fabric, and the durability, but also the country of origin, working conditions, and salaries of the people who produced the clothing. When inquiring how to invest their money, middle-class Christians will ask the banker about not only the rate of return, but also the justice record of the companies, even if it means lower returns. Again, availability of information concerning the justice record of companies is an absolute necessity.

Another way middle-class Christians can orient their daily lives toward justice is supporting shops which guarantee that all their goods are bought directly from the producers in the Two-Thirds World at fair prices (e.g., Ten Thousand Villages). Buying at such shops might include higher prices, limited choices, and in some cases a less processed, but frequently healthier, product.

Many middle-class parishes have large numbers of retired professionals who could put their knowledge and skills at the disposal of people in the Two-Thirds World. This would, however, presuppose careful training and preparation for involvement outside one's own culture and a readiness on the side of the service provider to learn from as well as befriend those whom they assist.

As we saw in the story at the beginning, the conscientization of Angela, Peter, and their family to the justice issues connected to their food and clothing had a profoundly transformative effect on them. They discovered worldwide solidarity. In addition they broadened the value of friendship to include people about whom they were previously indifferent or of whom they were afraid.

When people begin to understand and acknowledge the subtle and abrasive mechanisms of exploitation and oppression, they often feel guilty, powerless, or depressed. They feel caught in a tragic situation where they are doomed to collaborate in injustice no matter what they do. The road to justice seems like a road blocked by a series of insurmountable walls which make it difficult to significantly change the situation. Therefore mediating principles can show a direction and sustain hope. Individuals, families, or communities are involved in the struggle to end global economic injustice when:

- they are willing to invest time and resources to gather information and to gain knowledge about the economic policies of at least some of the companies they patronize;

- they are willing to invest time and resources to bring to bear their values on existing democratic processes in the sphere of economics (e.g., shareholders' meeting);

- they put faces to the people who are exploited and establish face-to-face contact with people in the countries of the Two-Thirds World;

- they connect with other individuals and groups who share similar values in order to counteract the structural superiority of the exploiters;

- they are willing to accept disadvantages and limitations (higher prices, lower quality, lower interest returns) for the sake of just economic conditions for all.

Even though middle-class Christians might realize that all their actions and decisions that touch on the economic realm have justice implications and even though they might become aware that often they cannot avoid participating in structural injustices, still they cannot step outside the system. They cannot stop buying food or clothes. But they can join forces with others, gather and exchange information, take new initiatives, or support existing ones. They will have to face severe limitations in what they are doing. They will invariably fail. They will never be able to do it all. But frequently they will be surprised that they can do something worthwhile and might have the role of a David against a seemingly invincible Goliath.

CASE STUDY: THE FAITH DIFFERENCE

St. Augustine's Catholic Parish resembles other urban parishes. Located in a large metropolitan area, its membership had shifted over the years from a homogenous to a heterogeneous population of European Americans, African Americans, Asian Americans, and Hispanic Americans. The transition had occurred with minimal white flight and racial hostility. Yet there were rumors that some parishioners refused to put money in the collection basket when African Americans passed it. Other parishioners would not receive from the communion cup when someone of another race drank from it ahead of them. The attitude that minorities ought to know their place surfaced when a vocal Indian American woman was labeled "obnoxious and out of line" for her contributions on the parish council, while a similarly vocal European American man was commended for his leadership. Two incidents brought existent racial tensions to the surface. Two young Hispanic men fiddling with a CD player in a car were accosted and questioned by local police officers for allegedly trying to steal the CD player. Their subsequent arrest made the headlines when it was learned later that the young men were in a car owned by a parent in front of their apartment near a local seminary that they attended. One of the police officers was a parishioner and one of the students arrested helped out in the parish religious education program. A couple of months later three teenage members of the parish were implicated in a hate crime directed toward African American students from the neighborhood school. The three young men had attended the parish elementary school and graduated from a Catholic high school in the area. After discussion, the parish Peace and Justice Committee made the following proposal to the parish council: (1) the parish council adopts a "zero tolerance" policy with regard to racial discrimination for all parish institutions and programs, and (2) through the Peace and Justice Committee, the parish collaborates with other religious groups, elected officials, and block clubs in the neighborhood in the implementation of an anti-racism education program.

In spite of their hatefulness, racist incidents effectively moved this local Catholic community to examine racism in its midst and in its neighborhood. The initial analysis by the Peace and Justice Committee and the parish council as described in Chapter 1 suggested some interlocking issues of which they were aware. In addition, the Catholic Christian traditions do provide a context in which to address racism. The image of God as Creator of all and not only of Catholic believers grounds a theology of collaboration with various religious bodies and of inclusion of all races. This same tradition provides visions of a city of God characterized by justice, inclusion, and community. Taken together these convictions provide a theological framework which supports an understanding of human persons as created in the image of God in their very difference. In other words, encounter with difference is encounter with God, the Creator of all.

A sacramental theology which understands Christ and the body of Christ today as the foundational sacraments of encounter with God makes it difficult to limit sacramentality to bread and wine. Rather, the local church in worship and in daily living, in the church and in the neighborhood, is the flesh and blood body of Christ. Normativity of the future challenges this local church to embody today these beliefs in God as creator of all, in a just and inclusive community, in the Church as body of Christ, and in difference as constitutive of human persons. Parish ministers and staff are challenged to make these theological, anthropological, and ethical foundations explicit and congruent in parish life, including worship, mission, programs, procedures, and interactions.

These theological, anthropological, and ethical convictions provide a context within which to address zero tolerance for racism. When justice is understood as participation, then racial discrimination must be recognized as the exclusion and marginalization of persons on the basis of embodied difference. Such exclusion and marginalization violates justice as participation. Consequently, discrimination must be publicly denounced and decried for what it is: sin in need of communal and personal conversion.

This public call for conversion is not enough. Rather, the local church, as a catalyst and in collaboration with other religious bodies and political officials, must work to transform conditions which allow the possibility of racism and racist incidents. Together these concerned groups search out ways to transform ignorance into informed appreciation, fear of difference into delight in diversity, and learned distrust into chosen acceptance. Patterns of hierarchy and domination divide persons into superiors and inferiors. Such a dualism promotes the creation of enemies as threats to one's social position in the hierarchy of domination. Consequently, patterns of hierarchy and domination which foster the creation of an enemy demand transformation into patterns of collaboration, inclusion, and participation.

Obviously, such conversion and transformation will not happen because religious bodies and civic structures decree it. An understanding of justice as participation proposes some concrete dimensions with which to begin. Churches can intentionally diversify their ministry teams, committees, teachers, councils, support staffs, and liturgical ministers. When adult and children's education, sacramental preparation, and liturgical rituals highlight the racial and ethnic background of saints and biblical characters, the difference and diversity of the Catholic Christian tradition is celebrated. A parish commitment to teaching songs, to using examples or stories, to acquiring statues or art works, and to purchasing library books which come from various ethnic groups legitimates diversity in the community. When these formative aspects of parish life reiterate Catholic Social Teachings, racism may begin to lose its power.

Since friends are less likely to become enemies, churches can create opportunities to meet and engage in face to face relationships which have a potential for friendship between persons of differing races and ethnicities. Churches can also devise ways for parishioners to work together with persons of other races and ethnicities. Employed parishioners and owners could routinely notify other parishioners of job or internship possibilities. Retired members could serve as mentors for new parents or for entrepreneurs or for students interested in a related career. The parish could tithe its income for incubation loans for small businesses which contribute to a just and inclusive community.

Conversion from racism to inclusion also entails the development of skills and a safe space for self-reflection. Local church communities need to teach and practice skills in cross-cultural and cross-racial communication. They can provide a safe space for group processes which explore issues, such as learned approaches to difference, socialization into racism, an affinity for stereotypes or racist jokes, the tendency to generalize from isolated incidents, and the inclination to create an enemy. More parishioners can be reached when the program is an extension of the worship service or when the skills and processes are offered immediately after racial incidents. Delight in difference requires comfort with ambiguity, which comes from resistance to evaluate sameness as good and to associate ambiguity with relativism. Ambiguity signals the complexity and not the relativity of difference.

Ending racism will not be achieved through a program or a policy. Rather, a comprehensive and integrated approach to all dimensions of parish life is required: worship, mission, programs, procedures, and interactions. The values which are threaded through parish life entail inclusion, participation, equality, difference, dignity and worth, friendship, self-reflection, and beauty.

A parish can recognize that it is on the way to embodying the city of God as an anti-racist just and inclusive community when:

- racial and ethnic stereotypes, jokes, and generalizations have vanished from the speech and writing of the local church;

- the songs, saints, statues, and stories from the diversity of the universal Church are routinely included in worship and education;

- parishioners seek more skills training in anti-racist behavior and more opportunities for cross-racial and cross-ethnic friendship;

- the church members teach and implement the skills and programs initiated by the local church in their neighborhoods, workplaces, and public agencies;

- the church and school attract persons seeking formation and education into an anti-racist, just, and inclusive community.

CONCLUSION

The responses to these dilemmas drew on justice as participation as a vision seeking present embodiment in each concrete instance. The comments also allowed the image of an incarnate, relational God and an essentially social anthropology to suggest ways of doing justice. Furthermore, the suggested just practices incorporated, as appropriate, the seven dimensions of the description of justice as participation: relationality, access to resources necessary for authentic human living, attention to structures and processes, concrete and transformative action, and accountable, responsible agency. The sections ended by highlighting some key values and pointing out some mediating principles which marked progress on the way toward just and inclusive community. It is our hope that this approach can be used in other situations as well.

Bibliography

Achtemeier, E. R. "Righteousness in the Old Testament." *The Interpreter's Dictionary of the Bible: An Illustrated Encyclopedia.* Ed. George Arthur Buttrick, 80–5. Nashville: Abingdon, 1962.

Aland, Kurt, and others, eds. *Novum Testamentum Graece.* Stuttgart: Deutsche Bibelgesellschaft, [27]1993.

Aquinas, Thomas. *Summa theologiae.* Latin text and English translation, introduction, notes, appendices and glossaries. London: Blackfriars, 1964–76.

Beauchamp, Tom L. "Distributive Justice and the Difference Principle." *John Rawls' Theory of Social Justice: An Introduction.* Ed. Elizabeth H. Smith and H. Gene Blocker, 132–61. Athens: Ohio University Press, 1980.

Berquist, Jon L. "Dangerous Waters of Justice and Righteousness: Amos 5:18-27." *BTB* 23 (1993) 54–63.

Bierhoff, Hans Werner, and others, eds. *Justice in Social Relations.* New York: Plenum Press, 1986.

Bieringer, Reimund. "'My Kingship Is Not of This World' John 18,36: The Kingship of Jesus and Politics." *The Myriad Christ: Plurality and the Quest for Unity in Contemporary Christology.* Ed. Terrance Merrigan and Jacques Haers, 159–75. BETL 152. Leuven: University Press and Peeters, 2000.

_____. "The Normativity of the Future: The Authority of the Bible for Theology." *Bulletin European Theology: Zeitschrift für Theologie in Europa* 8:1 (1997) 52–67.

Blank, Josef. *Krisis: Untersuchungen zur johanneischen Christologie und Eschatologie.* Freiburg: Lambertus, 1964.

Borgen, Peder. "God's Agent in the Fourth Gospel." *The Interpretation of John.* Ed. John Ashton, 67–78. Issues in Religion and Theology 9. Philadelphia: Fortress Press, 1986.

Boszormenyi-Nagy, Ivan. *Invisible Loyalties: Reciprocity in Intergenerational Family Therapy.* New York: Brunner/Mazel, 1984.

Brown, Raymond E. *The Gospel According to John: Introduction, Translation, and Notes.* 2 vols. Anchor Bible 29 and 29A. New York: Doubleday, 1966–70.

Brueggemann, Walter. "The Call to Resistance." *The Other Side* 26 (November/December 1990) 44–6.

Cady, Linell E. "Hermeneutics and Tradition: The Role of the Past in Jurisprudence and Theology." *Harvard Theological Review* 79:4 (1986) 439–63.

Carson, D. A. *The Gospel According to John.* Leicester/Grand Rapids, Mich.: Inter-Varsity/Eerdmans, 1991.

_____. "The Purpose of the Fourth Gospel: John 20:31 Reconsidered." *JBL* 106 (1987) 639–51.

Clinton, William J. "State of the Union Address." January 23, 1996, Washington, D.C.

Cohen, Ronald L. "Power and Justice in Intergroup Relations." *Justice in Social Relations.* Ed. Hans Werner Bierhoff and others, 65–86. New York: Plenum Press, 1986.

_____. "Procedural Justice and Participation." *Human Relations* 38:7 (1985) 643–63.

Coleman, John. "Discipleship and Citizenship in America Today." Video recording of a talk given on April 14, 1994, at Loyola University Chicago.

Crüsemann, Frank. "Jahwes Gerechtigkeit *(sedaqa/sädäq)* im Alten Testament." *EvTh* 36 (1976) 427–50.

Culpepper, R. Alan. *Anatomy of the Fourth Gospel: A Study in Literary Design.* Philadelphia: Fortress Press, 1983.

Curran, Charles. "The Changing Anthropological Bases of Catholic Social Ethics." *Directions in Catholic Social Ethics.* Notre Dame, Ind.: University of Notre Dame Press, 1985.

Dahl, Norman O. "Justice and Aristotelian Practical Reason." *Philosophy and Phenomenological Research* 51 (1991) 153–7.

Daloz, Laurent A. Parks, and others. *Commonfire: Leading Lives of Commitment in a Complex World.* Boston: Beacon Press, 1996.

Davis, Charles. "From Inwardness to Social Action: A Shift in the Locus of Religious Experience." *New Blackfriars* 67 (1986) 114–25.

D'Costa, Gavin. "Christ, the Trinity and Religious Plurality." *Christian Uniqueness Reconsidered: The Myth of Pluralistic Theology of Religions.* Maryknoll, N.Y.: Orbis Books, 1990.

Descamps, Albert. *Les Justes et la Justice dans les évangiles et le christianisme primitif hormis la doctrine proprement paulinienne.* Louvain and Gembloux: Publications universitaires and Duculot, 1950.

Descamps, Albert, and Lucien Cerfaux. "Justice et justification." *Dictionnaire de la Bible.* Supplément IV, col. 1417–510. Paris: Letouzey, 1949.

De Tavenier, Johan. "Eschatology and Social Ethics." *Personalist Morals: Essays in Honor of Professor Louis Janssens.* Ed. Joseph A. Selling, 279–300. BETL 83. Leuven: University Press and Peeters, 1988.

Donahue, John R. "Biblical Perspectives on Justice." *Faith That Does Justice: Examining the Christian Sources for Social Change.* Ed. John C. Haughey, 68–112.Woodstock Studies 2. New York: Paulist Press, 1977.

Dworkin, Ronald A. "Law as Interpretation." *Critical Inquiry* 9 (September 1982) 179–200.

_____. "'Natural Law' Revisited." *University of Florida Law Review* 34:2 (1982) 165–88.

Dussel, Enrique. *Ethics and Community.* Maryknoll, N.Y.: Orbis Books, 1988.

Epsztein, Léon. *La justice sociale dans le proche-orient ancien et le peuple de la Bible.* Paris: Editions du Cerf, 1983.

Farley, Margaret A. "New Patterns of Relationship: Beginnings of a Moral Revolution." *Introduction to Christian Ethics: A Reader.* Ed. Robert P. Hammel and Kenneth R. Himes, 63–79. Mahwah, N.J.: Paulist Press, 1989.

Folger, Robert. "Rethinking Equity Theory: A Referent Cognitions Model." *Justice in Social Relations.* Ed. Hans Werner Bierhoff and others, 145–60. New York: Plenum Press, 1986.

Forrester, Duncan B. *Christian Justice and Public Policy.* Cambridge Studies in Ideology and Religion 10. Cambridge: Cambridge University Press, 1997.

Gilkey, Langdon. *Catholicism Confronts Modernity: A Protestant View.* New York: Seabury, 1975.

Goizueta, Roberto S. "A Ressourcement from the Margins: U.S. Latino Popular Catholicism as Lived Religion." *Theology and Lived Christianity.* Ed. David Hammond, 3–37. The Annual Publication of the College Theology Society 45. Mystic, Conn.: Twenty-Third Publications, 2000.

Gottwald, Norman K., and Richard A. Horsley, eds. *The Bible and Liberation: Political and Social Hermeneutics.* Rev. ed. Maryknoll, N.Y.: Orbis Books, 1993.

Greeley, Andrew. *The Catholic Myth: The Behavior and Beliefs of American Catholics.* New York: Scribner, 1990.

Gutiérrez, Gustavo. *The Power of the Poor in History: Selected Writings.* London: SCM, 1983.

_____. *A Theology of Liberation: History, Politics and Salvation.* London: SCM, 1977.

Habel, Norman C. "The Future of Social Justice Research in the Hebrew Scriptures: Questions of Authority and Relevance." *Old Testament Interpretation Past, Present, and Future: Essays in Honor of Gene M. Tucker.* Ed. James Luther Mays and others, 277–91. Nashville: Abingdon, 1995.

Harrison, Beverly Wildung. "The Dream of a Common Language: Towards a Normative Theory of Justice in Christian Ethics." *The Annual of the Society of Christian Ethics* 29 (1983) 1–25.

_____. *Making the Connections: Essays on Feminist Social Ethics.* Ed. Carol S. Robb. Boston: Beacon Press, 1985.

Haughey, John C., ed. *Faith That Does Justice: Examining the Christian Sources for Social Change.* Woodstock Studies 2. New York: Paulist Press, 1977.

Hellman, John. "John Paul II and the Personalist Movement." *Cross Currents* (Winter 1980–81) 409–19.

Hendrix, Herman. *Social Justice in the Bible.* Quezon City, Philippines: Claretian Publications, 1985, 1988.

Hollenbach, David. "Justice as Participation: Public Moral Discourse and the U.S. Economy." *Justice, Peace and Human Rights: American Catholic Social Ethics in a Pluralistic Context.* New York: Crossroad, 1988, 71–83.

_____. "Modern Catholic Teachings Concerning Justice." *Faith That Does Justice: Examining the Christian Sources for Social Change.* Ed. John Haughey, 207–31. Woodstock Studies 2. New York: Paulist Press, 1977.

————. "A Prophetic Church and the Catholic Sacramental Imagination." *Justice, Peace and Human Rights: American Catholic Social Ethics in a Pluralistic Context.* New York: Crossroad, 1988, 181–202.

————. "Unemployment and Jobs: A Social, Theological and Ethical Analysis." *Justice, Peace, and Human Rights. American Catholic Social Ethics in a Pluralistic Context.* New York: Crossroad, 1988, 57–70.

The Holy Bible Containing the Old and New Testaments with the Apocryphal/ Deuterocanonical Books. New Revised Standard Version. New York/Oxford: Oxford University Press, 1989.

Howard-Brook, Wes. *Becoming Children of God: John's Gospel and Radical Discipleship.* Maryknoll, N.Y.: Orbis Books, 1994.

Irani, K. D. "The Idea of Social Justice in the Ancient World." *Social Justice in the Ancient World.* Ed. K. D. Irani and Morris Silver, 3–8. Westport, Conn./ London: Greenwood Press, 1995.

Janssens, Louis. "Artificial Insemination: Ethical Considerations." *Louvain Studies* 8 (Spring 1980) 3–29.

Johnson, Elizabeth A. "Theological Foundations of Catholic Social Teaching." *The Living Light* 28 (Fall 1991) 3–6.

Karris, Robert J. *Jesus and the Marginalized in John's Gospel.* Zacchaeus Studies: New Testament. Collegeville: The Liturgical Press, 1990.

Käsemann, Ernst. *The Testament of Jesus: A Study of the Gospel of John in the Light of Chapter 17.* Trans. Gerhard Krodel. Philadelphia: Fortress Press, 1968.

Kilpatrick, G. D. "What John Tells Us About John." *Studies in John Presented to Professor Dr. J. N. Sevenster on the Occasion of His Seventieth Birthday.* 73–87. NTSuppl 24. Leiden: Brill, 1970.

Langan, John P. "What Jerusalem Says to Athens." *Faith That Does Justice: Examining the Christian Sources for Social Change.* Ed. John C. Haughey, 152–80. Woodstock Studies 2. New York: Paulist Press, 1977.

Larmore, Charles E. "Review of *Whose Justice? Which Rationality?* by Alasdair MacIntyre." *Journal of Philosophy* 86 (1989) 437–42.

Lataire, Bianca, and Reimund Bieringer. "God the Father: An Exegetical Study of a Johannine Metaphor." *Gender: Tradition and Renewal.* Ed. Robert Platzner. Religions and Discourse. Frankfurt: Peter Lang, forthcoming.

Lebacqz, Karen. *Justice in an Unjust World.* Minneapolis: Augsburg Publishing House, 1987.

————. *Six Theories of Justice.* Minneapolis: Augsburg Publishing House, 1986.

Lips, H. von. "Anthropologie und Wunder im Johannesevangelium. Die Wunder Jesu im Johannesevangelium im Unterschied zu den synoptischen Evangelien auf dem Hintergrund johanneischen Menschenverständnisses." *EvTh* 50 (1990) 296–311.

Lummis, Adair, and Allison Stokes. "Catholic Feminist Spirituality and Social Justice Action." *Research in the Social Scientific Study of Religion* 6 (1994) 103–38.

MacIntyre, Alasdair. *After Virtue: A Study in Moral Theology.* Notre Dame, Ind.: University of Notre Dame Press, 1984.

————. "Précis of *Whose Justice? Which Rationality?*" *Philosophy and Phenomenological Research* 51 (1991) 149–52.

_____. *Whose Justice? Which Rationality?* Notre Dame, Ind.: University of Notre Dame Press, 1988.

Malina, Bruce J., and Richard L. Rohrbaugh. *Social-Science Commentary on the Gospel of John.* Minneapolis: Fortress Press, 1998.

Malinowski, Bronislaw. *The Ethnography of Malinowski: The Trobriand Islanders.* London and Boston: Routledge and Kegan, 1979.

Martin, Joanne. "When Expectations and Justice Do Not Coincide: Blue Collar Visions of a Just World." *Justice in Social Relations.* Ed. Hans Werner Bierhoff and others, 317–35. New York: Plenum Press, 1986.

Martyn, J. Louis. *History and Theology in the Fourth Gospel.* Nashville: Abingdon, 1979.

Mays, James Luther. "Perspectives from the Prophetic Tradition." *Interpretation* 37 (1983) 5–17.

Meeks, Wayne A. "The Ethics of the Fourth Gospel." *Exploring the Gospel of John: Essays in Honor of Dwight Moody Smith.* Ed. R. Alan Culpepper and C. Clifton Black, 317–26. Louisville: Westminster/John Knox, 1996.

_____. *The Prophet-King: Moses Traditions and the Johannine Christology.* NTSuppl 14. Leiden: Brill, 1967.

Meier, John. *A Marginal Jew: Rethinking the Historical Jesus.* 2 vols. New York: Doubleday, 1991–94.

Miranda, José P. *Being and the Messiah: The Message of St. John.* Maryknoll, N.Y.: Orbis Books, 1977.

_____. *Marx and the Bible: A Critique of the Philosophy of Oppression.* Maryknoll, N.Y.: Orbis Books, 1974.

Modras, Ronald E. "Karl Rahner and John Paul II: Anthropological Implications for Economics and the Social Order." *Religion and Economic Ethics.* Ed. Joseph F. Gower, 123–50. The Annual Publication of the College Theology Society 31. Lanham, Md.: University Press of America, 1990.

_____. "The Thomistic Personalism of Pope John Paul II." *The Modern Schoolman* 59 (1982) 117–27.

Moloney, Francis J. *The Gospel of John.* Sacra Pagina 4. Collegeville: The Liturgical Press, 1998.

Murphy, Charles M. "Action for Justice as Constitutive of Preaching the Gospel: What Did the 1971 Synod Mean?" *Theological Studies* 44 (1983) 298–311.

Murphy, Seamus. *The Many Ways of Justice.* Studies in the Spirituality of Jesuits 26. St. Louis: The Seminar on Jesuit Spirituality, 1994.

National Conference of Catholic Bishops. *Economic Justice for All: A Pastoral Letter on Catholic Social Teaching and the Economy.* Washington, D.C.: National Conference of Catholic Bishops, 1986.

Neal, Marie Augusta. "Part II: The Relation Between Religious Belief and Structural Change in Religious Orders: Some Evidence." *Review of Religious Research* 12 (1971) 153–64.

_____. "Social Justice and the Right to Use Power." *Journal for the Scientific Study of Religion* 23 (1984) 329–40.

_____. *Values and Interests in Social Change.* Englewood Cliffs, N.J.: Prentice-Hall, 1965.

Niebuhr, Reinhold. *Love and Justice: Selections from the Shorter Writings of Reinhold Niebuhr.* Ed. D. B. Robertson. Louisville: Westminister/John Knox, 1957.

Nissen, Johannes. "Community and Ethics in the Gospel of John." *New Readings in John: Literary and Theological Perspectives: Essays from the Scandinavian Conference on the Fourth Gospel, Arhus 1997.* Ed. Johannes Nissen and Sigfried Pedersen, 194–212. JSNTSS 182. Sheffield: Academic Press, 1999.

Nozick, Robert. *Anarchy, State, and Utopia.* New York: Basic Books, 1974.

Nussbaum, Martha C. *Poetic Justice: The Literary Imagination and Public Life.* The Alexander Rosenthal Lectures. Boston: Beacon Press, 1995.

O'Day, Gail R. "John." *The Women's Bible Commentary.* Ed. Carol A. Newsom and Sharon H. Ringe, 293–304. Louisville: Westminster/John Knox, 1992.

Okure, Teresa. *The Johannine Approach to Mission: A Contextual Study of John 4:1-42.* WUNT 2/31. Tübingen: J.C.B. Mohr, 1988.

O'Neill, Patricia. "Cognition and Citizen Participation in Social Action." *Journal of Applied Social Psychology* 18 (1988) 1067–83.

Perkins, Pheme. "Jesus and Ethics." *Theology Today* 52:1 (1995) 49–65.

Pettigrew, Thomas, and Ernest Campbell. *Christians in Racial Crisis.* Washington, D.C.: Public Affairs Press, 1959.

Pieper, Martha Heineman. *Intrapsychic Humanism: An Introduction to a Comprehensive Psychology and Philosophy of Mind.* Chicago: Falcon II Press, 1990.

Pippin, Tina. *Death and Desire: The Rhetoric of Gender in the Apocalypse of John.* Louisville: Westminster/John Knox, 1992.

Polan, Gregory J., and others. "Justice." *The Collegeville Pastoral Dictionary of Biblical Theology.* Ed. Carroll Stuhlmueller and others, 510–22. Collegeville: The Liturgical Press, 1996.

Preiss, Théo. "Justification in Johannine Thought." *Life in Christ.* Trans. Harold Knight. Studies in Biblical Theology 13. London: SCM, 1957.

Rawls, John. *A Theory of Justice.* Cambridge, Mass.: Harvard University Press, 1971; rev. ed. Oxford: Oxford University Press, 1999.

Rensberger, David. *Johannine Faith and Liberating Community.* Philadelphia: Westminster Press, 1988.

_____. "Love for One Another and Love for Enemies in the Gospel of John." *The Love of Enemy and Non-Retaliation in the New Testament.* Ed. W. M. Swartley, 297–313. Louisville: Westminster/John Knox, 1992.

_____. "Sectarianism and Theological Interpretation in John," *"What Is John."* Vol. 2, *Literary and Social Readings of the Fourth Gospel.* Ed. Fernando F. Segovia, 139–56. SBL Symposium Series 7. Atlanta: Scholars Press, 1998.

Reumann, John. *"Righteousness" in the New Testament: "Justification" in the United States Lutheran–Roman Catholic Dialogue.* Philadelphia/New York: Fortress Press/Paulist Press, 1982.

_____. "Righteousness. New Testament." *Anchor Bible Dictionary* 5 (1992) 745–73.

Roberts, Tyler T. "Michael Walzer and the Critical Connections." *Journal of Religious Ethics* 22 (Fall 1994) 333–53.

Robinson, Geoffry. "Do We Know What Justice Is?" *Origins* 23 (November 25, 1993) 423–30.

Ross, Susan A. "Extravagant Affections." *In the Embrace of God: Feminist Approaches to Theological Anthropology.* Ed. Ann O'Hara Graff, 108–21. Maryknoll, N.Y.: Orbis Books, 1998.

Sandel, Michael J. *Liberalism and the Limits of Justice.* Cambridge: Cambridge University Press, 1982.

Schillebeeckx, Edward. *God Among Us: The Gospel Proclaimed.* New York: Crossroad, 1983.

Schnackenburg, Rudolf. *The Gospel According to St. John.* 3 vols. New York: Crossroad, 1968–82.

Schottroff, Luise. "The Samaritan Woman and the Notion of Sexuality in the Fourth Gospel." *"What Is John."* Vol. 2, *Literary and Social Readings of the Fourth Gospel.* Ed. Fernando F. Segovia, 157–81. SBL Symposium Series 7. Atlanta: Scholars Press, 1998.

Schottroff, Luise, and Wolfgang Stegemann. *Jesus and the Hope of the Poor.* Trans. Matthew J. O'Connell. Maryknoll, N.Y.: Orbis Books, 1986.

Schneiders, Sandra. "History and Symbolism in the Fourth Gospel." *The Gospel of John.* Ed. Marinus de Jonge, 371–6. BETL 44. Leuven: University Press and Peeters, 1977.

———. *The Revelatory Text: Interpreting the New Testament as Sacred Scripture.* San Francisco: Harper, 1991.

Schnelle, Udo. "Johannes als Geisttheologe." *NovT* 40 (1998) 17–31.

Schüssler Fiorenza, Elisabeth. "Equality: A Radical Democratic Ekklesial Vision." *Spirituality Justice Reprint* (November/December 1998) 1–6.

———. "The Politics of Otherness: Biblical Interpretation as a Critical Praxis for Liberation." *The Future of Liberation Theology: Essays in Honor of Gustavo Gutiérrez.* Ed. Marc H. Ellis and Otto Maduro, 311–25. Maryknoll, N.Y.: Orbis Books, 1989.

Segovia, Fernando F., ed. *"What Is John."* Vol. 2, *Literary and Social Readings of the Fourth Gospel.* SBL Symposium Series 7. Atlanta: Scholars Press, 1998.

Segovia, Fernando F., and Mary Ann Tolbert, eds. *Reading from This Place.* Vol. 1, *Social Location and Biblical Interpretation in the United States.* Vol. 2, *Social Location and Biblical Interpretation in Global Perspective.* Minneapolis: Fortress Press, 1995.

Sing, Horst. "Eröffnet der Dialog zwischen Karl-Otto Apel und Enrique Dussel einen plausiblen Zugang zur Überwindung absoluter Armut in der Dritten Welt?" *Diskurs und Leidenschaft: Festschrift Karl-Otto Apel zum 75. Geburtstag.* Ed. Raúl Fornet-Betancourt, 285–304. Concordia. Reihe Monographien 20. Aachen: Verlag der Augustinus Buchhandlung Aachen, 1996.

Solomon, Robert C., and Mark C. Murphy. *What Is Justice? Classic and Contemporary Readings.* New York and Oxford: Oxford University Press, 1990.

Spohn, William C. "Jesus and Ethics." *The Catholic Theological Society of America: Proceedings of the Forty-Ninth Annual Convention,* 49. Ed. Paul Crowley, 40–57. Santa Clara, Calif.: University Press, 1994.

Stassen, Glen. "Michael Walzer's Situated Justice." *Journal of Religious Ethics* 22 (Fall 1994) 375–99.

Tanner, Kathryn. *The Politics of God: Christian Theologies and Social Justice.* Minneapolis: Fortress Press, 1992.

Taylor, Charles. "Justice After Virtue." *After MacIntyre: Critical Perspectives on the Work of Alasdair MacIntyre.* Ed. John Horton and Susan Mendus, 16–43. Cambridge: Polity Press, 1994.

Thompson, Marianne M. "'God's Voice You Have Never Heard, God's Form You Have Never Seen': The Characterization of God in the Gospel of John." *Semeia* 63 (1993) 177–205.

_____. *The Humanity of Jesus in the Fourth Gospel.* Philadelphia: Fortress Press, 1988; = *The Incarnate Word: Perspectives on Jesus in the Fourth Gospel.* Peabody, Mass.: Hendrickson, 1988.

Tyler, Tom R. "The Psychology of Leadership Evaluation." *Justice in Social Relations.* Ed. Hans Werner Bierhoff and others, 310–1. New York: Plenum Press, 1986.

Tyler, Tom R., and Kathleen M. McGraw. "Ideology and the Interpretation of Personal Experience: Procedural Justice and Political Quiescence." *Journal of Social Issues* 42:2 (1986) 115–28.

Van Belle, Gilbert. "The Faith of the Galileans: The Parenthesis in Jn 4,44." *ETL* 74 (1998) 27–44.

_____. *The Signs Source in the Fourth Gospel: Historical Survey and Critical Evaluation of the Semeia Hypothesis.* BETL 116. Leuven: University Press and Peeters, 1994.

Van Gerwen, Jef . *Denk-wijzen 6: Een inleiding in het denken van A. Schopenhauer, S. Kierkegaard, K. Marx en A. MacIntyre.* Leuven-Amersfoort: Acco, 1991.

Volf, Miroslav. "Eschaton, Creation, and Social Ethics." *Calvin Theological Journal* 30 (1995) 130–43.

Wahlde, U. C. von. "The Johannine 'Jews': A Critical Survey." *NTS* 28 (1982) 33–60.

Walsh, Michael, and Brian Davies, eds. *Proclaiming Justice and Peace: Papal Documents from Rerum Novarum through Centesimus Annus.* Mystic, Conn.: Twenty-Third Publications, 1991.

Walsh, William J., and John P. Langan. "Patristic Social Consciousness: The Church and the Poor." *Faith That Does Justice: Examining the Christian Sources for Social Change.* Ed. John C. Haughey, 113–50. Woodstock Studies 2. New York: Paulist Press, 1977.

Walzer, Michael. *Spheres of Justice: A Defense of Pluralism and Equality.* New York: Basic Books, 1983.

Weil, Simone. *Waiting for God.* Trans. Emma Craufurd, with an introduction by Leslie A. Fiedler. New York: Harper/Row, 1973.

Weinfeld, Moshe. *Social Justice in Ancient Israel and in the Ancient Near East.* Publications of the Perry Foundation for Biblical Research in the Hebrew University of Jerusalem. Jerusalem/Minneapolis: The Magnes Press/Fortress Press, 1995.

Welch, Sharon. *Sweet Dreams in America: Making Ethics and Spirituality Work.* New York: Routledge, 1999.

Wengst, Klaus. *Bedrängte Gemeinde und verherrlichter Christus: Ein Versuch über das Johannesevangelium.* München: Kaiser, 1990.

Index